KIERKEGAARD
The Descent into God

Walker gives a unified reading of Kierkegaard's later ethical and religious writings. He argues that these works present a single coherent account of the inner way to God—what Kierkegaard called "becoming a Christian." The starting points are Socratic ethics and sceptical epistemology. The individual who pursues truth and goodness in self-examination is led from subjective moral belief to vision of an objective and absolute Truth and Good. At the same time, the demands of morality are revealed with increasing depth as transcended in Christian love. In discovering the nothingness of the ego, the individual uncovers the reality of a self existing before God.

Walker displays Kierkegaard's writings as a systematic project of edification. As essentially practical philosophy, their aim is not just to instruct the reader but by provoking self-reflection to induce a psychological and spiritual activity that precisely reduplicates the inner way they analyse.

The method of the book mirrors its content. It is not a simple summary or analysis of Kierkegaard's views, nor is it a commentary on his writings. Its argument circles and recircles Kierkegaard's central ideas in a continuous creative inquiry. Walker's aim is less to solve problems than to expose questions and provoke reflective thinking.

Jeremy Walker, a member of the Department of Philosophy at McGill University, is the author of *A Study of Frege* and *To Will One Thing: Reflections on Kierkegaard's "Purity of Heart."*

KIERKEGAARD
The Descent into God

Jeremy Walker

McGill-Queen's University Press
Kingston and Montreal

© McGill-Queen's University Press 1985
ISBN 0-7735-0417-6
Legal deposit first quarter 1985
Bibliothèque nationale du Québec

Printed in Canada

Canadian Cataloguing in Publication Data

Walker, Jeremy D. B. (Jeremy Desmond Bromhead),
1936-
Kierkegaard : the descent into God
Includes bibliographical references and index.
ISBN 0-7735-0417-6.
1. Kierkegaard, Søren, 1813-1855—Religion.
2. Kierkegaard, Søren, 1813-1855—Ethics.
1. Title.
B4378.R44W34 1985   198′.9   C84-099551-2

Contents

A: pos
criterion

[B: neg]

vi   *Contents*

Acknowledgments

THIS BOOK owes much to many people. First, to Robert Perkins, who asked me to write a paper for a special Kierkegaard number of *Thought*. This sparked off a line of thinking which led eventually to this book. Next to Alastair McKinnon, who has shown me what a colleague can be. He has lent and given me useful material; read with patience several of my writings; answered my frequent questions; and helped me, through his own unique studies, towards a wider and clearer grasp of Kierkegaard than I could have got in any other way. To the articulate students in various of my classes in which I have talked about Kierkegaard or the relevant topics: classes in moral philosophy, where we have discussed self-knowledge and love; classes in nineteenth-century philosophy; and classes on Plato, where I have been able to explore the *Apology* in detail.

But, above all, I am indebted to the students in the seminar on Kierkegaard which I began to give in January 1980. These groups have met at my home, once weekly, in the evenings, and have shown me something new about what philosophy can be. We have read and talked about *Either/Or*, the *Concluding Unscientific Postscript*, *Two Ages*, *Purity of Heart*, *Works of Love*, and *The Sickness Unto Death*. So thanks to each and every one: to Miloche Barutciski, Stella Baza, Barbara Bryce, Rob Conrath, Allison Di Francesco, Susan Drummond, Brigitte Fefer, Dominique Leydet, Simona Massobrio, Neil Matthews, Grant McCrea, Lisa Moore, Claire Rothman, Jean-Pierre Sheppard, Tristan Tondino, Elliott Vizel, Bernard Vroom, Richard Westley, Andy Wheatley, and Cindy Yacowar. And special thanks to Ivan Khan, who shared his knowledge of Kierkegaard with me, as colleague and in my seminar.

I thank Mrs. Joy Chapman for her fast and efficient typing of my messy original.

Chapter 1 of this book appeared previously in *Thought* 55, no. 218 (September 1980) (New York: Fordham University Press, 1980), Copyright © 1980 by Fordham University Press. I am grateful for permission to reprint it here.

This book has been published with the help of a grant from the Canadian Federation for the Humanities, using funds provided by the Social Sciences and Humanities Research Council of Canada. It has also had the help of a grant from the Humanities Research Fund of McGill University.

Abbreviations

I HAVE TAKEN all quotations from the paperback editions of the standard English translations of Kierkegaard, except that I have used the new Princeton translations of *Two Ages* (formerly *The Present Age*) and *The Sickness Unto Death*. I have occasionally altered the translations slightly for reasons of clarity. All page-references are to the above editions (see the Appendix for full bibliographical information).

However, in identifying the works for quotation or discussion I have used the standard acronyms from the original Danish titles. For example, the book translated under the English title *Works of Love* is actually called *Kjerlighedens Gjerninger*, and so I identify it as *KG*, not as *WL* or *WOL*. Sometimes the English title of a work is quite different from its original Danish title. Thus, for example, the book translated under the title *Purity of Heart is to Will One Thing* is actually only the first part of a work consisting of three parts, the whole entitled *Opbyggelige Taler i forskjellig Aand* (roughly, "Edifying Discourses in Different Spirits"). Sometimes the English translation has a title where the Danish original had no title or no single title. Thus, the book translated as *Authority and Revelation* was never published by Kierkegaard, and never therefore acquired a publication title; though it is likely that he would have called it *Bogen om Adler* ("The Book on Adler"). The numerous articles and pamphlets published by Kierkegaard in 1854 and 1855 are translated together as the *Attack Upon Christendom*—yet another non-Kierkegaardian name. And so on.

This situation should not continue. It is in the interests of scholarship, in its widest sense, that we (*a*) pay Kierkegaard the elementary compliment of using his own chosen titles; (*b*) recall that he wrote and thought in Danish—just as Plato wrote in Greek, Aquinas in Latin, and Kant in German—and begin to read him in his own language; and (*c*) refrain from

using English titles which cut English-language scholarship partially off
from concurrent scholarly work in, say, French and German.

I now give the standard acronyms I have used, together with their
Danish sources and the English equivalent titles.

ACRONYM	DANISH TITLE	ENGLISH TITLE
AE	*Afsluttende uvidenskabelig Efterskrift*	*Concluding Unscientific Postscript*
BA	*Begrebet Angest*	*The Concept of Dread* (or *The Concept of Anxiety*)
BOA	*Bogen om Adler*	*Authority and Revelation*
B21	*Bladartikler 1854–55*	Articles in *Attack Upon Christendom*
CT	*Christelige Taler*	*Christian Discourses*
DS	*Dømmer selv!*	*Judge for Yourselves!*
EE	*Enten-Eller*	*Either/Or* (in 2 vols.)
EOT	*En opbyggelige Tale*	*An Edifying Discourse*
FB	*Frygt og Baeven*	*Fear and Trembling*
FV	*Om min Forfatter-Virksomhed*	"On My Work as an Author," in *The Point of View for My Work as an Author*
G	*Gjentagelsen*	*Repetition*
GU	*Guds Uforanderlighed*	*The Unchangeableness of God*
IC	*Indøvelse i Christendom*	*Training in Christianity*
JSK	*Papirer*	*The Journals of Søren Kierkegaard*
KG	*Kjerlighedens Gjerninger*	*Works of Love*
LA	*En literair Anmeldelse*	*Two Ages*
LF	*Lilien pa Marken och Fuglen under Himlen*	*The Lilies of the Field and the Birds of the Air*
OTA	*Opbyggelige Taler i forskjellig Aand*	1. *Purity of Heart is to Will One Thing* 2. *The Lilies and the Birds* 3. *The Gospel of Suffering*
Ø	*Øieblikket nos. 1–10*	"The Instant" in *Attack Upon Christendom*
PS	*Philosophiske Smuler*	*Philosophical Fragments*

ACRONYM	DANISH TITLE	ENGLISH TITLE
SD	*Sygdommen til Døden*	*The Sickness Unto Death*
SFV	*Synspunktet for min For-fatter-Virksomhed*	*The Point of View for My Work as an Author*
T	*Atten opbyggelige Taler*	*Edifying Discourses*
TAF	*To Taler ved Altergangen om Fredagen*	*Two Discourses at the Communion on Fridays*
TS	*Til Selvprøvelse, Samtiden anbefalet*	*For Self-Examination*
TTL	*Tre Taler ved taenkte Leiligheder*	*Thoughts on Crucial Situations in Human Life*
YTS	*Ypperstepraesten, Tolderen, Synderinden*	*The High Priest, the Publican, the Woman that was a Sinner*

KIERKEGAARD: THE DESCENT INTO GOD

Introduction

HERE ARE THREE REMARKS from Søren Kierkegaard's works:

The only analogy I have before me is Socrates. My task is a Socratic task, to revise the definition of what it is to be a Christian.... (Ø, 283)

In a formal sense I can very well call Socrates my teacher—whereas I have only believed, and only believe, in One, the Lord Jesus Christ (*SFV*, 41)

...I am and was a religious author...; the whole of my work as an author is related to Christianity, to the problem of becoming a Christian.... (*SFV*, 5)

My book consists of reflections on these claims. What has Socrates to do with Christ? How does Socrates point towards becoming a Christian? What can be Socratic about an essentially religious authorship? How can learning from a philosopher relate to religious faith? What do scepticism, logic, and metaphysics have to do with belief?

These questions have scholarly and historical dimensions. They might lead us into Plato and the New Testament, into the whole history of the influence of Greek philosophy on Christian theology, into the study of SK's own reading and training. But I am going in a different direction. For the questions have also quite general implications. They make us think about the relations between morality and religion, between moral thinking and religious reflection, between moral belief and religious faith, between moral philosophy and theology. Seen in this way, SK's writings raise deep and universal questions—and offer deep and coherent solutions to them. The questions are not scholarly or historical. They are questions which must raise themselves in the minds of everyone who reflects about morality or religion.

SK's writings are extraordinarily varied. Some were printed under pseudonyms, some under pseudonyms with SK's name added on the page, some under his own name. Their subjects are varied, too: from bedroom farce to the Atonement. They are diverse also in deeper ways. In genre, they range from the novella through the philosophical treatise to the unspoken sermon and the prophetic pamphlet—each often uniquely developed: in discipline and style, correspondingly. Now, the remarks I quoted above imply that this whole authorship holds together by some unifying principle. But of what kind? It can be a unity only of *intention* or purpose. The authorship holds together as a single project. It is what SK is trying to bring about in his reader that remains constant and single. Indeed, he says as much: "Corresponding to this authorship there is an originator who, as author, 'has only willed one thing'" (*FV*, 143). That one thing is "the religious." It is to this single-minded intention that "Socratic task" and "the problem of becoming a Christian" refer us. The sense in which SK always was a religious author is this: his authorship was essentially *edifying*. It is unified as a single huge project of edification, manifest as much in pseudonymous, critical, or prophetic works as in the simply and directly edifying discourses. It is aimed at his contemporaries— and at himself. And it is *both* Socratic *and* Christian.

I

What, then, does SK mean by "Socrates"? Two things, primarily: the ethical and the individual. SK saw Socrates as the inventor (discoverer) of both conceptions. And it is in this light that his grand project of edification is Socratic. For edification is an essentially ethical project, and it goes from individual to individual. What does SK mean, then, by the "ethical"? The *absolute*, and the *inward* (notions associated with Kant, but equally central in Plato's *Apology*—which is for SK the paradigm of ethical writing). "Absolute" has a double sense. The demands of morality are seen increasingly clearly to be absolute, and they are given a correspondingly absolute priority in one's existence (thus *OTA1* and *SD*). At the same time, the locus of the ethical is inward, not external. Its demands are given only to the individual's self-examination, to conscience. (The Good is an intentional concept, as it is in Aristotle.) And the ethical is realized only in an individual's inner self and acts: his willing, truth-seeking, loving.

The ethical, in this sense, is a formal notion, *not* to be confused with the pseudonymous idea of ethics as a "stage," or way of existing, between "the aesthetic" and "the religious." In the formal sense, religion and even Christianity can be—indeed must be—essentially ethical. This is why we find the notions of absoluteness and inwardness *everywhere* in SK's works, and why they are stronger and clearer the more rigorously Christian his writings become. Of course, these notions change their forms as their context alters and deepens. But to show this is a crucial part of SK's aims. For, in particular, the way the notions of the absolute and inward work out depends on the conception of *truth* they are associated with; and this conception is systematically deepened throughout SK's work.

Then what is the heart of the ethical—that which Socrates discovered? What is the essential in Socrates? The name "Socrates" is associated in SK's works with many things. Thus: irony, the maieutic method, the doctrine of recollection, the theory that knowledge of the Good entails virtue, and the consistency of belief and life which led him to stake all for the immortality of the soul. (This is historically the Socrates of Plato's early dialogues: the *Apology*, *Phaedo*, *Gorgias*, and *Meno*; though we can detect also the *Symposium* in SK's works.) But the essential in Socrates is none of these; it is, rather, a dictum, an ethical dictum. It is the dictum "Fear most of all to be in error." SK repeats this over and over, more and more urgently. "It is far from being the case that men regard the relationship to truth, relating themselves to the truth, as the highest good, and it is very far from being the case that they Socratically regard being in error in this manner as the worst misfortune. . . . No, to be in error is, quite un-Socratically, what men fear least of all" (*SD*, 42). Or this:

Fear most of all to be in error. This, as everyone knows, is a saying of Socrates: he feared most of all to be in error. Doubtless in one sense Christianity does not teach men to fear, it even teaches them not to fear those who are able to kill the body; yet in another sense it inculcates a still greater fear than that of Socrates. . . . First, however, that which is first, namely, to become mindful of the Christianity of the New Testament, and to this thou wilt be helped by the Socratic fear, fearing most of all to be in error. (Ø, 188)

"Fear most of all to be in error." But what error, and why fear? Error is correlative with truth; one's conception of error—what it is, how it is possible, why it matters—is given in one's conception of truth. At the same time, in principle, is given a method for reaching truth, a method for dissolving error, and a method for distinguishing between them. These are matters, technically, for metaphysics and epistemology. It is one of the fascinations of Plato's work to constantly show the connections (e.g., in the *Phaedo*). But it is there throughout SK, too. There is a constant, systematic, and explicit concern for the metaphysical and epistemological principles of the ethical, in each of its forms.

For Socrates himself, as SK saw it, "truth" was eternal and universal; accessible by "recollection," which is in fact a process of reasoning. "Error" was conversely ignorance; and the method was the maieutic method, a kind of questioning which exposed to the listener his own ignorance—illusion of knowledge—and incited him to start searching for the truth himself. Discovery of the truth would be a sufficient aim. For from knowledge action follows; from knowledge of the Good, virtue. *This* whole picture of the ethical is rejected, not just by SK himself as a Christian, but already by his pseudonym Johannes Climacus speaking for a non-religious "ethics." As Johannes Climacus expounds it in *AE*, the truth—in the sense relevant to ethics—is "subjective": accessible again only inwardly, but this time not through "recollection" but through a deepening *passion*. Error in its primary sense simply means lack of subjectivity, or passion, or decisiveness. The method? The method of searching for truth is simply a deepening of subjectivity, of "ethical pathos," appropriation; and the method of exposing error (and communicating truth insofar as it can be communicated) is the famous "indirect communication." Here already the Socratic picture is decisively rejected. For there is no goal of knowledge, from which action may start out. In fact, there is no *goal* at all for this process. There is only a constant striving.

SK himself, as a Christian, rejects both these accounts. A Christian conception of truth must start, puzzling though this is, from the saying in the Gospel of St. John: "I am the way and the truth and the life." "The truth" is first Christ himself; then his life, the way we are to imitate and follow. And, in a transferred sense, "the truth" may then be identified with the message and teaching of the Gospels: what SK repeatedly refers to as "the Christianity of the New Testament." "Error" means, in the first instance, *sin*. But, by derivation, it means a set of illusions about the truth. (There is, of course, sheer ignorance of the truth, i.e., of Christianity and Christ. But SK is not so concerned with this in his writings, since the contemporaries he was writing for were at least nominally Christians.) It means illusions about what Christianity demands, what a Christian life is, and what Christian faith consists in. If so, the "method" becomes simply *the way*. The only method of seeking the truth is following Christ (i.e., *loving*). And what about the Christian correlative for "maieusis" and "indirect communication"? That is *edification*, the edifying. Of this there are many kinds, from apostolic teaching, "witnessing for the truth," and ordinary authoritative preaching to the kinds of writing in SK's authorship.

2

What is edification? The word "edify" has acquired in English dreary and repulsive connotations: preachifying, rhetoric which is essentially dishonest—Dickensian and Pharisaical. We have to wipe these out of our minds. We can do so by going back to etymology. "Edify," like the Danish *opbyggen*, literally means *build*. Both words are exact equivalents of the Greek *oikodomein*, which St. Paul uses, and which SK is translating. So edification is a kind of building, not just of the intellect or the psyche in general, as in education and psychotherapy, but specifically of the moral and religious in us. We might say it is a building of the moral self, of the self in us as a moral (religious) self. SK, following St. Paul, calls this *spirit* (*Aand*)—sometimes "will" or "heart," "inwardness," "continuity," or "passion." And he explains it as being *love*.

The activity of edification is both practical and reflective. It is practical, not purely theoretical, because its final aim is action, not contemplation. But it is also reflective, because it works through the listener's (reader's) understanding. For in a nutshell, it means getting the listener, through his understanding, to reflect on the ethical implications, the application, of what he is hearing and to be moved thereby to new or renewed resolution for his own life. Each part of this definition is crucial. If I do not try to appropriate what I am hearing to my own life, then my thinking is either frivolous or hypocritical. If I do not move towards a resolution, it has been merely imaginative (in either case, not genuine moral thinking). And if the movement does not operate through my reflection, then it bypasses my freedom, autonomy, and rationality: so whatever emerges cannot be a moral resolution or action.

It belongs to this picture that edification—moral teaching—must be specific, differential. What you say and how you say it must depend on who you are speaking to. For it depends on how intelligent the listener is, how literate, how educated; on how he sees things, on what his deep beliefs are; in particular, on where he stands morally. (SK does not think that moral teaching can *make* anyone moral. Unlike other kinds of teaching, edification works only by presupposing that the listener already has within himself the essence of what one is trying to build up.) This general principle shows why edifying writing is so various. At one end, serious literature, from tragedy and moral fiction to satire and farce (Moliere,

Rabelais, Aristophanes, Swift). At the other, pure moral philosophy—regarded, following Aristotle, as a practical, not a theoretical, pursuit. In between, many genres of the directly edifying: sermons, parables, treatises on prayer or devotion, wisdom collections, books of popular morality, and so on. Each is needed, to do its specific work. Aristotle thought that "the young" would not benefit from ethics; puritans will get little from Rabelais, sceptics, from St. John of the Cross; or those who cannot read, obviously, from books.

Still, every genre of the edifying involves reflection of one sort or another. This means that *theory* is present within all edification; though in different mixes, in different aesthetic guises, and with different connections to practice (resolution, the will). Only in pure moral philosophy is it presented purely and nakedly, and in its full logical rigour and coherence. In all other genres, it is bedded in the specific rhetoric and structure. *Rhetoric* is the key concept. It stands for everything which unites "content" and "form"—everything which makes the aesthetic features of a text a necessary part of the expression of its (ethical) message. This concept is basic to literary criticism, and without it we cannot understand edifying writing.

Thus, suppose we think of "rhetoric" in the popular modern sense: as ornamental decoration, empty of sense and content, plastered on a text's surface. "Rhetoric" now looks like a mere set of devices for turning the audience on. The message, the statement, gets only to the understanding and so is powerless by itself to stir resolution, whereas rhetoric—being an emotive use of language, a use of emotive language—evokes an emotional response and so moves the listener to act. In this picture, edifying writing is interpreted as ethical theory dressed up persuasively, a bitter pill disguised under sugar. Simply and directly edifying writing has suffered most from this distorting picture; for example, the central edifying discourses of SK (*T, TTL, OTA, KG, CT, LF, GU*). It has often been found difficult to read these discourses seriously, because both their form and their rhetoric are unfamiliar and misunderstood and then, naturally, are felt as artificial and deceiving. Now, my book is greatly concerned with just these writings. It is one of my aims to recapture this part of SK for moral philosophy, to show that these discourses are not windy literature but deep fine thinking, crammed full with sharp conceptual analyses and powerful arguments *of a most respectable kind*—that is, to start digging out the *theory* they contain.

I now quote at length a striking passage out of *IC*, for this can lead us from the reflective element in edification to the practical.

Say not that this stress upon words is hair-splitting pedantry, at the remotest remove from edification; and believe me it is highly important that a man's speech be accurate and true, for so then will his thought be. And furthermore, although to understand and to speak rightly is not everything, inasmuch as one is also required to act rightly, yet in relation to action the right understanding is like the spring-board from which the jumper makes his leap. The clearer, the more exact, the more passionate (in a good sense) one's understanding of a matter is, by just so much does it lighten one's weight for action, or just so much easier is it for one who has to act to render himself light for action.... (*IC*, 158)

These words are a powerful defence of what is now called "analytical philosophy"—a phrase which rightly names not a particular modern school but a practice common to all serious philosophers since Plato. They are a defence of *theory* within even edifying contexts (the passage itself occurs in one of the discourses of pt. 3). At the same time, they defend it because of its practical function. SK defends clarification for the sake of right action.

Another, still later, remark will illustrate further. "This is the task; but the task has a double direction. It is in the direction of seeing what can be done by way of clarifying men's concepts, teaching them, moving them by means of the ideals, bringing them by pathos into a state of suffering, stirring them up by the gadfly-sting of irony, derision, sarcasm, etc., etc." (Ø, 97). It is the theoretical function of edifying discourse to clarify and present a right conception of the Good. Without this, our whole picture of morality and practice must be a confused mess. (Analogy: with an inadequate conception of truth, our picture of knowledge is confused.) *And so will our moral practice be, too.* (Analogy: our knowledge will be a mess, too.)

In this light, edifying writing is primarily an attack on (rational) barriers and defences against right action. (This is the *ethical* element in Christian edification.) The edifier aims at a particular close relation between thinking and doing. For it is a mark of Christian reflection—the proper use of practical thinking in a Christian existence—to be immediately active. It is central in SK's understanding of Christianity that a Christian need not be clever, learned, worldly-wise. Its teaching is not difficult. It is not profound (like say Plato). It is fearfully simple. Thus, "Give all thy goods to the poor" (see *TS*, 59). We like to think that this is hard to understand, but the truth is that we are reluctant to understand—for then we would be obliged to obey! Now, the edifier aims at the state in which understanding is translated immediately into action. For delay causes poor translation. And this is the real deep aim of most practical thinking: to create "interpretations," difficulties, complex calculations, excuses, etc., etc.

I want to stress this idea of practical reason, for it is central in SK's whole picture of ethics and ethical teaching. The psyche is seen primarily as an organized system of defences: defences against looking inwards at oneself, against searching the deeps, against admitting reality, against genuine passion. They are manifold: the habit of objective reflection; losing oneself in the external; apathy, even death, of the spirit; diverting pathos into the aesthetic (physical pleasures, art, fantasy, romance); ordinary self-delusion and self-deceit; and so on. Within this picture, by far the most serious disorders of the human psyche are not active but passive: denials, rejections, avoidings—loss, waste, coldness, emptiness, barrenness. SK actually speaks of Christendom as laying waste the significance of life for us (Ø, 141). It is consistent with this picture that SK sees the ethical as analogous to medicine. He even calls Christianity a "radical cure" (*B17*). The analogy goes right back to Plato, in whose thinking it is quite fundamental (the *Gorgias*, the *Republic*). But it is also traditionally Christian. It is in these contexts, not in the much narrower derivative context of Freudian psychoanalytic theory and practice, that we ought to read SK's psychology. (In fact, SK foresaw that psychoanalysis would be used to try to resolve spiritual problems—disastrously: see the passage on *DS*, 210, about the doctor's attitude to a guilty conscience.)

But of course the "radical cure" is so only in relation to the Christian diagnosis of spiritual sickness. And this is relative to the Christian conception of the human spirit, which is radically different from psychoanalytic theory and moral philosophy, even Plato's. We must put another point beside this. Edification, and the spiritual cure, work only through the individual's own efforts. And these must be inward, since what is to be clarified and cured is itself the inward: the will, the spirit, the deep self. So self-examination is necessary. But self-examination is not just a condition for the cure, a means to it; it is the central part of the process itself, of the edification, the clarification, the spiritual healing. Self-examination is the ethical in the whole process.

But, as we must distinguish Christian edification from moral teaching (Johannes Climacus or Plato-Socrates) and psychotherapy, so we must distinguish SK's Christian understanding of self-examination from ethical and psychoanalytical ideas. Self-examination begins in *fear*. SK writes of himself: "I have worked to awaken *disquietude* with the aim of effecting inward change" (*TS*, 45; my emphasis). "For what is the edifying? The first answer to this tells what the edifying first is: it is the *dismaying* (*CT*,

101). For the edifying is for the sick, the spiritually sick. "To the supposedly healthy and strong it must therefore in the first instance appear as the dismaying." It is dismaying to be shown that although I thought myself healthy, I am really "sick unto death," and that what I thought was my health in reality is my sickness. For the edifying is the Good in-and-for-itself: the inversion of our "healthy" conceptions of the Good. So edification can begin only in *contrition*. *This* is the kind of self-knowledge at issue, and the matching self-examination is *contrite* self-examination: shame, humility, remorse; not narcissism, not interest in myself, not even the demands of science (Freud's self-analysis).

This links up with love, because the spirit's health is loving, its sickness unloving. To edify is to build up love; but this cannot begin until the "ground" is cleared, the self emptied of rubbish. The first task of edification is to tear down, destroy, empty. For this is also the first part of ethical and spiritual growth. After that, the growth of love. And thus SK explains the apparent paradox that the honest teaching of Christianity— which is a doctrine of *love*—must be so much more rigorous and severe than any other ethical teaching. For Christianity locates far deeper in the self than any other doctrine does the springs of the self's vision of, and assent to, absolute Good. These springs cannot be unlocked except by an act of self-penetration correspondingly deep, painful, annihilating. (But *after* that "the consolation and the comfort and the cure".)

3

This, then, is my picture of SK's authorship—without the Attack literature. It is about these themes that I am going to reflect in the studies that follow. Their central thesis is easily stated. In SK's view, the essence of the ethical existence is self-examination. But self-examination leads—given the nature of the human self and reflection—towards revelation of the self's nothingness and acceptance of it; that is, towards a self-annihilation before the absolute. At this point, the individual is prepared for the reality of God. Why does the process go like this? Because inwardness, conscience, is the locus not only of ethical claims but also of religious ones (a view Johannes Climacus ascribes already to Socrates). This gives the inner life, the life of self-reflection, its danger and its promise. Once an individual has penetrated himself so deeply that he can hear the true voice of duty speaking to him, he has opened a breach in the wall between himself and God, and he can no longer control the consequences. The more strongly and clearly he hears that voice, the more absolute, so to speak, will its demands appear. For there is lying in wait for him at last, deep within himself, that real Absolute whose voice conscience is, and which a Christian knows as God.

I begin with an account of SK's central ideas about ethical belief. Two issues dominate these analyses. First, I have tried to bring out various intertwined strands in the complex idea of "subjective truth" to show how SK deliberately relates logical and epistemological ideas to psychological and ethical issues. I have tried to display some of the enormously intricate thinking which underlies his constant insistence that the right answer to the question, What ought I to believe? is Love!—and then believe what love believes. And, second, I have tried to show where the essential connection between ethical belief and self-examination lies. In SK's view, as probably in Socrates' too, no "ethical belief" really deserves the name unless the individual who claims it actually tries to live by it, to shape his decisions and acts by it. He must be constantly trying (not necessarily succeeding) to apply it rightly to himself. SK usually calls this "appropriation" (*Tilegnelse*). Now, a constant attempt to appropriate my ethical beliefs entails a constant self-accounting, in ethical terms: a constant effort to judge myself clearly and honestly, and in turn a constant striving to open myself as transparently as I can to my own sight and understanding. The ideal must be a perfect self-transparency. In SK's view, this is humanly impossible. It is a very important step in the process of self-uncovering to recognize that (and why) I cannot reach perfectly clear and honest self-judgment. At this point, we are left with either despair or faith.

Now, recall that SK's writing is intended for *edification*. This means that it is not just theory. It is intended to be appropriated and used by its readers—by each one of us, for his or her unique ethical and religious growth. Self-examination is not, therefore, simply an interesting theoretical topic *within* the authorship (though it certainly is that). It is at the very heart of the *purpose* of the authorship. In analysing the relations between self-examination and the ethical and Christian existences, SK is writing to provoke his readers to individual self-examination *of* their unique ethical or Christian existences.

The shape of the authorship clearly mirrors this intention. SK did not think that there was just one (one correct) conception of self-examination or self-knowledge. There must be as many distinct conceptions of self-knowledge as there are of the self. Roughly speaking, to each ethico-religious level of understanding there answers a specific conception of self-knowledge. There may also be "ethical" systems in which the idea of self-knowledge plays no particular role; but that, for SK as much as for Socrates, would itself say something damning about such systems and world-views. (Nor, significantly, would such systems strike most people in our time as serious.)

If so, it is an essential part of SK's project, for both theoretical and practical reasons, to construct a series of accounts of self-knowledge and self-examination. This is part of the task of leading the reader through the relevant series of ethical and religious positions. And indeed we do find, in the edifying as well as pseudonymous works, a constant preoccupation with the ideas of self-examination and self-knowledge. But we also find a constant progressive deepening in the analysis, just as there is a deepening in the ideas themselves. Suppose we begin, hypothetically, with the picture sketched by Socrates in the *Apology*—which is precisely where we are actually meant to begin. From there, we go on to the deeper and more complex—but still "Socratic"—account developed by Judge William in *EE2*. Then there is the whole theory of subjectivity and ethical reality given by Johannes Climacus in *AE*. Next, we leap to the religious understanding, displayed in *OTA1*, which turns on the notion of confession and the eternal. Beyond that lies Anti-Climacus and *SD*. At last, there is the specifically Christian doctrine: self-knowledge is truly available to an individual only insofar as, being conscious of himself as in bondage to sin, he has won faith in the forgiveness of sins, mysteriously offered on the Cross.

My book does not contain any serious study of SK's theology. The two last chapters are meant only to suggest that his "ethics" points towards a "theology," without which it is incomplete. In chapter 9, I survey from a great height some of the conceptual terrain which needs to be explored, philosophically and reflectively. In chapter 10, I offer a brief sketch, from one angle, of the heart and centre of SK's thought and existence—the figure of Jesus Christ. I would like to add one remark. If we think of SK in theological, not philosophical, terms, then we can substitute for his phrases "becoming a Christian" and "what it is to be a Christian" the word *prayer*, or perhaps *worship*. SK's authorship is all about worship, the life of worship, and the place of worship in life. Certainly it is decisively post-Cartesian, post-Kantian, and post-Hegelian. SK regarded each of these thinkers as disastrously wrong. Still, he accepted the evident fact that they had altered the terms for epistemology and metaphysics, and so also for any philosophical engagement with ethics or religion. But he did not imagine that it followed that the *truth* had altered (nor could this be possible for one who accepted the Christianity of the New Testament). So his theology, if I may speak out of ignorance, remains almost wholly orthodox and traditional—non-sectarian. He uses contemporary idioms to restate familiar themes of Christian teaching, as found, say, in Thomas a Kempis's *Imitation of Christ*, St. John of the Cross's *Ascent of Mount Carmel*, P. de Caussade's *Abandonment to Divine Providence*, or William Law's *Serious Call*.

In a now famous poem, St. John of the Cross wrote:

> To come to be what you are not
> you must go by a way in which you are not.

And these lines express neatly the doctrine of the necessity of absolute self-abnegation that is central in Christian thinking and practice. Central no less in SK's writings. What is original, perhaps, is that he boldly sets out to construct a system (and theory) of edification which begins *before* the beginning of a genuine spiritual life, and proceeds rigorously through the subsequent stages up to the life of ordinary Christian devotion— though not beyond, to the life of religious, for whom many of those earlier books were written.

4

This book consists of a number of essays. "Essay" means "attempt," and each essay paints an attempt to reflect about an idea within SK's work. The essays will form a coherent set if the ideas they analyse are interrelated. And they will form a series if these ideas are nodal points of a real, though unstated, theory. But if there is a theory within SK's edifying literature, why do I not treat it as philosophical theories are usually treated? Because the theory belongs within a context of edification. Because the method of my analysis matches methods of SK's exposition of his theory. And because his methods of exposition express both the *content* of the writing and its *intention*.

These essays have two distinct characters. Sometimes they are dialectical. These are argumentative—and self-argumentative—attempts to make sense out of various passages and themes from SK's works. Here I ask questions, suggest possible lines of thought, open conceptual complexities. At other times the essays are more straightforward, expositions of text or statements of theory, as I understand it.

In part, this distinction of character reflects a division of topics or depth of treatment. The dialectical passages deal with relatively elementary treatments, which are in general "Socratic." Here, the approach tends to be logical or epistemological: what is belief, what is knowledge, what is self-knowledge, what is the self, what is truth? The more directly expository passages have to do with SK's specifically Christian reflections. I am in particular concerned to begin the analysis of SK's conception of love, *agape*, and of the relation between the concepts of love and selfhood. But only begin, for I have consciously stopped short of penetrating SK's metaphysics. It is a profoundly important and characteristic idea of his that the self—its nature, even its reality—is a function of its object; not simply the object of reflection, but the object of willing (what I essentially *am* is a function of my conception of the Good). In consequence, the human self is fully realized, becomes its true self, only in accepting the full rigours of Christian faith. I stop short of these matters, since I am here analysing a way, not its goal.

But there are more general reasons for the dialectical method of my analysis and argument. The first is just that the central concept is self-examination. Now, I am concerned not just with explicating this concept, in some of its forms, but also with exploring its place and role within moral philosophy generally, that is, the place and role of self-examination in the ethical existence. And, beyond that still, I am concerned with *the bearing of moral philosophy on self-examination*. (As my book will show, I find this term vastly preferable to the more common "self-knowledge".)

Certainly there has been a good deal of writing about the self and self-examination in recent philosophy—both phenomenological and "analytical." This has not been independent, obviously, of contemporary theorizing in psychoanalysis. But these discussions have not on the whole addressed the moral and ethical issues. They have rather plainly contributed little to moral philosophy. It is a very great merit of SK, regarded strictly as philosopher, to have placed the topic of self-examination firmly at the centre of ethical theorizing, by replacing the activity of self-examination firmly at the heart of the ethical existence. He has only one predecessor—Socrates—and only one worthy successor—Simone Weil. Yet it is clear that self-examination is a basic constituent of any authentic existence in the modern world (varieties of explanation: Heidegger, Philip Rieff, Erving Goffman). If one thinks about self-examination, a wholly new light shines on every important issue in moral philosophy, and in the ethical life too. No wonder there is such a gap between our psychological and ethical understanding! Moral philosophy has just been left behind by the understandings of human nature and the self developed by Freud and later psychoanalysts, or for that matter, too, by modern writers: Dostoyevsky, Chekhov, Proust, Henry James, Conrad. It is really in this sense that moral philosophy today needs a new psychology and that, lacking a deep account of self-reflection, moral philosophy remains pathetically thin, unrealistic, ungripping, unedifying.

It is one aim of my book to suggest that this is not just a question of choice but one of conceptual connections and so of necessity. (But only suggest, for my book is not that rigorous treatise which is required here.) I mean that a moral philosophy without self-knowledge is not just an impoverished but still viable option. It is not an option at all, for it cannot offer a coherent analysis of its central concepts: moral standards, principles, goals; moral decision, criticism, self-assessment; "ought"; "good." Nor can it give any account of edifying literature, moral fiction, the relations between psychology and morality, the role of the idea of mental health in relation to morality, or the idea of moral growth. It cannot give any convincing account of evil, temptation, or sin. And, to the objection that these are topics of theology, not moral philosophy, I reply that it takes a deeply impoverished moral philosophy to lose connection with moral theology. But all these are matters for further study.

No, the point I want to make here concerns the nature of the concept of self-examination, the nature of the concept of self-knowledge. There are vast intrinsic difficulties and complexities in this concept. Some are of a kind common to all moral concepts, and some of a kind common to all concepts having to do with the idea of self and self-reflection. But there are also difficulties of quite another sort. In general, it is a basic feature of all ethical concepts (widest possible sense) that they are not the sort of thing we can recognize, identify, grasp, understand, discuss, analyse, explicate *objectively*—from *outside*. They are concepts which can be grasped only through and in one's own experience and existence. They can be grasped only through and in one's actually *using* them in one's moral existence. "Experience" and "existence" mean *individual* experience and existence. Thus, *my* understanding of the concept of temptation depends essentially on my having come across this concept—that is, having seriously *used* it—in my own life and of my own life. No quantity of reading, listening to sermons (or confessions), giving counsel, and the like, can do anything to fill the gap which only personal appropriation can fill. (Debt here acknowledged to Iris Murdoch, who once wrote illuminatingly that moral concepts are *concrete universals*.)

It is a direct consequence of this *logical* feature that one's understanding of a moral concept—just like one's understanding of a moral issue—essentially has a *level*. The level corresponds to one's morally reflective experience (appropriation). Another way of making this point: people *necessarily* have differing conceptions of virtue, duty, temptation, and so on, including necessarily different-level conceptions of self-knowledge and self-examination.

Now, it is clear, as a matter of fact, that people do have very different conceptions of self-knowledge and self-examination and that these match very different habits of self-examination and degrees of self-knowledge (if any). Aristotle has reason on his side, for example, when he says that young people cannot be a good audience for moral philosophy. For they simply cannot yet have had, with rare exceptions, the kind of experience that is needed to give a deep, or even a real, insight into, say, commitment, or patience, or lasting happiness—or self-knowledge. Yet age is not the only variable, and not the most important. Advancing years do not by themselves bring self-knowledge or an understanding of what self-knowledge is and what it requires; no more than they bring of themselves virtue, commitment, patience, or a lasting happiness. Middle-aged and old people are not intrinsically wiser or better than their juniors. All too often, in fact, the years, and bitter experience, bring not more light but less: a growing narrowness, defensiveness, hostility, superficiality, self-delusion. This is one of SK's most constant and penetrating themes. He writes, for one example, about Socrates: "He had perceived that young men still had a receptivity for the divine, a receptivity which is very easily lost in the passage of the years, in trade and commerce, in erotic love and friendship, in subjection to merely human judgement and the demands of the times" (*KG*, 131).   In *CT*, he returns several times to the theme: "He desires now to sink down in the inanity of worldliness, there to seek forgetfulness, forgetfulness of the most dangerous thought..., the thought of existing before God.... Then the spirit's light goes out...." (*CT*, 91). Such a man has lost himself; he his literally no longer a self, no longer a man, but—however successful, admired, or famous—only a number. So, like Dostoyevsky, SK continually urges his reader to heed the gospel message to "turn and become like children," not to "cut away all communication with childhood" (*AE*, 311).

There are, then, other important variables: vanity, egocentricity, superficiality, all the forms of block and defence and escape from self-insight. All give a shallow or, worse, distorted conception of self-knowledge and self-examination. A clear and deep conception depends wholly on the individual's practice of self-examination, just as clear and deep self-insight does. Both can be won only through practising the disciplines of self-knowledge through a lifetime, continuously, truthfully, deeply. If "the light of the spirit" has gone out, then however cultivated and intelligent, one will have only an obscure, confused, and dark picture of what self-knowledge is and what it demands. Conversely, the more we seriously try to know ourselves and see ourselves, the more we look into ourselves questioningly and critically, the more obvious it becomes that we do not in fact know ourselves well or see ourselves clearly. The more visible become the operations of blocking, defence, escape. The more clearly do we recognize the *intrinsic* (and often purposive) inadequacy of earlier self-examinations and self-judgments. And the more it grows on us that both self-examination and self-deceit are essentially *ethical* projects, that self-knowledge is essentially an ethical goal and ideal. In sum, as we know ourselves more deeply, we see self-knowledge as deeper and more demanding. The depth of our understanding of self-knowledge corresponds to the depth of our self-knowledge.

I will put the general point schematically, and to that extent unilluminatingly. A man's conception and practice of self-knowledge depends on how he conceives "right and wrong" and "truth." It depends, first, on his understanding of notions (phenomena) like these: his own wrongdoing, guilt, need to make reparation; the place of suffering in human existence; humility; temptation, self-control, weakness, "really trying"; excuses, flattering pictures, and so on; the depth and pervasiveness of evil in himself, that is, his will not to do good or be good. It depends, second, on his understanding of notions like these: truth, in relation to claims about actions, motives, character, and so on; objectivity of vision, especially about himself; a "will to truth," or its lack; perspective; and breadth. ("Understanding" here means, of course, understanding through, in, application and practice, not external analysis.) It is not accidental that in the *Apology* two qualities stand out as intrinsic to self-knowledge: humility and wisdom. Over much of this ground I shall be going, in a highly unschematic way, in the essays that follow.

How, then, may we philosophize about, analyze the concept of, self-knowledge, self-examination? Three points, again briefly. First, "analysis" of a concept which has the general logical nature I have indicated must be *phenomenological* (rather non-technical sense). It must consist of a series of richly constructed paradigms, each an imagined type, showing levels of self-knowledge in full complexity. That is, a series of realistic pictures of individual human existences. *This is exactly what SK's "experimenting" and "psychological" mean.* My book is not such an analysis. It is a discussion pointing to one, namely SK's. Second, the "analysis" must be reflective, so argumentative. (I entirely accept Gilbert Ryle's view that philosophy, which is essentially conceptual analysis, is essentially experimental logic.) Reflective, for this reason: the topic of self-examination, and the others with which it is connected, are in their nature constant and permanent subjects for our individual reflective exploration. Certainly, my thinking about, say, self-deceit or love or God is likely to change with the years. But these are not notions about which I can ever be justified in saying, Now I have thought enough about this, it is time to go on to something else. And of course my reflections, I hope, move. They move because of my experience, but also because of my thinking: my clarifyings, distinguishings, connectings, inferrings, reasonings. So, to have written my book as a linear treatise would have obscured and denied, in its form, this basic feature of the ideas which are its subject. Third (we cannot avoid the embarrassing admission), to write about self-knowledge involves the writer in revealing his level of understanding of the whole matter. At the same time, it should make him reflect about this, and thus reflect about his own self-knowledge—such as it is. For in writing about self-knowledge, he must use his understanding of it. And so he must use his own self-knowledge. These facts are embarrassing, because we like to keep philosophy distinct from autobiography, literature, the perspectival. But it seems that we cannot.

5

The second general reason for the dialectical method of my analysis is that all philosophical thinking is essentially dialectical. For it is essentially argument, that is, arguing: making up, destroying, and rebuilding arguments. Here, I shall take two points. First, philosophical arguments very rarely have conclusions. Second, philosophical arguing is a kind of dialogue.

Philosophical arguments very rarely, perhaps never, have anything like an accepted conclusion. I do not mean that they consist just of premises. I mean that if you look at the actual history of philosophy, you will find few or no arguments which are accepted as conclusive: as finally proving some thesis, establishing its truth beyond all question, giving it henceforth the status of takeable for granted. Certainly we often find *within* particular systems or treatises arguments which are intended to be conclusive in that way, these intended (perhaps believed) to be conclusively established. (This is especially true of modern philosophy: think of the aims of Descartes, Hobbes, Spinoza, Kant, or Hegel.) But in practice these arguments and claims are immediately and almost universally disputed. And rightly, not just out of contentiousness. For there exists *no* philosophical argument—except possibly Zeno's paradoxes—which is anywhere near to obvious soundness. What first looked like an odd historical fact now begins to look rather deeper and stranger. It is not just a sociological oddity that philosophers always dispute all philosophical claims. It lies in the nature of *assertions* in relation to philosophical thinking. And this means that it lies in the nature of the ideas of *truth* and *knowledge* as they relate to philosophical thinking.

Assertions have a peculiar role in philosophical thinking. As Plato saw, they never have the role of an axiom or assumption, except for the artificial purposes of teaching or debate. They always have the role of topic for analysis and argument. Now this is not, in fact, as peculiar as it appears. For something very similar, *mutatis mutandis*, holds also for history and even for science. It is a common picture that historians and scientists discover truths, which they add to a growing body of established knowledge. What actually goes on in libraries and laboratories is quite different, which suggests, again, that the ideas of truth and knowledge play quite different roles in historical and scientific thinking from the roles they are commonly supposed to. Still, despite this convergence, philosophy remains unique. This is because philosophical *method*—the proper methods and forms of philosophical arguments—is itself a permanent central topic for philosophical argument. (And this is in turn because the very ideas of truth and knowledge are themselves subjects of philosophical analysis.)

Now it is open for any philosopher, if he likes, to issue a statement about any topic. But this has little to do with the activity of philosophizing as I understand it. For philosophizing is exploring, exploring difficulties and darknesses. When we think philosophically, we think about a number of ideas and claims which are usually only *vaguely* distinct and *vaguely* related to each other. And almost all of them are also intrinsically complex. Philosophical exploration is above all an attempt to discover and throw light on the complexities and vaguenesses. The kinds of ideas and claims philosophers discuss do not exist, so to speak, on their own. They are what they are only in virtue of their relations with other ideas and claims. It makes no sense, then, to imagine philosophy as explanation or theory in anything like the senses of science—still less, mathematics or logic. There, one aims at the linear: at clarifying elements one by one, at defining their relations, at moving step by step from the primitive to the derived. Thinking which resembles that is not philosophical. Philosophical thinking means, rather, circling around a piece of conceptual terrain, approaching its parts now from one side, now from another. The ideas and claims start revealing their complexities only when looked at from many different perspectives. Wittgenstein once wrote, "A perspicuous representation produces just that kind of understanding which consists in seeing connections." And it is intrinsic to this sort of exploration that it can have no *rules*, no single universal pattern, method, theory.

Now my second point: philosophical arguing is a kind of dialogue. Here again, we seem to have just an empirical fact—and one that is not always so, either. There have been famously solitary and independent philosophers: Descartes, Spinoza, Rousseau, Schopenhauer, Wittgenstein. But against such exceptions we must set these three generalities. First, almost all thinkers think within a community of thinkers. The sciences provide an extremely good example for this rule. And even solitary and independent thinkers communicate with their peers or contemporaries: how vital correspondence was to Descartes, Spinoza, Rousseau. Second, all thinkers think within or in engagement with a tradition of thought (the sciences again here). Both of these apparently empirical generalities have a *necessary* ground. It is simply this: no one could have any thoughts at all unless he belonged to a community, in which he had learned to think such thoughts. Further, philosophy, like the sciences, begins in questioning, not asserting or hypothesizing. And no one could have any questions, unless he had learned something out of which they arose.

Now these truisms do not imply that philosophers must do their thinking out loud in public. But this does not refute my point about dialogue. For dialogue need not be carried on with only the present or living. Much philosophical thinking consists, in fact, of reading other philosophers' writings critically; that is, arguing with them, and also for them, as one reads. However, we perhaps still need my third generality. Philosophers philosophize within communities of teachers and learners, that is, communities of students. Where is philosophy paradigmatically *done*? Where to go if you want to see and hear philosophizing going on? Without doubt, a philosophy classroom in a university. Now, I mean this claim to connect with my earlier claim that within the philosophy all assertions and arguments are essentially disputable. For it is certainly the working practice of all teachers of philosophy to teach their pupils, by example and argument, that in philosophizing *nothing must be taken for granted*. (Which returns us, in a curious way, to Socrates.)

So all attempts to philosophize, or present philosophical thinking, as if it were an individual performance are more or less dishonest. More important, they misrepresent the essence of what is going on and so may mislead the audience, and perhaps also the philosopher himself. This danger can affect teaching; but it is usually not too damaging, since the teacher can lecture in a way that encourages radical questioning. But the *writing* of philosophy is a much more dubious project. Now, in practice, philosophers usually send out copies of their early drafts to each other, asking for criticisms, questions, comments, etc.: and then rewrite those drafts accordingly, often many times over. So there is a real, even if not face-to-face, dialogue. It is with publication, as realized in our time, that the danger strikes. For a printed book or an essay in a journal inevitably has the character of a monologue. And, worse still, its form—the form of its argument—is quite unlike anything that happens while actual philosophizing is going on. (I am told that scientific papers usually have the same essential defect of character—falsity to the subject.)

There is only one way of avoiding this disaster: it is to construct artificial dialogues in one's writing. Thus the dialogues of Plato, Augustine, Berkeley, Hume, and the later Wittgenstein, with his many voices. But today, and always unless he is a true artist, the philosopher had better leave the writing of philosophical dialogues to novelists (Dostoyevsky, Mann, Iris Murdoch) and dramatists (Ibsen, Beckett, Stoppard). Only two men have reached greatness in both thought and art: Plato and SK. For the rest of us, there is really only the apology that publication, too, is in its way a contribution to a continuous dialogue that today extends, thanks to the technologies of communication and preservation of knowledge, around the world and across the centuries.

6

One can read and write about a thinker in the spirit of detached and objective scholarship. One may read, and more dubiously write about, him for personal and private edification. I have not intended, in my book, to do either of these things. I have aimed, so to speak, to fall between these two stools. My book is an attempt to think appropriatively about SK in such a way as to throw my reader back constantly into SK, and into his or her own appropriative thinking about SK.

Everyone who has penetrated *AE* as far as the Lessing chapter will see what I am trying to do as a clumsy transposition of the procedure Johannes Climacus ascribes to the "subjective existing thinker." (It is worrisome writing about SK; for he wrote so much about the subtleties of writing that you always feel, while you are writing, that he is peering over your shoulder and asking, somewhat ironically, why you think you are writing *in that way*.) I suppose that it is open for a subjective existing thinker to do more than just think—that is, to talk or write. And I imagine that the author of *AE* must have counted himself as a subjective existing thinker; so, if we understood exactly how the techniques of that book tend to throw its reader back appropriatively into self-reflection, we should understand a great deal about what the Socratic can mean in the context of a literary culture, even a professionalized one. I have tried, then, to write this book in something like a genuine Kierkegaardian way (which is *not* claiming unusual rationality, passion, transparency, or maieutic skills). In particular, I have tried not only to *say* what edifying writing is but to *show* it by showing what it is to read an author as edifying, that is, what it is to read appropriatively.

There is a note later in *AE*, in which Johannes Climacus (who is, let us remember, not SK) analyses the notion of a religious discourse. "What counts in this connection is the manner in which the speaker and the listener are related to the discourse or are presumed to be related. The speaker's relation to the discourse must not be merely through the imagination, but as himself being what he speaks about, or striving toward it in his own experience and continuing to have his own specific mode of experience in relation to it" (p. 374). My book is written, not spoken; and philosophical, not religious. But Johannes's words are apt enough. I should like to hope that his next remark fits too: "The listeners must be informed and assisted in becoming that of which the discourse speaks."

I

Ethical Beliefs

IN THIS CHAPTER I try to anatomize SK's theory of ethical belief. I do so only sketchily and partially, for the theory is complex and extensive.

I

First, the general theory of belief. This has two parts. One is an argument that all empirical propositions are logically detachable from their evidence. The other is an argument that a proposition becomes a belief only in an act of assent.

The first idea is not original. SK found it in the sceptics. It is just a form of the idea that there can be no necessary truths about contingents. SK argues for this thesis in *PS*. But he wants to add a positive point to the familiar negative one. So he (Johannes Climacus) writes, "The organ for the historical must have a structure analogous with the historical itself..." (*PS*, 100). This organ is faith. Just as even the most probable empirical proposition may be false, so even the least probable may be true and can therefore be believed without that belief's being necessarily erroneous.

For "faith" we need the second idea. SK wants to distinguish between beliefs and mere propositions. A proposition is a belief only if some individual believes it. But believing is a mental act distinct from "entertaining" and reflecting. A proposition entertained becomes a hypothesis; a proposition reflected on becomes a link in a chain of reasoning. Believing is giving assent to a proposition, and for empirical propositions is assigning the value "Truth." But this is a genuine act and requires a genuine decision. Thus Johannes Climacus writes, "Reflection can be halted only by something else, and this something else is something quite different from the logical, being a resolution of the will" (*AE*, 103). He does not commit the error of identifying the assignation of truth-value to a proposition with asserting the proposition; his "believing" means the same as Frege's late "judging."

A proposition *P* may evidentially ground another proposition *Q*. And, if I believe *P*, I may come to believe *Q* on the ground that *P*. Now, between the propositions *P* and *Q* there is a logical gap; this is bridged by the logical relation of probabilification. But between the beliefs *P* and *Q* there is a psychological gap. And this can be crossed only by an act of the individual mind in real time. Then what is coming to believe *Q* on the ground that *P*? It is to believe *P*, to believe that *P* logically probabilifies *Q* to a reasonable degree; and to decide therefore to assent to *Q*. Each stage in this process is itself a result, the result of a process of the same sort. So not only does no result determine any later result; no earlier result has support of a sort different from the support available for later results.

These arguments do not imply that we can believe propositions only as the results of processes of inference, for example, proofs. Some propositions can be believed immediately. But Johannes Climacus writes, "The 'what' of a happening may be known immediately, but by no means can it be known immediately that it has happened" (*PS*, 101). Even when believing *Q* does not require crossing the psychological gap in a process of inference, it still requires crossing it in an act of assent. To be aware of an event's "what" is not assent or belief; it is just "entertaining" (Frege's "thinking"). So all empirical belief whatever requires performing an act of assent, that is, faith.

This general theory of belief has two roles in SK's theory of ethical belief. It brings the ideas of belief and action into a certain relation. And it detaches the idea of belief from a certain idea of rationality.

The idea of action is roughly distinguishable from the ideas of process, event, condition, state, and so on. Part of the distinction is that action verbs can be intelligibly qualified by certain modal phrases. These include "can," "try to," the deontic "ought," and so on. We ordinarily feel strain in attaching such phrases to "believe." Now, SK's arguments show that belief must involve a certain action. So they imply that these modal phrases, through being applicable to the action verb "assent," are applicable also to "believe." SK uses this part of his theory to clear logical space for the thesis that there may be propositions we ought (ought not) to believe, or to try to believe. And this thesis is important in the edifying works.

The idea of rationality is roughly this: rationality requires us to believe any empirical proposition *Q* with a degree of strength ("certainty") matching the degree of *Q*'s probabilification by its evidence. Rationality then forbids us to pretend certainty about any empirical proposition; and it forbids us to assent to any such proposition *Q* when *Q*'s probability is less than not-*Q*'s.

SK's first criticism consists in reaffirming the distinction between logic and psychology ("existence"). We often imagine that evidence which makes a proposition *Q* more probable than not-*Q* thereby also makes believing *Q* more rational than believing not-*Q*. But this cannot be so. For the nature of contingency is such that, to cite Wittgenstein, "there is no possible way of making an inference from the existence of one situation to the existence of another, entirely different situation" (*Tractatus*, 5.135). Whatever has happened earlier, *Q* and not-*Q* have an equal chance of happening in the future. This is why SK speaks in *KG* of being faced with truth and deception "as two equal possibilities" (p. 215). If the ordinary idea of rationality involves confusing logic and psychology, it is irrational to follow it.

SK's second criticism concerns the idea of error in belief. In its straightforward sense, this just means believing a proposition which is false. Error is distinct from irrationality, since a proposition may be well supported by the evidence but false. If so, rationality sometimes requires us to believe a proposition that is false (hence one ground for Feyera-bend-like views on the role of reason in the progress of knowledge).

Now we ordinarily distinguish between the ideas of error in belief and error in action. If SK's theories are sound, this distinction must be re-drawn. We may still allow a sense of error in belief relative just to truth-values. But we must admit a second sense, derived from the action status of beliefs. Error may now be located not in proposition's falsity but in an individual's decision to assent to it. It becomes conceivable that I may "err" in believing *Q* even though *Q* is true or may not "be in error" even if it is false.

The role of these arguments is mainly to clear logical space for a philo-sophical theory of belief in propositions that lack truth-values, especially ethical propositions. They clear space for constructing a coherent idea of error applicable to such beliefs. Truth-valuelessness is no longer a bar; error in an ethical belief may be now taken as a sort of error in action, that is, error in deciding to assent.

Very roughly, a theory of error in action is a theory of the right and wrong thing to do, and the right and wrong ways of doing it, for a particular individual in particular circumstances, and so on. It is a theory of what we ought and ought not to do; and this "ought" ranges, as in

Aristotle, from the purely technical to the moral. So *SK*'s basic theory clears logical space in which we can intelligibly ask, What ought (ought not) a man to believe? And it clears space for the possibility that this question can be asked, and answered, with moral force. It becomes conceivable that in the ethical realm, the "right" and "wrong" beliefs may be those beliefs it is morally right and wrong to adopt. And this thesis is central in *KG*.

2

Next, there is the theory of essential knowledge. Here SK describes a central feature of ethical beliefs. Ethical propositions, propositions ordinarily used to express ethical beliefs, have two semantic peculiarities. They lack truth-values and they are not grounded on empirical evidence. They are not contingent propositions.

If ethical propositions are truth-valueless, then assenting to an ethical proposition is not assigning to it the value "Truth." Still, the fact that we speak of "assent" and "belief" in the ethical does suggest possible use for some idea of truth here. And if ethical propositions are not contingent truths, the rationality of assent in the ethical is not the rationality of probabilification. Then the ideas of right and wrong belief in the ethical can be understood, if at all, only through the idea of error in action, that is, through the idea of right and wrong decision. And "decision" here must mean decision to assent to (or away from) an ethical principle.

What are ethical principles? Consider these words: "All essential knowledge relates to existence, or only such knowledge as has an essential relationship to existence is essential knowledge. All knowledge which does not inwardly relate itself to existence, in the reflection of inwardness, is, essentially viewed, accidental knowledge" (*AE*, 176).

The Socratic dialogues of Plato often illuminate SK's more playfully Hegelian remarks. So here. It is plain that "essential knowledge" recapitulates the discovery Socrates narrates in the *Apology*. There is a kind of knowledge that is unconditionally required for all existence—self-knowledge. "Existence" always means some particular individual's existence. So a belief about existence is a belief about the believer's own existence. Now, a belief is about oneself only if one makes a certain proposition to be about oneself, that is, if one applies the proposition to oneself. Thus essential knowledge is knowledge that an individual has about himself, in virtue of applying some proposition to his own existence. Johannes Climacus is plainly thinking not of any sort of knowledge that we can have about ourselves but of knowledge about our own actions and decisions. But whether or not a piece of knowledge is essential does not depend on the meaning of the proposition that is used to express it; it depends only on whether the individual relates that proposition inwardly to himself.

In *AE*, Johannes Climacus gives four examples of items of possible essential knowledge: death, immortality, Providence, and marriage. But what sort of knowledge? Knowledge only in a Pickwickian sense. For the subjective existing thinker knows about such items only in the sense that he raises about them a certain sort of self-reflective question. The question has the form What does it mean that I . . .? So he asks not just, What does it mean to die? (*AE*, 147) but, What does it mean that I shall die? and, What does it mean to me that I shall die? Essential knowledge is having an answer to a question of this sort.

But precisely what sort of answer? On the purely propositional level, the answer must take the form The fact that I shall die means . . . to me. But qua proposition these words do not yet express a belief. What is required is that this answer should "inwardly relate itself to existence" and "have an essential relationship to existence" (*AE*, 176). The meaning of my death to me lies in a relation between my death and my existence, between my actions and my life. And that meaning is expressed in my existence. So it is I, and I alone, who set meaning to my death in building my past and present life reflectively, and my future intentions decisively, around the reflection that death awaits me.

Surely SK should now replace the Pickwickian idea of knowledge by choice? Yes; and he does. In *EE2* Judge William writes: "The ethical individual knows himself, but this knowledge is not a mere contemplation . . ., it is a reflection upon himself which itself is an action, and therefore I have deliberately preferred to use the expression 'choose oneself' instead of know oneself" (p. 263).

SK therefore analyses ethical principles as principles of meaning. They are principles that an individual uses to give sense to his actuality and direction to his potentialities. The relevant ideas are "recollection," "resolution," and "continuity." There are no ethical propositions as such (Fregean "thoughts"). For no proposition can express an ethical principle except in the act of use by a particular individual as a self-applied meaning-principle. And there are no universal or universalizable ethical principles. For even if two individuals adopt the same propositions as their principles, these principles must differ in virtue of yielding sense and direction for two actually different lives.

To acquire an ethical belief is to come to reflect on one's own life through the idea of commitments that have content in terms of one's actual existence, give shape to that existence, and give direction, coherent with the past, to one's projected decisions. To have an ethical belief is to reflect continuously on one's existence in those terms and to strive continuously to exist in terms coherent with that self-reflection. It is tempting to try to sharpen this account; it would not be useful.

The theory of "essential knowledge" complements SK's basic arguments. For here he identifies a class of beliefs that fill the space those arguments cleared, beliefs whose criterion of error lies not in their propositional content but in a feature of the believer's act of assent.

SK's point is not that all beliefs about oneself are truth-valueless. They are not. There is a simple sort of error about oneself that consists in just getting the facts wrong. But this cannot be the whole story. Consider, briefly, self-deceit. Self-deceit is certainly a sort (genus?) of error about oneself. But it is quite distinct from just getting facts wrong about oneself. If self-knowledge involves choice, so does self-deceit. SK writes: "There is an ignorance about one's life that is equally tragic for the learned and for the simple, for both are bound by the same responsibility. This ignorance is called self-deceit. . . . But there is only one thing that can remove that other ignorance which is self-deception. . . . The ignorant man can gradually acquire wisdom and knowledge, but the self-deluded one if he won 'the one thing needful' would have won purity of heart" (*OTA1*, 52). Self-deceit is "impurity of heart." Now the self-deceiver is an individual who makes a certain sort of error in his choice of beliefs about himself. This error cannot be corrected by right information, nor even by conversion of one's angle of vision, but only by purification of the organ of vision. And this organ is "the reflection of inwardness." But it is an organ of will as much as of thinking. And it is the self-deceiver's will that requires purification. For he has a will to obscurity of vision, and hence to ignorance about himself; his ignorance and factual error are products of this impure will. (SK also calls this "illusion," "shutupness," "double-mindedness," or "distraction.")

It is important that self-deceit involves an engagement of the will in self-reflection. In this it differs from the "objective" attitude and the aesthetic alike. The self-deceiver, no less than the ethical individual, has chosen to adopt ethical principles to set meaning to his existence. But why? Why choose to adopt principles that will obscure his existence? We must not reply: because he wills not to see the facts right. Rather: because he wills not to set such a meaning to his existence as a pure heart might set to it.

3

I now turn to the theory of "subjective truth." This theory makes a two-way identification: truth is *subjectivity*; but at the same time subjectivity is *truth*.

Johannes Climacus writes: "When subjectivity, inwardness, is the truth, the truth becomes objectively a paradox; and the fact that the truth is objectively a paradox shows in its turn that subjectivity is the truth.... The paradoxical character of the truth is its objective uncertainty" (*AE*, 183). He adds, speaking of Socrates: "But the eternal essential truth is by no means in itself a paradox; but it becomes paradoxical by virtue of its relationship to an existing individual." (We can grasp these ideas without considering Christian faith.)

The idea of paradox here refers not to a belief's propositional content but to what is implied in an individual's deciding to give assent to the belief. It may be "paradoxical" simply because it is counter-rational to assent to a proposition known to be possibly false; still more plainly, if probably false. This point applies universally, but especially to ethical beliefs. For here assent is adopting a principle of practice. To assent intellectually is to risk one's rationality. But to assent practically is to risk much more—oneself and one's existence. So in the ethical realm "the truth becomes objectively a paradox." If we examine ethical beliefs through the objective question, But is it true? we shall necessarily see all ethical commitment as paradoxical, counter to practical rationality. Much safer to stick to probabilities and prudence! But if we convert the inference, we may equally well conclude that the question of truth cannot have an objective force for ethical beliefs.

So much for the identification of truth as subjectivity. This is well known and suggests the popular opinion of SK as a sort of early existentialist or irrationalist. But now for the other identification. In *JSK*, SK writes: "The curious thing is that there is a 'how' which has this quality, that if *it* is truly given, then the 'what' is also given.... Here, quite certainly, we have inwardness at its maximum proving to be objectivity once again" (p. 355). This is strong and unambiguous writing. SK says there is an exemplary act of assent that is possible if and only if the internal object of that act is also in some sense "objectivity." And therewith, presumably, some sort of "truth" once again. But in what sense? How is this claim intelligible?

Consider a second claim from *JSK*: "Immanently (in the fantastic medium of abstraction) God does not *exist*, he only is—God only *exists* for an existing man, i.e. he can only exist in faith" (p. 173). Abstraction is the medium of pure thought, of propositions and ideas. The idea of God can be contained therein, also the proposition that God exists. But not God Himself, nor his existence. Now the existence of God is certainly not provable empirically. But that point does not count against God. For nothing's existence can be empirically proved; there can be no empirical proofs of existence. (Recall the *PS* distinction between the "what" and the "that-it-is" of things.) Still, might not God's existence be provable in "abstraction," that is, a priori? Might not logical analysis of the bare idea of God reveal lurking within the idea that God necessarily exists? SK thinks such a proof could at most conclude within abstraction. First, he could always appeal to Kant's famous refutation of the ontological argument. Second, he adds that the whole inference lies within the hypothetical. This is generally so for everything abstract. Thus, whatever can be abstractly proved, existence is the one thing that cannot. "Necessary existence" is a contradiction in terms if "existence" means what it means when we speak of cabbages and kings.

Consider another *JSK* remark:

> Socrates did not first of all get together some proofs of the immortality of the soul in order then to live in that belief, on the strength of the proofs. The very reverse is the case; he said: "the possibility of there being an immortality occupies me to such a degree that I unquestionably stake my whole life upon it as though it were the most certain of all things." And so he lived—and his life is a proof of the immortality of the soul . . . ; his life is the proof, and only with his martyr's death is the proof complete. (P. 367)

Even if theoretical proofs were available in the ethical realm, they could not by themselves determine practical assent. For assent here means "staking my whole life upon it." On the other hand, the unavailability of theoretical proofs is no bar to ethical assent. By analogy, even if there was a valid a priori proof of God's existence, it would still be one thing to give intellectual assent to its conclusion, quite another to live as if living before God.

But how could Socrates' life be a "proof" of the immortality of the soul? One popular reading of SK must be rejected out of hand. It may be said that such a life is a "proof" simply because what we mean by the "immortality of the soul" is that such a life is possible. D. Z. Phillips once wrote: "In learning by contemplation, attention, renunciation, what forgiving, thanking, loving, etc. mean in these contexts, the believer is participating in the reality of God; *this is what we mean by God's reality.*"* No, it is not. Nor is such a position SK's; for the whole point of "objectivity once again" is that God's reality is not reducible to the believer's act of faith and love.

Sometimes SK speaks like Phillips. So, in *CT*, he connects the idea of existence with the idea of prayer. But his point is just the opposite to Phillips's. SK does not mean that "God" denotes a non-detachable part of the worshipper's intentional object, that is, an idea. He means that it is the worshipper himself who becomes real in his act of prayer before God. So he could have replaced Phillips's italics by *"this is what we mean by the self's reality."*

What is a proof? A proof, generally, is the establishment of a proposition on premises, where the premises are known to be true and the method of establishment is known to be valid. Now what relation does all this have to belief? What is it to believe a proposition *Q* because of a proof that *Q*? A proof, as that because of which a man assents to a proposition, must be a proof for him; it is irrelevant that others accept it as sound. So, as before, a proof can work to determine a man's belief that it is sound. (Proofs compel belief only if we decide to allow them to.)

Can there be proofs, and if so, what sort of proofs, in the ethical realm? Here I want to make a somewhat unusual distinction. Philosophers often [distinguish between the realms of theory and practice;] I want to distinguish, along with SK, between the realms of abstraction and existence. The usual distinction separates ethical beliefs from empirical ones; SK's puts them together in the same box, separated from the mathematical and metaphysical. (maybe metaph., 34)

We characteristically "live in" many of our ordinary empirical beliefs, for example, that tables and trees are real. But we do not live in them on the strength of proofs. There are no such proofs. And even if there were, they would not be determining for our practical lives. The "proofs" that determine our lives are pragmatic, not theoretical: the testing of everyday experience. Now what criteria of soundness can there be for such "proofs"? Plainly not formal criteria. These "proofs" cannot be adequately modelled by deductive structures. The proof of a pudding is, rather, in its eating (a central motif of *Alice in Wonderland*). But we cannot claim

* *Death and Immortality* (London: Macmillan, 1970).

eating as a "sound proof" of a pudding's reality without once again falling foul of the sceptics. Yet just this is what we do ordinarily accept as sound proof that puddings are real, except that we do not ordinarily require that proof be given *before* we start to eat.

Reconsider Socrates now. His decision to live in the belief that the soul is immortal was not grounded on a proof. No more is our everyday life, concerned as it is with tables and trees and puddings, grounded on proofs. We can say it is the other way round. Our everyday living, our ordinary experience, is "proof" of the reality of tables, etc. But for whom? Certainly not for others. The Azande mode of life is no proof for anthropologists that their magic beliefs are true. Nothing I say or do can be a proof for you that tables or puddings are real. Our existence can constitute "proof" of reality only for us. So, if by "proof" we mean "what can work by convincing a man that it is a sound proof to help determine him to assent to its conclusion," that is the only sort of proof that the empirical affords. Complaining only betrays failure to distinguish the existing from the abstract.

So, now, the *JSK* claim about Socrates does not look outlandish. If empirical "proofs" of reality are thought not to impugn the objectivity of tables and puddings, why now should Socratic "proof" of an ethical position be thought inconsistent with the objectivity of the ethical?

Reconsider, again, the *JSK* claim about God's existence. Surely the phrase "exists in faith" is Pickwickian. Is not "existing," whatever it may be, something public, independent of our minds? Yes; but also no. Even empirical existing is actual only to some actual existing individual. The "what" may be objective in the required sense, but the "that" can be conferred on a thing only in some individual's act of assent. The idea that empirical existence is *not* "existence in faith" is again a product of confusing the existing and the abstract.

But surely the idea of empirical existence ties up with the idea of truth-valuedness, where the idea of God's existence or the soul's immortality does not. And surely this distinction is crucial. But consider the following argument. "Proof" that something exists, insofar as possible, can only be the proving of individual experience. Certainly there can often be many experiences purporting to be of the same thing; agreement of a sort can often be reached about tables and puddings. (If you take a slice, I discover one less slice left for me.) It is just this fact that encourages us to call empirical propositions "objective" and that thus underlies our habit of using the idea of truth-value for propositions asserting empirical existence. Insofar as we tend to agree that particular tables and puddings are real, we are encouraged to think of propositions asserting their realities as true or false. And our agreement, in each particular case, tends to function as our criterion of truth-value. Still, where does all this leave the sceptic, or the eccentric? By the logic of the case, nobody else's purported experience can serve by itself as satisfactory proof for me that anything exists. Only my own experience can do that. "The opinion of all mankind minus one" that a particular pudding is real cannot be by *force majeure* a proof for me of its reality. I may, of course, decide to accept their opinion as part of a proof for me; if so, it is only through accepting that as a relevant part of my own experience.

Now the apparent distance between assertions of empirical existence and assertions of God's existence diminishes further. Here, too, there can be and often are agreements of a sort. (It is a central feature of the orthodox understanding of mysticism that there exists a growing science of mystical experience: detailed, precise, agreed-on, and used as criterion to verify and locate claims to mystical experience.) And if it is the fact of basic agreement that gives sense to the use of the idea of truth-value in the empirical realm, why should its analogue not do the same in the ethical?

I have in these pages only touched the surface of SK's theory of subjective truth. I have tried to dissipate much of its air of paradox, by suggesting that much of what SK says about ethical beliefs can be said also about a large class of "objective truths," that is, empirical beliefs. Does there then remain a contrast for "truth as subjectivity"? There does, but in the abstract, not the empirical. Propositions of mathematics and logic, and maybe metaphysics, may still be allowed wholly non-subjective truth-values.

4

Finally, and briefly, the theory of upbuilding (edifying) belief. In *AE*, Johannes Climacus writes: "Only the truth which *edifies* is truth *for you*. This is an essential predicate relating to the truth as inwardness; its decisive characteristic as edifying *for you*, i.e. for the subject, constitutes its essential difference from all objective knowledge" (p. 226).

The idea of upbuilding is crucial and central in SK's whole thought. For it links his arguments about belief with his idea of spirit and so also with his doctrine of spiritual qualities. What upbuilding belief builds up is just spirit; but spirit is essentially communication (*CT*, pt. 2, no. 3), and the form of spiritual communication is love. Thus SK writes: "Spiritually understood, what are the ground and foundation of the life of the spirit which are to bear the building? In very fact it is love; love is the origin of everything, and spiritually understood love is the deepest ground of the life of the spirit. Spiritually understood, the foundation is laid in every person in whom there is love. And the edifice which, spiritually understood, is to be constructed, is again love..." (*KG*, 204–5). "Spirit" is therefore "love"; and the potentiality of becoming spirit, which is man's essence, is the capacity for loving.

All upbuilding belief, therefore, is belief that builds up love in the believer: no more, no less. It can do this only by building upon the love that is already in him. And it can be this only by itself being a manifestation of his love.

SK's epistemology can be understood only if put into proper relation with his metaphysics of spirit. Having said that, I return to the main theme of this essay. In chapter 2 of the second part of *KG*, SK proffers a puzzling thesis: "Love believes all things—and yet is never deceived" (p. 213). He gives arguments. But they do not seem adequate. I suggest that they may seem less inadequate if taken in the wider philosophical context. In particular, this chapter contains a puzzling idea of error in belief. Thus: "And yet, even if one is not deceived by others, I wonder whether he is not deceived anyway, most terribly deceived, precisely by himself, by believing nothing at all, deceived out of the highest, out of the blessedness of devotedness, out of the blessedness of love!" (*KG*, 221–22). But we can now see how SK might say this. The criterion of error for ethical beliefs is, finally, whether the belief upbuilds or not. To be in error in an ethical belief is just to have adopted it unlovingly. The "right" belief, here, means just the loving belief.

There is in ethics a very simple argument form that runs as follows. All men ought to be good (say, loving). But to be good is necessarily to have certain typical beliefs *B*. So all men ought to believe *B*. SK's epistemological arguments are mainly designed to clear away the rubbish that prevents us from seeing the validity of that general form of argument. His metaphysics is largely meant to give it a sound filling.

II

Belief, Understanding, and Proving

BELIEF AND UNDERSTANDING

IT IS QUITE PLAIN from *PS* and *AE*, as well as from many other passages in later works, that SK never intended to reject the ordinary concept of truth completely. He could well have found this concept outlined in Aristotle's *Metaphysics*, in remarks such as: "For to say that what is is not or what is not is is false, and to say that what is is and what is not is not is true"; and "The false and the true are not in things (as the good is true and the bad false), but in thought." It is this ordinary concept of truth which Hegel often refers to disparagingly as mere "correctness," which J. L. Austin discussed in his essay "Truth," and which Tarski analysed and Popper accepted. This is the conception that truth is correspondence—in SK's term "reduplication." It is the correspondence between a belief or a proposition (sentence, statement, etc.) and external objective reality (the world, the facts, etc.). This general conception has, of course, many variant interpretations. *Inter alia*, SK's clear retention of the classical conception of truth is intended explicitly as a rejection of the non-classical conception introduced by Hegel and central to Hegel's whole idealism—central indeed to idealism of this variety in general (e.g., Bradley's).

I

I want to begin by considering a passage from *IC*. "Christ is the truth in such a sense that to *be* the truth is the only true explanation of what truth is.... That is to say, the truth, in the sense in which Christ was the truth, is not a sum of sentences, not a definition of concepts, &c., but a life.... And hence, Christianly understood, the truth consists not in knowing the truth but in being the truth" (p. 201). Speaking through the thin pseudo-nym "Anti-Climacus," SK makes first a relatively weak point. *Besides* the classical conception of truth, there is another conception of truth. This is the conception that is used in the Gospel according to St. John: "I am the way and the truth and the life" (14:6). (The Greek word is the ordinary word for truth, *alétheia*.) So SK's first point is this: Christ, in saying that, and Christians, in believing it, are not using the classical conception of truth, which would make simple nonsense out of the utterance. Rather, "truth" here has a different sense, which allows the utterance to be mean-ingful, (perhaps) true, and (certainly) important. So what is this other, non-classical, conception?

To uncover this conception, we must analyse in turn the following ideas: reduplication; a life, striving, and "approximately"; being and existing. Reduplication of what in what? SK's words suggest, at first, that we have to do here with a reduplication of some belief in the indi-vidual's life. That is, we are dealing with the idea of a life that expresses a certain belief. Then the belief might be said to be reduplicated in the individual's life. "Life" means, primarily, the individual's actions. So a first reading yields the idea of a reduplication of belief in action or in a pattern of action.

So far, we should have no more than the familiar, and rough, theory that the individual's manner of action is the criterion for his belief. Pre-sumably throughout we are intended to concentrate on moral or religious beliefs, so that we can ignore problems which arise when this theory is generalized over all kinds of belief. Now, SK shows that he is aware of the very obvious facts about belief that make a simple theory of this sort untenable: weakness of will, insincerity, self-delusion, and so forth. Belief in ordinary human beings is expressed not just in a complete and perfect mirroring in one's actions of belief, but in a mirroring that is "approxi-mate." Better, this is an approximation of a particular sort—not just a random hit-or-miss process, for instance. It is the approximation which expresses that the individual is "striving" and which allows for the failures and approximations typical of all human striving. We must not, on the other hand, go to the extreme of supposing that it is the striving—willing—alone that is the criterion and expression of belief. For striving and willing themselves require criteria; and what the individual visibly does, or visi-bly strives to do—that is, his life—constitutes these criteria. The inner, as SK often puts it, is not perfectly commensurable with the outer; but still it requires an outer. For example, there is no "love" without "the works of love."

Then, by "the being of truth" SK means the fact that a life exemplifies a moral or religious belief. But this can at best be a first step in argument. For it does not satisfactorily explain why SK should think that the conception of *truth* is in question. Certainly there is some concept of correspondence at work here. But we do not yet seem to have the reference to some external objective reality that a concept of truth additionally requires. Crudely, this kind of reduplication of belief in life seems more like "the being of belief" than "the being of truth."

Let us now look at a further passage from the same part of *IC*, in which the general doctrine is set out further.

But when one is the truth, and when the demand is to be truth, this knowing the truth is an untruth. For knowing the truth is something which follows just of itself from being the truth, not conversely: and precisely for this reason it becomes untruth when knowing the truth separates from being the truth, or when knowing the truth is made one with being the truth, ... and Christ would never have known the truth, if He had not been it; and no man knows more of the truth than he is of the truth. Indeed, one can not really know the truth; for if one knows the truth, one must know that the truth is being the truth, and so in one's knowing the truth one knows that knowing the truth is an untruth.

This passage clearly contains the following theses:

A. If X "knows" the truth but does not exemplify it in his life, then X does not really know the truth.
B. If X thinks that "knowing" the truth is knowing the truth, then X does not really know the truth.
C. If X really knows the truth, then X knows that "knowing" the truth is not really knowing the truth.
D. If X really knows the truth, then X knows that exemplifying the truth in one's life is really knowing the truth.

Here I have used "knows" to indicate the individual who pays lip service, apparently sincerely, to some proposition of morality or religion but whose life does not exemplify the proposition nor, apparently, any attempt to do so. He claims to be a Christian, but his life is not an attempt to follow the teachings and demands of Christ.

Now, what can "knowing," "knowing the truth," and "the truth" mean in connection with moral or religious propositions? According to the classical conception of truth, the concept of truth is essentially related to some idea of an external objective reality. Thus, the idea of a true belief imports the idea of an external reality which the belief is about and which it correctly corresponds to. Can this general theory be applied to moral and religious beliefs?

In SK's view, the answer is clearly no. If the classical conception of truth applied in such contexts, that could only be so because there existed some external objective reality which was the measure of truth for ethico-religious propositions; and truth could be assigned to moral or religious beliefs just insofar as such a belief consisted in assent to a true ethico-religious proposition. But SK clearly thinks it absurd to suppose there is any such ethical or religious reality, that is, an external objective ethical-religious reality which can be used as a criterion of truth and falsity for our moral and religious beliefs.

Although there are many passages in SK's writings—typically, and significantly, in the pseudonymous works—which imply that "good" and "God" do not name external objective realities, I take the force of such arguments to be not metaphysical but epistemological. It is plain from the later works that SK does believe in the external and objective reality of "the Good," that is, God. But his belief follows Aristotle, not Plato. The Good is not to be sought or found by looking *outside* ourselves; it is to be found precisely by looking within, by purifying our minds and our wills, that is, by purifying our conceptions of the good. Conceptions of the good can quite certainly, for SK, as for Aristotle, be more or less adequate to the reality of the Good. But for both this is not the same as being more or less adequate in relation to a *given* external objective entity (the Form of the Good). It is rather conceiving of the good in a more or less adequate way. And this means, for example, having a conception of the good which is embodied in one's self-examination, humility, charity, etc. The deeper, more sincere, and clearer these qualities are, the more adequate one's conception of the good.

The distinction between metaphysics and epistemology is crucial in SK's theory. For it allows him to say, as he was saying in theses B, C, and D, that even if people believe that the classical concept of truth applies in morality and religion, they are mistaken. The real question is not what people say or think the proper concept of truth for ethico-religious propositions is, but what it actually is—which may be quite different. Against those who want to say that the classical conception of truth still applies, SK suggests, we merely have to insist repeatedly that whatever any individual *believes* to exist, in the way of an external objective criterion for the truth of moral or religious propositions, such propositions are not and cannot be measured against any such objective reality. It makes no difference whether an individual thinks he is measuring his beliefs *for truth* against some external objective reality, for example, God's revelations, or the Bible, or moral intuitions. The fact is that he is not and cannot be measuring his beliefs *for truth* against anything we can identify as an external and objective entity.

2

SK's rejection of the classical conception of truth for moral and religious beliefs seems to form part of a grand rejection of several classical positions, which he takes to be intrinsically connected.

First, there is the propositional theory of belief. This is the theory that belief is constituted by a certain relation between a believer and a proposition. Whatever exactly the relation is, it involves two conditioning relations: understanding (apprehension, entertaining) and assent. So, among other things, the propositional theory of belief involves also a propositional theory of understanding. The classical theory here is again Fregean. Understanding a proposition is just understanding that proposition's sense or meaning (in the ordinary sense of this word). And understanding a proposition's sense is precisely understanding in what conditions it would be true, in what false. So, on the classical theory, belief is analysed as a believer's relation to a proposition, which relation involves (*a*) understanding the proposition's truth-conditions and (*b*) assenting to its truth.

SK rejects this whole general position for two reasons. One is that he rejects any explanation of the *meaning* of moral or religious utterances in terms of the classical conception of truth. The other is that he rejects any account of *understanding* such utterances which introduces the concept of a proposition. These two reasons are not, of course, independent of each other. To borrow slightly from Wittgenstein, "meaning" means "what we understand when we understand the meaning of." For unless we allow this kind of connection, we must accept the possibility that a proposition has a meaning that is distinct from and independent of our understanding of the proposition—objective in the same way that the proposition's truth-value is classically supposed to be. Therefore, the weight of SK's position rests on his account of understanding—what it is to understand an assertion in morality or religion.

For SK, the central feature of moral and religious propositions is that they have the form of demands, of requirements (injunctions, prescriptions, prohibitions). Now what is it to understand a proposition as a demand? It is to understand, among other things, that believing that proposition *P* is expressed in trying to conform to *P*. That is, it is to understand and accept the four theses I listed above. Whether or not an individual actually accepts a given demand *P*, he shows that he understands that *P* has the form of a demand in understanding that *if* he were to accept *P*, he would do so in trying to conform to *P*, and that if he rejects *P*, he does so in not trying to conform to *P* or trying not to conform to *P* or trying to conform to not-*P*.

When *P* expresses a demand, it is not possible to believe *P* but not try to exemplify it in one's life or to disbelieve *P* and not try to exemplify *that*. So the phenomenon of an individual's seeming to believe *P* but not trying to exemplify it (or vice versa)—what SK calls taking the "objective" point of view—is not so much mistaken as impossible. The best we can say about such an individual, if he is not insincere, is that despite appearances he does not understand the proposition in question as a demand.

So far, what I have said is merely a development of SK's version of the familiar theory of belief and its criteria. To this SK adds a further and extremely surprising idea. This is the idea that understanding a demand is possible only *through* trying to conform to it. It is the idea that one can fully and clearly understand a moral injunction, or a religious belief, only through trying to shape one's life in conformity with it. (Compare *The Imitation of Christ*, bk. 1, chap. 1.)

There is an apparent, but not serious, paradox about this thesis. If trying to follow *P* is a necessary condition for understanding *P*, it may be asked, then how is it possible to try to follow *P*, seeing that I cannot do this unless I already understand what "following *P*" is, that is, unless I already understand *P*. The solution is to reject the all-or-nothing interpretation of the thesis. Before trying to live by a certain moral principle I may certainly have some understanding of it, simply in virtue of understanding the words in which it is stated. But this understanding will necessarily be vague, partial, and blurred. We all have some partial grasp of what might be meant by "Thou shalt love thy neighbour as thyself." But on SK's view it is only when, and in the measure in which, we are actually engaged in trying wholeheartedly to conform our acts and lives to this injunction that we begin to grasp fully and clearly what it is that is enjoined on us—on you, on me, on him, in SK's useful expansion.

Trying to conform to a moral principle means trying to exemplify a general injunction in various different particular situations. Among other things, it means trying to see which injunctions are applicable in this or that particular situation, and how. Thus, after a point the individual is able to see that in *this* situation the injunction upon him that he is to love his neighbour as himself amounts to the particular injunction to perform certain quite particular acts towards quite particular individuals, and also in a quite particular spirit. But it is not immediately self-evident that in *this* situation the Dominical injunction amounts to the demand to perform just *those* acts. Yet how can the individual be said to understand the general Dominical injunction if he cannot infer its particular qualifications? This is analogous to claiming to understand a general proposition but not knowing what particular propositions it entails. Now it seems clear that the ability to grasp what, in any particular situation, the general injunction requires is and can only be a product of experience and learning. This process of learning *is* also the process of coming to understand more clearly and fully what the general injunction means.

However, there is a different and deeper point. I cannot understand the injunction "Do *P*" unless I can understand the meaning of "trying to do *P*"; and I cannot understand the latter without actually trying, in various situations, to do *P*. Again, there is of course a vague preliminary understanding, which I have simply through understanding in general and vaguely what is meant by "try-ing" and "do-ing *P*." But I cannot understand a priori what it is to be trying to do *P* (because I believe that I ought to do *P*) in this or that particular situation.

I do not mean simply that we cannot understand the meaning of the words "trying to do *P*" until we have some experience of the thing—of trying to do *P* in various situations. I mean that we cannot begin to understand what it is like to try to do *P*, what trying to do *P* demands of us, what difficulties and sufferings it involves, what temptations it presents, what resistance it faces, what alternatives it rejects. Trying to love my neighbour, in *this* situation, is among other things at the same time trying to see his position justly and fairly; to grasp his true needs; to forget or discount my own feelings of anger, or resentment, or dislike, or contempt; to overlook the calls of my own comfort, convenience, and self-indulgence; to hear the voices of generosity, compassion, mercy, pity; and so forth.

But this point is not, after all, independent of the former point. For if I cannot understand these kinds of things, surely I cannot be said to really understand what "trying to do *P*" means. For understanding what "trying to do *P*" means is understanding what sorts of activity exemplify that description and what sorts of activity exemplify the description "not trying to do *P*." Suppose that trying to do *P* necessarily involves trying to discount my resentment and hear the voice of compassion. Then if I do not understand this fact, and if I do not understand what these efforts are like, I cannot be said to understand what trying to do *P* is. "Trying" is not a verb with a once-and-for-all meaning, so that by learning what "trying" means, and adding that to my knowledge of what "doing *P*" means, I can simply deduce what "trying to do *P*" means.

Both the inevitable difficulties and the possible successes involved in trying to do *P* are essential ingredients in the process of experience needed for coming to understand what "trying to do *P*" and "doing *P*" mean. The difficulties, largely because they reveal *that* there are alternatives to "trying" and *what* these natural alternatives are (e.g., anger, resentment, self-indulgence, injustice) and so reveal by negation what "trying" means. And the successes, because they reveal, in their measure, what "doing *P*" actually is, for instance, what loving my niehgbour as myself actually is—something I cannot know except in the measure in which I have succeeded in my attempts to do so.

Now for some tentative corollaries of this account of what it is to understand an ethico-religious assertion. First, the classical picture of the relation between belief and understanding must be rejected. It is essential to this picture that understanding is prior to belief, for believing is analysed as giving assent to a proposition that is already understood. But on the view I have ascribed to SK, this relation does not hold. It is not the case that we first understand an assertion, *then* decide to give (or withhold) assent to what we understand; for understanding the assertion comes only through trying to follow it. But trying to follow such an assertion means having given one's assent to it, for the former *is* the criterion for the latter, that is, is the mark of "believing" the assertion. So assent, belief, is a precondition for understanding—to put the point epigrammatically. Transposing into the terms of religion, we might say that faith is a precondition, not a possible consequence, of understanding.

Next, the classical theory of understanding as holding a certain relation to a proposition must be rejected. This is not so much because ethico-religious assertions cannot usefully be analysed as assertions of propositions. It is because the experiential process of learning to understand such a proposition more clearly and fully is not a process of learning to distinguish a proposition's truth-conditions more sharply. On the classical theory, the sense of a moral injunction would be given by distinguishing, for every imaginable situation, the class of acts whose performance would exemplify the injunction and the class of acts whose performance would fail to exemplify it. Then learning to understand an injunction better would simply mean learning to make such discriminations more sharply and more accurately. But this picture contains a serious misrepresentation of what it is to come to grasp a moral injunction's sense, or indeed of what it is to try to conform to a moral injunction, and therefore also of what a moral injunction is essentially like.

Let me use once more as an example the Dominical injunction "Thou shalt love thy neighbour as thyself." How are we to understand the sense of this injunction? On the classical theory, understanding the injunction's sense means being able to distinguish, for any situation, acts which would exemplify the injunction and acts which would fail to exemplify it. So the criterion for understanding the injunction as clearly and fully as possible would be knowing, in any situation, what act or acts the injunction in fact enjoined.

Yet, as SK himself makes almost tediously plain in *KG*, the Dominical injunction cannot be understood simply as an injunction to perform certain acts or certain kinds of act. Its sense, whatever this may be, is not to be identified with the sense of a possible injunction to perform certain acts or certain kinds of act. There may well of course be injunctions of the latter sort. Here is one: "Sell whatsoever thou hast, and give to the poor." The injunction is to be understood as enjoining a certain *spirit* in one's actions, a certain spirit which will inform and direct one's actions. Coming to understand the Dominical injunction, then, is coming to grasp more fully and clearly what this spirit is—what love is.

The reason is very simple. I cannot fulfil the injunction to love my neighbour as myself unless I do actually love my neighbour as myself. Unless I love my neighbour as myself, I will not be able to see, in any particular situation, what act the injunction requires of me. Only my love for my neighbour can enable me to discern what, in this situation, will count as fulfilling the injunction "Love thy neighbour as thyself." If I do not have that love, then no matter how good my intentions and will in other respects, I will not be able to respond to the situation in the way that expresses and exemplifies love for my neighbour. And even if I hit on an action which is just the action I would have done *if* moved by the spirit of genuine love of my neighbour, still, if I do so without being moved to do so by love—for whatever other reasons, however honourable—my performing that action is not a fulfilment of the injunction to love my neighbour. It is not one of the "works of love." "Love is the fulfilling of the law, *for in spite of all its many provisions the law is still somewhat indeterminate. . . .* In love all the provisions of the law are even more definite than in the law" (*KG*, 110, 112).

3

Some moral injunctions can be taken as injunctions to perform a certain act or a certain kind of act. "Sell whatsoever thou hast, and give to the poor" is one; "Render therefore unto Caesar the things which are Caesar's; and unto God the things that are God's" is another. It may well be the case that injunctions of the former sort can be fulfilled without the need for any spirit in the performance. But for many, and probably most, moral injunctions this is not so. For it is characteristic of a moral injunction that it cannot be consistently and constantly exemplified unless you possess corresponding inner virtues. This is true even for act-injunctions of the general sort. So it is at least a necessary condition for exemplifying such a moral injunction that the individual come to acquire those virtues. Again, it is typical of moral injunctions that we discover gradually that it is not really possible to fulfil them perfectly, that the best we can hope to achieve is to set our wills on fulfilling the injunctions we accept, and thus to try to fulfil them. But, as we learn by experience, failures of many sorts are inevitable. Setting one's will on fulfilling a given injunction, that is, coming to will to fulfil it, *is* acquiring the inner virtues, the spirit, that correspond to this injunction. And then trying, given the general will, to fulfil the injunction simply is the external expression and exemplification of this general set of the will, these virtues.

In fact, as the quotations from *KG* show, the argument of that paragraph can be simplified exceedingly. In SK's view, it is impossible to fulfil the injunctions of morality unless one is inspired by love. And experience teaches us that the closest we can come to success in obeying these injunctions is to acquire the spirit—the will—of love.

So we can now put forward the following general picture of what it is to come to understand a moral injunction. It is to come to understand that the injunction cannot be fulfilled just in any set or pattern of external acts. It is to understand that failure is inevitable, unless I am strengthened and armoured with an inner will and spirit, which in the end can be summed up in the concept of love. It is to understand that the injunction can be fulfilled only in and through a spirit of love. This spirit is not single, even if it is simple. SK himself lists some of its constituents in an earlier work: "It is faithful, constant, humble, patient, long-suffering, indulgent, sincere, contented, vigilant, willing, joyful" (*EE2*, 142). The process of learning through experience to understand the demands of morality more fully and clearly, therefore, is a process in which the individual learns that the real demands are for those virtues and their like.

So what is the mark of a deeper understanding of a moral injunction? It is coming to understand that one can fulfil the injunction only by acquiring certain inner virtues. It is coming to understand that fulfilling the injunction really consists not so much in performing this or that act but in acquiring a certain moral character. Of course, the individual whose understanding has deepened in this way may also acquire a clearer grasp of what acts the injunction calls for in this or that particular situation. He may become clearer in seeing what would count, in this situation, as loving his neighbour as himself. In this sense, then, he becomes clearer about what he should do, what he should try to aim at. But all this is merely a consequence of his primary understanding. And that is marked in his becoming a more loving person. Nor can others use his choices and acts as criteria for deciding how good his understanding is, or whether it is deepening and clearing. For if *I* am not loving, how can I tell whether this or that act is the loving act, the act which fulfils the injunction to love one's neighbour as oneself?

If we return for an instant to the Wittgensteinian idea about meaning, it is clear that the classical theory of sense simply does not fit moral injunctions. I do not mean that moral injunctions are senseless. I mean only that the Fregean concepts of sense and reference fail to play any primary role in explaining what it is for a moral injunction to have a meaning, to be intelligible—explaining what it *is* to understand a moral injunction. Whatever we mean by "the meaning of a moral injunction," if this is "what we understand when we understand the meaning of the injunction," then explaining that meaning is plainly very different indeed from laying out truth-conditions. Indeed, as I have argued, we begin by talking about truth-conditions—the identification of acts which conform and acts which do not conform to the injunction in various situations—precisely to show that all such talk misses the real point.

BELIEF AND PROOF

I

Now I want to turn to the notions of knowledge and proof. For these notions, too, have close logical connections with the ordinary conception of truth. And a crucial part of SK's work is to enforce a divergence here, too, between the way these notions operate in moral and religious contexts and the way they operate in other contexts.

This divergence is especially significant. For the classical concept of truth is marked, *inter alia*, by its peculiar connections with the notions of knowledge and proof. The connections, roughly and briefly, are these. First, since a proposition's truth consists in its correspondence with fact, proof of a proposition, which is proof of the proposition's truth, is proof that the proposition corresponds with fact. (It may be said that this is a realist statement. Very likely it is, but the man in the street *is* a realist in this way.) Second, knowledge of a proposition is knowledge of the proposition's truth. And knowledge of, as distinct from belief in, a proposition implies and requires proof of the proposition's truth.

No conception of truth at all like *that* can play a role in connection with moral and religious assertions. If "true" is taken to have its classical sense, then, dramatically, we can put the divergence as follows:

A. Knowing that *p* (where "*p*" expresses a moral injunction) is not, and does not imply, knowing that *p* is true.
B. Knowing that *p* does not imply (require) a proof that *p* is true.

For example, assuming that the injunction "Love thy neighbour" is true—in whatever sense actually intelligibly fits moral injunctions—it is possible to know that one ought to love one's neighbour without this meaning or implying that one knows that "Love thy neighbour" is true (classical sense). And it is also possible to know that one ought to love one's neighbour without having a proof of this injunction's truth (classical sense).

However, it is quite another question whether the notions of knowledge and proof are thereby shown to be irrelevant. Plainly they are not. For we do speak of "knowing that" and "proving that" in connection with ethico-religious assertions. The question is how these ordinary notions diverge from the classical ones, or what kind of conception of truth can be at play in these contexts.

Here is an important remark out of *JSK*:

Socrates did not first of all get together some proofs of the immortality of the soul in order then to live in that belief, on the strength of the proofs. The very reverse is the case; he said: the possibility of there being an immortality occupies me to such a degree that I unquestionably stake my whole life upon it as though it were the most certain of things. And so he lived—and his life is a proof of the immortal-ity of the soul ... ; his life is the proof, and only with his martyr's death is the proof complete. (P. 367)

How can a *life* be a proof of any such assertion? How can a life be a proof, for example, that we ought to love our neighbours as ourselves? SK does not imagine, and is not saying, that Socrates' life constitutes a proof of immortality for you or me. It can be a proof at most for Socrates himself. "The fact that he lives in accordance with the doctrine does not prove that it is right" (*BOA*, 10). SK is here speaking of the teacher who lacks *authority*. Second, and just as important, certainly I cannot get a proof of any ethico-religious assertion unless and until I understand it. But I cannot understand such an assertion except by trying to fulfil it in my life and so coming to grasp what the spirit and sense of the require-ment expressed within the injunction is. So, it follows, there can be no question of my proving such an injunction before I have shaped my life into conformity with it. That is, at least, a necessary condition for my being able to get anything like a proof of the injunction. The same is, plainly, the case for "proofs of the existence of God."

Then suppose that someone—Socrates or SK—claims that by trying to live according to some injunction all his life he has gained a proof of it. How can we interpret this claim? Not in the sense that he has come to see that the injunction corresponds with "moral fact" or "necessity." This form of intuitionism is clearly untenable and rests on mistakenly wanting to hold on to a classical concept of truth in the wrong context. Nor, again, in the sense that his life has worked out in a certain way, which constitutes a proof of the injunction; for example, that his life has been successful or happy. Certainly the individual's life may work out successfully or hap-pily. And no doubt this event proves something about the way the indi-vidual has chosen to live—always allowing for the element of chance and luck, which is there to allow fools and knaves to sometimes escape the consequences of their choices and to prevent the wise and good from being rewarded with whatever we think they deserve. Success, and even happiness, can at best be evidence that the individual has tried to live according to sound, reasonable principles of prudence. They are in no way evidence that he has been following the right moral principles—or that he has followed any moral principles at all.

So what sort of feature of a man's life is it that can serve as evidence that he has been trying to follow the right moral principles? Well, what sort of feature of a man's life can serve as evidence that he has been trying to follow *moral* principles at all? What sort of feature can serve as evidence that he has been striving towards *moral* ideals and goals? (Recall that we are not asking what can be evidence for other people; we are asking what can be evidence *for the individual himself.*)

The answer is, nothing. There can be nothing in the man's life—his deeds, his pursuits—which displays and demonstrates the moral principles and ideals at work therein. Alternative interpretations, and self-deceit, make a kind of scepticism inevitable here. On the other hand, it is plainly not by looking inwards, at one's private intentions, avowals, desires, hopes, etc., that one can find evidence in any acceptable sense that one has been trying to live by a moral code, by moral notions.

If so, the conclusion is plain. There can be *no evidence* (even for the individual himself) that a life has been governed by morality. So, if by "proof" we mean "establishing on the basis of reasonably conclusive evidence," there can be no proof of the same. So, assuming that SK realized all this, what could he have meant by his remark that a man's life can constitute the *proof* of his belief?

2

The exception proves the rule. But how? Because it is a *test* of the rule; it *tests* the rule; it is an *experiment.* When SK talks about "proof" in the context of morality and religion, he has in mind this, the older and more general, sense of the notion of proof. The "proof " of a moral or religious assertion is its "testing," its *proving.* As he remarks in *KG*, love has to undergo a proving, "must survive the test (*prøve*) of the years" (p. 47).

When SK talks about Socrates, he is saying that Socrates put the belief in the soul's immortality *to the test* in his life, that his life was and is a test of that belief and that his death was and is the completing of that test. The belief that the soul is immortal in the Greek sense at least can be "tested" only by living in a certain way and dying, or being ready and able to die, in a certain way. By analogy, presumably, for moral injunctions. So the injunction to love one's neighbour as oneself can be *tested* by trying to live according to it, and quite possibly to die for it too—and tested only so. There is no other test the individual can make of this injunction. In particular, it cannot be "tested" by any theoretical procedure, such as trying to deduce it from even a theology—still less a history, psychology, or biology.

Now the question must be faced: what is it for a belief to *pass the test?* In what sense, if any, did the belief that the soul is immortal pass the test for

Socrates—or perhaps for us also, who read about Socrates? And what would it be for such a belief to *fail* the test?

The classical conception of truth does not fit ethico-religious assertions. None the less, there is strong pressure to suppose that we cannot simply give up use of the concept of truth altogether in these contexts. Not only is there the fact that we do ordinarily speak of knowledge and proof here, but there is also a quasi-realist point. We do ordinarily suppose that it makes sense and is important to hold apart the ideas of (*a*) what I or anyone happens to believe is good, right, and so on, and (*b*) what actually, really, is good, right, and so forth. We suppose that some moral injunctions, some moral beliefs, are wrong and that some may be right. So in a very elementary sense a moral injunction "Op" would be ordinarily considered "right" if and just if in fact—independently of what anyone believed—Op. And it is a strength of intuitionism that it stresses the fact that we do think like this and that we do argue about moral injunctions and moral beliefs.

So, for the most general injunctions and beliefs, like Socrates's belief in immortality or the injunction "Love thy neighbour as thyself," we do ordinarily suppose that it makes sense and is proper and urgent to ask, *Ought* I to follow this, to try to live according to it? And the "ought" here expresses what used to be called "objective" duty.

The crucial question can now be put as follows. Is it possible for an ethico-religious belief to *pass the test*, the test which consists in a man's trying to shape his life in conformity with that belief, in such a way that—the test being a test of whether it is right to believe and act thus—his life shows to him that it was and is right to believe and act so? Could the sense in which Socrates's life and death "tested" his belief in immortality provide a sense for that belief's *passing* the test, meaning a demonstration that Socrates was right to hold that belief, that it was the right belief for him to live by? Allowing that a man can test in his life the injunction to love his neighbours, can there be a sense in which this injunction passes for him the test of life, in such a way that he is shown that he ought to love his neighbours and was right to have tried to do so? Can a man come to *know*, through testing a moral or religious injunction by following it, that it is *right*?

The answer to this question must be no. And that is also plainly SK's answer. The concept of knowledge cannot be helpfully used in connection with moral and religious assertions *at any point*. If so, the argument of the last few pages must have run off the rails at some point.

Let us reconsider the notion of a test for, say, a moral injunction. If moral injunctions were simply commands, there could be no sense in the concept of "testing" a moral injunction. For there is no sense in the idea of testing a command. Commands are obeyed or disobeyed; but neither procedure can count as any sort of "test" of the command. Of course, if obeying a command produced disastrous or unwanted results, that might well show that the command was foolish. In this sense a command might be revealed to have been *the wrong* command to give in the situation: a military manoeuvre, perhaps, or a play called in a football game.

But this sense of "wrong" for commands is simply the familiar sense for hypothetical imperatives, technical and prudential "oughts." And for these there is again no problem about the idea of testing. Since imperatives of these kinds are thinly disguised empirical assertions, they can be tested quite simply for truth and falsity in the ordinary and classical sense. Plainly, however, moral injunctions are not hypothetical imperatives.

I want here to go back to a point made but understressed earlier, for this will prove crucial. However the notion of testing works for moral assertions, it works differently, in one important respect, from the way the notion works for empirical or mathematical propositions. For these, there is a sense in which the test or tests are essentially objective: public, open to any individual. For moral and religious assertions this does not seem to be so. A test within morality or religion is a test for me—or for you, or for him, or for Socrates. For such an assertion to face and pass a test is for that assertion to face a test that I (you, he) subject it to and pass that test in my (your, his) eyes. When the assertion that the soul is immortal was tested by Socrates, it was tested by Socrates alone—and not also, simultaneously, by or for Phaedo or any other individual. And when it passed, it passed for Socrates, not for Phaedo or anyone else.

This point has two implications. (*A*) The whole issue of testing arises only for a certain kind of person. It arises only for the kind of person who is seriously inquiring into the assertion to be tested, the kind of person who is already seriously concerned with and about that assertion. Thus, the issue of testing the belief that the soul is immortal arises only for a person for whom this already *is* a serious issue, for a person who is concerned about the immortality of the soul, that is, about the possible immortality of *his* soul. Lacking that concern, the assertion's testing is not a real issue. (*B*) So the kind of test that is appropriate for moral and religious assertions is the kind of test that the person who is seriously concerned with such assertions accepts as a test and would accept as "proving" such assertions as passed the test. The question of what sort of test is appropriate for ethico-religious assertions cannot be answered in the abstract, nor by just anyone. It is the view of Socrates that is decisive;

the view of individuals who are concerned as Socrates was, or as a would-be moral individual is, or a would-be Christian.

Then the question can be put as follows. What sort of "test," what sort of "proving" and "proof," for the assertion that the soul is immortal would seem fitting to a man who, like Socrates, was seriously concerned with this assertion—thought that it might be true, and that if it were, he should have to order his life in accordance with it? What sort of test and proof would seem appropriate for the injunction "Love thy neighbour as thyself" to a man who seriously thought that he might be bound to love his neighbour as himself, and that if so, he would be bound to live according to that principle?

But *this* question is extremely strange. For it is impossible to make sense of the frame of mind it presupposes or of the enterprise it describes. We are being asked to imagine a man who seriously thinks that it *might* be the case that he ought to live in a certain way, but also might not. And he is supposed to think that he can find out which by trying to live in that way, this constituting the "test" and proof of the belief at issue. He is supposed to think that if he lives it in a certain way, his life can reveal to him whether he is (was) right to live in that way or not. We are being asked to imagine a man, for example, whose thoughts can be pictured thus: I do not *know* whether I ought to love my neighbour as myself. But I know that whichever is the case, I ought to order my life correspondingly. Now I can make the test only by putting that principle to the test within my life, as my life's ordering principle. And living so will reveal to me whether I ought to love (ought to have loved) my neighbour as myself, will reveal to me either that I was right to think that I ought to love my neighbour as myself or that I was wrong.

But this frame of mind is not intelligible. The enterprise, the decision, it presents is self-contradictory. For it is impossible to decide to follow a moral injunction, to live by a religious belief, *in order to test it*. It is impossible to decide to adopt a moral (religious) belief *in order to discover whether it is right or wrong*. If that were a man's reason for adopting the belief, then it would be sufficient to show that he had not really adopted the belief at all. It would be sufficient to show that he did not *believe* the injunction, assertion, at issue.

So, paradoxically, by the act of adopting a moral injunction or religious belief *in order to test it*, a man makes it quite impossible that his life should be a test of that injunction or belief. A life can be a test of such a belief if and only if the belief be genuinely adopted, that is, adopted as true for its own sake. It is said of Evans-Prichard that at one time when studying the Azande, he quite deliberately decided to run his own household for a year on Azande principles—not the Western principles of reason and science that he, of course, believed in. And he found it an effective and successful way of running his household. Evans-Prichard was following the Azande principles hypothetically—to test them. And they passed the test. Moral and religious beliefs are absolutely not like that. They are incapable of being adopted hypothetically, in a pragmatist spirit.

3

There is, however, a sense in which moral and religious beliefs might themselves be called "tests." In exactly this sense, too, even a command might be a test. For it might well be a test of one's obedience, courage, faithfulness, trust, etc. In this sense, moral principles might well be re-garded as tests. Certainly the injunction to love one's neighbour as oneself can be seen as a "test." For it tests everyone, by existing as a standard against which the life and acts of every individual can be measured.

But in this sense, it is not we who can or should put moral injunctions and religious beliefs to the test. It is they that exist *as tests for us*. And they are tests whether or not one is aware of this, or even of them. A man's life can still be measured against the injunction to love one's neighbours or against the principle of a life lived under the belief in the soul's immortal-ity, even if he does not accept either and even if he has not heard of either.

I quoted earlier SK's remark that love can and must "survive the test of the years" (*KG*, 47). But what exactly is this test? Presumably, the very simple test of love's constancy and endurance; not only the fact that it survives, but the fact that it is *love* that survives. And this means that the years test, and may reveal, love's fidelity, patience, humility, etc. Without these virtues, one's love would be at best a very poor sort of love—the sort of love, perhaps, that the aesthetic individual knows, but certainly not any sort of love that is acceptable from a moral or religious stand-point. What the years primarily test is whether one's love embodies these virtues. And the years test love precisely by revealing either that love does embody the virtues, in which case it survives, or that it does not, in which case it dies.

We might just as well invert SK's words. If love survives the test of the years, then it has been *proved* (just as a love which fails this test has been, we might put it, disproved—and proved false, as we ordinarily say, or superficial, spurious). We also ordinarily speak of such a love as *true*: "true love." In passing the test of the years, then, love is *proved to be true*, although obviously not in anything like the sense in which a proposition might be proved to be true. At the same time, the test of the years is a test of the individual who loves or claims to love. In proving the individual's love, the years also prove the individual; and here, too, we ordinarily say "prove him *true*, a *true lover*."

But the proving of a love is not a process in which a love that is given and complete from the start is gradually tested and revealed over the years. For love develops with the years; a love that does not so develop is not true love, does not become true love. Love cannot be true love at its beginning. This is because true love involves the virtues or many of them. And the virtues can be developed and displayed only over the years. Not even the lover can know at the beginning whether his love is true love. For at the beginning it cannot be true love; although equally it cannot yet be a false superficial love either.

So the test of the years is not the kind of test that consists in trying to answer a question whose terms are given already at the beginning: Does he love or not? It is not like, say, a complex intelligence test which might take several weeks to complete, yet which as a whole answers only one question, and that about a presumably unchanging and constant fact. At least one question posed by the test of the years is, Will his love become true love? Will he *become* a true lover?

Of course, it is not only love that is tested and proved by the years. All the moral qualities have the same feature, and is precisely this fact which underlies SK's point about love. So the years are just as much a test, a proof, of a man's fidelity, patience, humility, long-suffering, and so on.

The years test *the man*; they prove the man. For "the years" we can write "life." So we can now say, life tests a man. "To live is to be examined" (*IC*, 184). But two points must be made about this general claim. (*A*) There are examinations and examinations. His own life constitutes for an individual a test, a proof, of many different sides of his character, and by no means only his moral qualities or his religious faith. So one's life also, for example, reveals how prudent, self-seeking, worldly-wise, and trimming one is. It reveals one's capacities for getting rich or powerful. (*B*) Not every examination is recognized by the individual as such. There are, in life, not only unexpected examinations but also *unsuspected* ones. These are much more devastating and revealing. For, crucially in morality, the very fact of not suspecting an examination may well itself be a way of failing the examination. If I am set a moral problem but fail to recognize it as a moral problem, then, in a very profound and comprehensive way, I have failed. SK writes: "So little by little it becomes for the individual a serious truth that to live is to be examined..." (*IC*,

184). Or it does *not* become a serious truth for him; in which case he reveals that he has failed, or is failing, the examination of his life. Its *becoming* a truth for the individual that his life is an examination is itself a profound way of passing the test—of being proved by the examination. For the examination is an examination of what a man *becomes*, has become, is becoming; not of what he *is*.

Can we now reinvert the concepts of testing and proving and say that the years can reveal to the faithful lover that he was *right* to love, that his principle (the principle of loving faithfully) was and is right? The years can prove a man and his love. Does it make sense to say that they can prove, to him, the rightness of the principle of his love?

A man may say, as the years pass, "I was right to do this, to choose this." He may say this of a way of life, a commitment, a resolution such as love embodies: "I was right to choose this life, to choose to follow this way of life." And in saying this, he is saying that he was right to follow the architectonic principle or principles expressed in that way of life. But that is to say that the principle was the right one for him to have followed, to have striven through his life to follow and conform to.

It is one thing for a man to pass the test of the years himself, in respect of some commitment or principle, and quite another for him to come to believe that his commitment or principle has passed the test. For with the years he may come to see that he has failed, is failing, the test, but at the same time come to believe that the principle has been "proved." Thus, for example, a man may come to see simultaneously that the principle of faithful married love was the right one for him, that his decision to try to live by it was the right one, but that he himself has failed, when measured against this principle and this resolution.

This distinction can be applied not only to moral principles and injunctions but also to injunctions of religion and religious beliefs. For with these we never succeed, and never can succeed. But human failure, even if inevitable, does not in SK's view invalidate the corresponding requirements and ideals. The fact that no individual can possibly hope to imitate Christ successfully does not show that this ideal requirement is not a requirement, or a requirement only if relaxed. The point can be put like this: the fact that, if measured against a certain principle or faith, a man fails, even necessarily fails, does not show that the principle or belief itself fails the test.

The distinction also holds the other way round. A man may come to believe that, measured against the principle he has chosen to live by, he has passed or is passing the test of the years; but as the years pass it is ever clearer to him that the principle itself is wanting. This might happen, for example, if a man chose to set out in life with pragmatic and prudential principles alone. He might well become a success in terms of these principles, a worldly success, but at the same time grow increasingly aware that these principles themselves are and always have been inadequate and wanting. There are many senses for "the wrong life"; but it is quite possible for people to discover as the years pass that they are living the wrong life—meaning not that they are failures, in the terms set by the principles of their lives, but that the principles of their lives are *wrong* principles to live by.

Of course, a man may never become aware in this kind of way of the inadequacy, failure, wrongness, of the principles of his life. He may live quite successfully by worldly standards and never come to suspect that these standards are wrong. He may, equally well, live unsuccessfully by worldly standards—remain poor, powerless, unknown, despised—without abandoning these standards and still believing them to be right. And these kinds of unawareness can themselves be seen as ways of failing the test of the years, the test of life. But if we say so, it can only be because we assume that a man can be measured against and tested by principles and ideals which he himself does not accept, and of which he may actually be unconscious.

However, of course, moral principles and ideals, like religious beliefs, do not present themselves as objects for testing. I argued earlier that this enterprise is not conceivable: here I just add that, as a matter of psychology, ethico-religious ideas do not occur to us *hypothetically*. And it is one of the marks of SK's "aesthetic" individual that for him moral and religious ideas occur as possibilities. So his attitude to them will quite consistently be experimental. But just for this reason they cannot appear to him as moral principles or religious beliefs.

For SK, the real position is this. At every moment in an individual's life, the individual has some conception of moral principles and ideals, some conception of the measure and standard by which he is measured. SK sometimes refers to this summarily as "the Good." He has in mind that particular principles and ideals can all be regarded as derivatives of a general conception of the Good or as specifications of it: not necessarily as deducible from that concept, nor as related to that concept in a species-genus way, but as referrable to, intelligible in the light of, that general conception—as particular principles of the life that can be understood as lived under that conception of the Good.

SK's view is derived historically from Aristotle. The actual thesis is stated in the *Nicomachean Ethics*. For each person there is an "apparent good": to the truly good man the truly good appears as good. This thesis seems to be derived from a view stated in Plato's earlier dialogues, especially the *Symposium* and the *Republic*, although deprived by Aristotle of Plato's peculiar realism. It is crucial to the moral philosophy of these dialogues that we typically move from one conception of the Good to another. And this movement is presented as, at least sometimes and potentially for all of us, *upwards*, that is, towards a real goal, in a real direction. This is what Plato calls "the Good Itself," the Form or Idea of the Good.

For SK, it is by differing general conceptions of the Good that we can distinguish the stages discussed in the pseudonymous works. Roughly, the aesthetic individual identifies the Good as this or that natural good— beauty, pleasure, power, and so on. The ethical individual identifies the Good with the moral good, itself understood in a variety of different ways, ranging from the ethical existence described in *EE* to the neo-Kantian conception of the moral good latent in *AE* and explicit in *OTA1*. And at the level of religion, the Good is identified with God, according to one's particular conception of God. The final and true concept of the Good, for SK, is given in the Christian conception of God. And it is exemplified and embodied for us in the person of Jesus Christ. This theory is plainly very different from Aristotle's or Plato's or Kant's.

4

I want finally to try to put together two themes: the idea of coming to understand a principle or belief as a result of experience, and the idea of coming to see that life is an examination, a test, of oneself. Surely these ideas are connected.

They are connected, because it is at the heart of coming to understand more deeply what a moral principle really requires, what it really means, and in general what a moral principle *is*, that a man comes to see it more and more clearly as itself constituting a requirement on him—and so an implicit test of his life.

On a shallow understanding of morality, and moral principles and ideals, this aspect will not be grasped. At such a stage, moral principles may hardly be distinguished from "my beliefs" or "my opinions." As in the case of aesthetic ideals and standards, a man may think of his moral ideals and standards as just certain ideas which he happens to have adopted or happens to approve, as if it were up to him to decide which moral ideals and standards to adopt and approve. At this stage, the individual is likely to think of other people's moral principles and ideals as "their opinions," for example, as their taste. If so, the whole conception of one's moral beliefs as constituting an examination of oneself is still wholly alien, incomprehensible, unguessed at.

Coming to understand moral demands is coming to grasp the real demand that is implicit within what may at first sight look like a requirement for certain kinds of action. It is coming to see that the real requirement is to acquire a certain kind of spirit—certain virtues—and to act in that spirit. For SK, the general spirit of moral requirements is identified as love: first in its moral form as described by Judge William, but ultimately in its Christian form as charity. And this requirement is identical with the requirement that we follow, imitate, Christ. Which is *not*, to repeat, a requirement to perform any specific actions.

Then the movement from an "external" to an "internal" understanding of what is required and the gradual recognition that there are requirements, tests, on one will tend to go together. The more deeply a man understands that moral demands are demands for a certain spirit and not just for certain external acts, the more strongly he will tend to feel these demands as requirements on and tests of himself. It is the individual for whom morality appears to be no more than a set of command-like injunctions to external performance who is likely to think of morality as arbitrary, "subjective," a matter of opinion and taste.

The man who regards the requirements as external injunctions can scarcely have a deep conception of their rationale. He is very likely to have at best only that conception of their rationale which we call "conventionalist"; some variety of a social, or utilitarian, conception. This is to say that his conception of the Good is virtually non-existent; at best, shallow and superficial. It cannot appear to him as something that really stands over against him, strongly compelling, in whose light all his life is to be seen and judged.

In contrast, a man who deeply grasps that the requirements of morality can be understood only as pointing towards spirit, virtue, will have a deep conception of the Good. For he will have a deep conception of the rationale behind moral requirements. At the same time, the requirements appear to him more clearly as tests—tests of himself. They appear as tests of his character, his inner self, including his desires, feelings, and intentions. The more strongly morality appears as a test of oneself, the more its requirements must appear as real, independent of one's own opinions and wishes—as "objective."

III

Paradox and Passion

IN THIS CHAPTER I want to try to explain a couple of sentences out of the chapter "Truth is Subjectivity" from *AE*.

> When subjectivity, inwardness, is the truth, the truth becomes objectively a paradox [*objektivt bestemmet P.*]; and the fact that the truth is objectively a paradox shows in its turn that subjectivity is the truth. For the objective situation is repellent [*Objektiviteten støder fra*]; and the expression for the objective repulsion constitutes the tension and the measure of the corresponding inwardness. The paradoxical character of the truth is its objective uncertainty [*P. er den objektive Uvished*]; this uncertainty is an expression for the passionate inwardness [*Inderlighedens Lidenskab*]; and this passion is precisely the truth. (P. 183)

I am going to follow two principles of interpretation. The first is that these sentences are not nonsense, not a silly philosophical joke. The second is that although they are written in a kind of post-Hegelian dialect—which is just as far from plain Danish as from plain English, or German either—they have a sense which can in principle be stated in plain English (Danish). I am going to try to explicate this sense and to show that these sentences express a perfectly serious, intelligible, and important theory.

I

First, I offer a paraphrase in reasonably plain English of what Johannes Climacus is saying. From the objective point of view, "the truth" is a paradox. Looked at objectively, that which is claimed as truth is in fact a paradox. But of course the truth cannot be a paradox, paradoxical. A proposition might be simultaneously true, in fact, and also paradoxical in the common weak sense of "paradox," the sense in which, for example, Aristotle uses the term when he says that "Might is right" is a paradox. But paradoxes in this weak sense are (*a*) not in any logical sense paradoxical and (*b*) paradoxical only in relation to what we normally believe or expect. That is to say, they are paradoxical only "subjectively." As a first approximation, Johannes Climacus is distinguishing propositions which are merely "at an angle to common sense" (*paradoxon*) from propositions which are resistant to classification as true because of features objectively within them, for example, self-contradictions and talking at first, explicitly, about propositions of the first kind.

Now to say that if looked at from the objective point of view, a certain proposition is both true and paradoxical is to say something that is itself paradoxical, self-contradictory. It follows, therefore, that the objective point of view (in relation to such a proposition) must itself be internally incoherent in some way. That is to say, in relation to truths, propositions, of a certain kind or class, the objective point of view cannot be taken coherently. And to say this is to say that in relation to these truths the subjective point of view, whatever that may be, is the only point of view which can coherently be taken.

Presumably, using and applying the concepts of objective truth and falsity are a function of adopting the objective point of view. Part of what "an objective point of view" in relation to a proposition *means* is a point of view from which the objective truth-value of propositions is in question, a point of view from which propositions are regarded as having objective truth-values and in which their truth-values are among the chief objects of that point of view. That is, the question, Is this proposition (objectively) true or false? is askable only from an objective point of view, and its asking is a mark of the questioner's taking the objective point of view.

Whatever exactly Johannes means by "subjectivity," presumably it is a mark of a subjective point of view *not* to ask about the objective truth-value of the propositions one is concerned about. Taking a subjective point of view with regard to a proposition means, among other things, *not* asking about its truth-value; it means that the proposition's objective truth-value is *not* a concern. We can put this dramatically: if one adopts a subjective point of view concerning a proposition, the concept of that proposition's truth-value vanishes from one's mind. If so, the concept of a proposition's strong paradoxicality, self-contradiction, vanishes too. So it becomes just as impossible to raise the question, Is this proposition a paradox? as it is to raise the question of its truth-value.

Now Johannes presumably has before his mind, as an example of the subjective point of view, religious faith; in particular, Christian faith. By "faith" I mean not a set of propositions, doctrines, dogmas, but the faith of some particular individual who is a Christian. Faith is expressed by a creed, a statement expressing the individual's beliefs. Suppose an individual's expression of his faith takes the quite normal form of his saying "I believe that *P*," where *P* can be represented as a set of propositions. Johannes's point is that if such an utterance is the genuine expression of faith, it is because it is the expression of an attitude or point of view from which objective questions concerning *P* do not arise.

He is not of course denying that it is possible to take up an objective stance towards *P*; to do so is among other things to take a stance towards *P* regarded as a set of propositions. And this implies regarding *P* as a set of truth-valued entities. His remarks, indeed, begin with the possibility of an objective stance towards what the believer (subjectively) believes. For he begins precisely by pointing out that if one looks at the content of faith objectively, it will necessarily appear to be a paradox. If one supposes that the believer is expressing intellectual assent to a set of propositions, then necessarily it must appear to one that this set of propositions is logically incoherent or inconsistent, or otherwise semantically defective in a very serious way.

On the other hand, Johannes is not in the least suggesting that to the believer the content of his faith is non-paradoxical. The believer is not the individual whose point of view is such that he can legitimately and truthfully say, "The propositions that are the content of my faith are *not* paradoxical." He cannot say this, because even denying the paradoxicality of one's beliefs is using the concept of paradoxicality in relation to them; and even this is already a move within an objective point of view. The question whether one's faith is or is not paradoxical cannot arise within the subjective standpoint—that is, for faith as such—any more than can the question, Is this true or false, or neither true nor false?

So, whatever Johannes wishes to say about the standpoint of faith, it cannot at least be that faith is the recognition of the non-paradoxicality of belief. *Fides quaerens intellectum*: but for Johannes, at least, the *intellectum* that faith seeks and acquires cannot be objective, or theoretical, for it cannot be concerned with issues of truth and falsity, consistency and inconsistency and self-contradiction. Whatever its concern, *that* whole range of questions and concepts lies forever outside the scope of faith.

2

Now I want to consider Johannes's weak concept of paradox. This concept is partially expressed in his remark, "The paradoxical character of the truth is its objective uncertainty." The point Johannes is making here concerns the weak concept. He writes a few lines further down: "The external essential truth is by no means itself a paradox; but it becomes paradoxical by virtue of its relationship to an existing individual."

To say that a "truth" is objectively uncertain is, in Johannes's language, to say that a proposition, looked at from the objective point of view, is uncertain. Now this word is ambiguous. But Johannes is talking epistemology, not psychology. He does not mean that we cannot feel certain of the proposition's truth; he means that its truth cannot—whatever anyone feels or believes—be known with certainty. (Hence the "objectively.") This is because the proposition is of a certain very general kind, where, because of something intrinsic to that kind of proposition, all propositions of that kind are essentially vulnerable to sceptical doubt—epistemologically vulnerable. In this whole argument Johannes is concerned with epistemologically vulnerable "truths"; specifically ethical and religious propositions, as objects of a man's belief.

At the same time, he speaks of such propositions as "eternal and essential truth." How is this consistent with saying that they are "objectively uncertain"? The answer is that "eternal" is a characterization of a quite different kind from "objectively certain or uncertain." For whatever exactly Johannes means by "eternal" in *PS* and *AE*, it is clearly a *metaphysical* and not an epistemological character. "Eternal" is a characterization of the same kind as "necessary," whose contrary is "contingent." The key to the puzzle is that metaphysics and epistemology do not coincide. Speaking metaphysically, Johannes classifies ethical propositions together with "logical" (i.e., metaphysical) and "mathematical" (including logical) ones, as "eternal" truths. "Historical" (i.e., empirical) propositions take the opposing box. But speaking epistemologically, Johannes puts ethical propositions into the same box as empirical ones, as "objectively uncertain," whereas logical and mathematical truths are objectively certain, invulnerable to sceptical doubt. This is possible because a proposition can be metaphysically "eternal," or necessary, without thereby being epistemologically invulnerable to sceptical doubt. Moreover, Johannes also uses a distinct pair of *semantic* characterizations: "analytic" and "synthetic." These reduce neither to metaphysics nor to epistemology. Thus, Johannes's "logical" truths are both necessary and synthetic—in this dimension, classified together with empirical and ethical propositions, and leaving out only "mathematical" ones (which also shows that it is not because they are synthetic that ethical truths are "objectively uncertain").

Now, what is *paradoxical*, even in the weakest sense, about a proposition's being epistemologically vulnerable ("objectively uncertain")? What is paradoxical about the fact that ethical truths are sceptically questionable? Obviously, nothing at all. Paradoxicality does not attach to vulnerable truths as such; there is nothing paradoxical, for instance, about an empirical truth. There is no paradox in the fact that a proposition is sceptically questionable. So, an additional element in the situation is needed if the concept of paradox is to get any sort of grip. Now, Johannes does name this: it is the "relationship to an existing individual." So paradox, in his sense, is a function not just of a proposition but also of some actual ("existing") individual. It is a function of the individual's being related to the proposition in a determinate way. The way is belief (not, for example, disbelief, doubt, suspension of belief, failure to understand, and so on). So, paradox is a function of (*a*) a proposition not of a kind ever to be known beyond doubt to be true and (*b*) someone who believes this proposition.

But now what and whence the paradoxicality? The key is in the following sentence:

The eternal and essential truth, the truth which has an essential relationship to an existing individual because it pertains essentially to existence (all other knowledge being from the Socratic point of view accidental, its scope and degree a matter of indifference) is a paradox.

Here Johannes is referring to the argument developed by Socrates in the *Apology*, where the latter distinguishes the life which is unexamined from the "examined life." The examined life is a life spent in attending to virtue, wisdom, and the perfecting of one's soul, rather than to anything else, such as money or fame or honour. So, we are concerned with propositions (beliefs) which have an "essential" relation to our existence as individuals, in a sense in which no proposition of science, or art, or politics can have an "essential" relation to our existence. Johannes clearly takes over from Socrates the idea that ethical propositions are the paradigm examples of "essential truths."

We can therefore develop the formula for paradox further by adding a third condition. Paradox is a function of (*a*) a proposition not of a kind ever to be known beyond doubt to be true, (*b*) someone who believes this proposition, and (c) the holding of an essential relationship between b and a.

Johannes is talking here about moral principles; he is also talking about matters of religious belief, but I shall pass this over. He is, then, saying that there is an inescapable paradox generated by a certain general feature of belief in a moral principle. The paradox lies in putting together the two facts that moral principles are essentially epistemologically vulnerable— cannot be known with certainty to be true—and that someone who holds a moral principle holds it as something essential to his existence. He may, like Socrates, be prepared to stake his life on this principle; but at least he is prepared to *live* according to it. Now, where exactly does the paradox lie in this situation?

We might say (a) that it is paradoxical that a proposition could simultaneously be objectively uncertain and essential to a human existence. But this does not seem obviously true, and even its sense is not plain.

We might say (b) that to believe that a proposition has those two features is to believe that there is something paradoxical in the human condition. But this is no more helpful or clear.

We might say (c) that there is something paradoxical in the situation afforded by an existing individual's adopting as a moral principle a proposition he simultaneously knows to be less than indubitably true, that is, objectively uncertain. The paradox is that he both recognizes that in itself the proposition calls for a degree of assent less than 100 per cent and at the same time chooses to believe it, that is, adopt it as a principle by which to live and perhaps to die. For to believe a proposition in this way, this strongly, this decisively—in Johannes's word, "passionately"—is to believe 100 per cent, if this qualification means anything at all.

An example of this situation is given by SK in *JSK*, writing about Socrates.

Socrates did not first of all get together some proofs of the immortality of the soul in order then to live in that belief, on the strength of the proofs. The very reverse is the case; he said: the possibility of there being an immortality occupies me to such a degree that I unquestionably stake my whole life upon it as though it were the most certain of all things. (P. 367)

The paradox is a paradoxicality in the believer's belief; that it is counterrational to give absolute assent to a proposition known (or believed) to be not 100 per cent certain. (On the other hand, we are not at this stage concerned with the paradoxicality of believing in propositions themselves paradoxical. The proposition that we are immortal is not in itself a paradox, i.e., self-contradictory. It states a possibility.)

Johannes thus in effect distinguishes two pairs of possible stances towards any proposition of the kind in question. One is the pair believing *P*–doubting *P*. The other is the pair adopting *P* as a principle–not adopting *P* as a principle. We can now say that for Johannes the first pair of ideas operates only within the objective point of view, the second only within the subjective. Indeed, it is precisely this second pair of concepts that characterizes a "subjective" point of view towards such a proposition.

The individual cannot simultaneously stand in both the objective and the subjective position with respect to one and the same proposition. Yet he may move from one point of view to the other. This move seems to be what Johannes indicates when he writes that "the truth is precisely the venture which chooses an objective uncertainty with the passion of the infinite" (*AE*, 182). Here the individual is imagined as *first* standing in the objective position, from which he can evaluate the proposition as "objectively uncertain," *then* moving over into the subjective position—in this case, choosing the proposition. This example shows that Johannes's weak paradoxicality is not generated by *simultaneously* believing *P* to be objectively uncertain (objectively) and living according to *P* (subjectively)—a feat that is miraculous indeed, seeing that it is impossible to stand simultaneously in both positions. The paradoxicality is generated simply by the move from an objective understanding ("uncertain") to the rationally inappropriate subjective stance ("choose to adopt and live by").

Now, an important qualification must be made. I have talked of certain kinds of choice as being counter-rational or irrational. This idea might be taken to allow that other choices of the same general sort might have been by contrast rational, supported by reason. As if paradox is generated only sometimes by the choice of moral principles for one's life; by choosing others, paradox might have been evaded. But of course from Johannes's point of view this is not a possibility. For it is not a differential feature of some moral principles that their adoption is counter-rational because they are uncertain. This is an essential feature of all moral principles, of all conceivable moral principles, of all plausible candidates for moral principleship. There are and can be no moral principles whose choice would be other than paradoxical, in Johannes's sense of the word. Johannes's point is not that paradox is generated in some cases of the adoption of moral principles, as if there might be other moral principles whose adoption did not give rise to paradoxicality. The point holds for all moral principles whatever.

If so, anyone who holds any moral principle whatever must, in a sense, stand in this paradoxical situation. I qualify the generalization for this reason. Suppose I do not recognize the essential epistemological features of moral principles—of all propositions which might be adopted as moral principles. I might, for example, imagine that a particular proposition I have adopted as one of my principles is an indubitable truth. If so, of course, I do not consider it to be objectively uncertain. I am quite certain of it, albeit mistakenly and confusedly. Hence the paradoxicality of my actual situation will not, at any rate, strike me. And what strikes others cannot so much be anything paradoxical in my situation as something merely irrational. If this argument is correct, then paradox strictly speaking is a function of what the individual is conscious of about his situation, not just a function of that situation. Paradox is *for the believer*, not for any outside observer nor there in itself. However, in the light of a distinction drawn earlier, we can be still more precise. The believer is a believer, not both a believer and an objective observer of his own principles. Hence, as I said earlier, for the believer, with his subjective point of view, there can be no question of paradoxicality in respect of his principles. So, the feature of paradox in relation to beliefs can show itself at one point only: the point of choice, of decision, the point at which the individual moves from his objective stance to the subjective stance of a believer.

How, then, can such paradoxicality be avoided in one's existence? There is only one possible answer. It is to avoid coming to hold, that is, to avoid choosing, any moral principles whatever. That is, to remain firmly within the objective point of view. It is precisely this fact which explains why Johannes finds it essential to spend so much time considering and attacking the objective life.

But just here the concept of an "essential" truth reveals part of its force. For one way of describing the individual who passes his whole life entirely within the objective point of view is to say that he has failed to do something in his life which is "essential." Essential to what, for what? Essential, I suppose, (*a*) for living a genuinely human life, for existing in the characteristic way of human beings, and (*b*) for being or becoming the particular human individual he had it in him to become (or any one of the individuals he had it in him to become). Sometimes SK expresses the same point by saying that such an individual either has never gained or has lost his "spirit."

SK is careful to make it quite explicit that these kinds of failure do not by any means necessarily entail other kinds of failure, or loss. On the contrary. The whole-hearted objective scholar or business man is by no means the individual who is likely to lose his material goods, his job, his self-contentment, his reputation, etc. The loss of one's essential humanity is not always *noticeable*; and this is precisely one of its most essential features, and its most dangerous and alarming. The penalty, the punishment, lies largely in the very fact that one is unconscious that one's mode of life is itself a penalty and a punishment. The characters Socrates recalls in the *Apology* were not dissatisfied with themselves for not leading an "examined" life. On the contrary. The only kind of person who can be dissatisfied in Mill's way is Socrates. A pig is by its nature incapable of that sense of self-dissatisfaction.

3

I stress once more that we are here concerned only with weak paradoxicality, not with the strong objective paradoxicality of self-contradiction. Roughly, the latter typifies Christian faith alone, the former the whole of ethics as such.

Consider again the opening sentence from the passage quoted at the beginning of this chapter. "When subjectivity, inwardness, is the truth, the truth becomes objectively a paradox; and the fact that the truth is objectively a paradox shows in its turn that subjectivity is the truth." An important implication of this doctrine can be revealed by rewriting Johannes's words in the following way.

For many propositions—many kinds of propositions—there are two available stances from which the proposition can be considered and assessed: the objective and the subjective. But there is a large and important class of propositions for which, in their very nature, objective assessment can generate no final or certain truth-value. Among these are propositions of ethics. Unlike other kinds of dubitable truth, these have the further features of being essential to decisions and actions and of being *capable* of being followed in decisions or actions. That is, they are capable of functioning as Aristotelian major premises in practical reasoning, which other kinds of contingent proposition are not. But if they are looked at in this light, an inescapable paradoxicality (explained in section 2 above) is revealed. This can be put in a nutshell: We *must* follow some such injunction, although we *cannot* know that it is *true*.

But plainly this remark expresses an intellectually unsatisfactory, not to say paradoxical, point of view. Hence some assumption behind this remark must be relaxed. But what assumption? We might suggest relaxing the general assumption that ethical propositions—the stuff of moral principles—have truth-values. But in one way this goes too far. There is nothing wrong with saying that, objectively, such propositions may have truth-values but truth-values that are undecidable by us. The point is that "undecidable." For this brings out the question, Why should we want to decide the truth-values of such propositions?

Presumably, we want to decide truth-values for ordinary factual propositions, roughly enough, in order that we may know what the facts are: to know what we should believe and what not. So why do we want to decide truth-values for ethical propositions? Perhaps in order that we may know what is right and what is wrong, what we ought to do and what not to do. If an ethical proposition has the general form OP (e.g., "Thou shalt not kill"), then deciding the truth-value of OP amounts to deciding whether one should kill. Similarly, to believe an ethical proposition—say, to hold a certain moral principle—amounts to believing that there is something one should do (or not do).

But if objective truth-values cannot be decided for ethical propositions, then we are faced with two alternatives. Either (a) since we can decide what we ought to do only by first deciding the truth-values of various ethical propositions, and since such truth-values are undecidable, therefore we can never be in a position to decide what we ought to do. Or (b) since we cannot avoid having to face the decision about what we ought to do—unless we take the wholly objective way out—but since we cannot make this decision by means of settling truth-value questions for relevant principles, it follows that there must be some other way in which such decisions—moral decisions—should be made by us.

There is a third possibility which I mention only to ignore. It is the possibility that it does not matter what we decide. I ignore this because Johannes does, too. For his words "when subjectivity, inwardness, is the truth" indicate that he is precisely *not* prepared to take this third way out. He is effectively saying here that the concept of truth does apply within the ethical (and the religious), even though not an objective concept of truth, a concept of objectively decidable truth-value. And what he means, in part, is that there is a real and important difference between doing P and not doing P (or doing not-P).

Let me return for a moment to the idea of an "essential" truth. Part of what Johannes means by calling moral principles essential is that they are not unnecessary to a human life in the sense of being optional. By contrast, one might suppose that aesthetic opinions and tastes are optional for a human life; it does not matter deeply what aesthetic opinions you have, or whether indeed you have any aesthetic opinions at all. (This point is certainly arguable; however, it may bring out the point at issue.) The general claim that morality is essential to a human life can, of course, be made from very many different philosophical standpoints. In itself it does not indicate a Socratic, or Kantian, or Kierkegaardian position.

So it is essential for the individual, every individual, to have moral (and religious) principles—a moral point of view. This does *not* mean that it is impossible for any individual to avoid having a moral point of view. It means that any individual who contrives to avoid having a moral point of view thereby misses in his life something that is essential to him. And here a deep explanation is required.

But any conceivable moral point of view has two connected features which strongly evoke the general idea of truth. First, from within any moral point of view, some things are right and others wrong; some acts (kinds of act) ought to be done, others ought not to be done. "Ought" and "ought not" (and "not-ought") are concepts which necessarily go together; just so, "right" and "wrong" (and "permitted," etc.). Summarily, the concept of negation necessarily applies *within* moral thinking, within the use of moral concepts. Just as empirical propositions require the concept of negation, so do moral principles. Second, from within one moral point of view, other divergent points of view must necessarily appear wrong. This is for the same general logical-semantic reason.

We can express the point in terms of belief. If OP states a moral principle, then to believe that OP is inconsistent with believing that $-OP$ or believing that $O-P$. (Moral principles, unlike ordinary factual ones, allow for two kinds of negation.) Of course, as is well known, human beings often are inconsistent in their beliefs, even for empirical propositions. Inconsistent moral belief is betrayed by inconsistent decision and action; if it does not emerge there, we can take what the individual says as merely confused. The person who says "I believe that OP and also that $-OP$ (or that $O-P$)" cannot be understood as expressing an intelligible moral point of view.

This point is even clearer for particular moral judgments, for example, decisions. I cannot simultaneously decide that I ought to do P and that it is not the case that I ought to do P (or that I ought not to do P). I am not here denying the existence of moral dilemmas. But in a moral dilemma the "ought" and the "not ought" (or "ought not") conflict at the prima facie level alone, at the level of relevant considerations and principles. The decision by which I resolve a dilemma, however, cannot have the form "I ought and I ought not."

It is impossible to have a moral point of view and at the same time not to believe that there is a difference between right and wrong. It is impossible to have a definite moral point of view and not to believe that one's own principles are the right ones, alternatives wrong. It is impossible to make a moral decision and simultaneously *not* believe that one's decision is the right decision. These are the very general, and obvious, facts which I had in mind when I said earlier that the wholesale view that the concept of truth simply does not apply to the ethical goes too far. Whatever account we finally give, it must do justice to the fact that an individual cannot make, or be in a position to make, moral decisions without (necessarily) thinking of his decisions in terms of "correct" and "incorrect."

Another point needs to be added. In thinking of a moral decision of one's own as right or wrong, one cannot be thinking of it as simply "what I think or call right" (or "wrong"). To use the distinction between right and wrong for moral decisions is also to distinguish between "right" and "what I think right," or "what appears right to me" (similarly for "wrong"). To think of a moral decision as "right" is to think of it as "really right" (even though one's thinking of it so is acknowledged to be possibly mistaken).

Something like this shows why Johannes, while arguing that ethical propositions cannot be decidably assessed for truth-values within the objective stance, refuses to infer that the concept of truth simply does not fit ethical propositions at all.

4

There are two concepts of truth. One applies within an objective point of view, the other within the subjective point of view. The former goes with assessing a proposition objectively; the latter is connected rather with the ideas of adopting a principle and deciding on an action. If an individual thinks of his principles (and decisions) as right, then he is thinking of them as true in the subjective sense. He may believe that in thinking a principle or decision is right, he is actually thinking of it as objectively true; if so, he is mistaken. He may well not believe, or not know, that in thinking of P as right he is in fact thinking of it as true in the subjective sense; however, this is in fact what he is thinking. Now what is truth as "subjectivity, inwardness"?

I want to reconsider an argument from the passage quoted at the beginning of this chapter. This time, I shall substitute my own translation for the standard translation, in order to bring out what I take to be the logical structure of the sentences in question.

The fact that objectively truth is a paradox shows that subjectivity is the truth; for the objectivity repels, and the objectivity's repulsion (or the expression for it) is inwardness's tension and a measure of its strength.

These sentences present a syllogistic argument, whose premisses are (*a*) "Objectivity repels" and (*b*) "The objectivity's repulsion, etc.," and whose conclusion is (*c*) "Subjectivity is the truth." The conclusion is derived from *a* and *b* by means of deriving from the latter (*d*) "Objectively truth is a paradox." Presumably *c* follows immediately from *d*. Now what does all this mean?

The first proposition is simply a way of saying that the objective uncertainty of the proposition in question makes that proposition correspondingly hard to believe, that is, to give assent to. This profoundly important objective feature of the proposition repels belief.

The second proposition can be rephrased in some such way as this. The more strongly or deeply a proposition's objective uncertainty "repels" the would-be believer, the stronger or deeper his inwardness is shown to be. Conversely, the less a proposition's objective epistemic status concerns or offends the individual, the weaker or shallower his inwardness is revealed to be. SK's standard term for this range of phenomena is "passion" (*Lidenskab*).

Now in several of his works SK introduces the concept of offence in connection with belief, particularly religious belief. These works include pseudonymous books (*BA, PS,* and *AE*), quasi-pseudonymous but Christian works (*IC, SD*), and acknowledged works (*KG, DS*). Sometimes the concept of offence is introduced in close relation with the concept of paradox (see, e.g., *IC*). Offence, more specifically offence at Christianity or at Christ, is the deepest form that can be taken by the *repulsion* of a strong and deep inwardness. (Christian faith is the deepest form of an inwardness that does not allow itself to be repelled or that overcomes the objective repulsion.)

Let us ask, very crudely, when a proposition's epistemic status concerns an individual. When can its epistemic status be for him a cause of concern, tension, anxiety perhaps, offence possibly? We may be inclined to start by saying not, at least, if the proposition be inherently "objective"; if, for example, it belongs to history, or one of the sciences, or metaphysics, in contrast with ethics or religion. But we *do* encounter the phenomenon of individuals concerning themselves with the truth and falsity of such inherently objective propositions. Johannes does not fail to notice this phenomenon. But he regards it as a form of profound alienation, even a form of madness. He does so by playing on the ambiguity of the concept of indifference. In one sense, indifference is precisely a mark of objective truth-value and the objective standpoint as a whole. For here it simply means independence of all individual and subjective attitudes to a proposition's objective truth-value. The exact date of Caesar's crossing of the Rubicon is quite independent of anyone's beliefs, wishes, or hopes. In a second sense, however, the investigator or believer may well not be indifferent to this truth. And, in so far as his non-indifference is the scholar's desire for accuracy, the historian's desire for full understanding, etc., it is wholly praiseworthy. Yet there is a kind of non-indifference which is inappropriate in this case: the non-indifference of the individual who takes the truth or falsity of the proposition in question as bearing personally on himself and his existence and worth. That is what Johannes calls objective madness.

Conversely, it is possible and even common to find individuals who are indifferent about propositions that are not inherently indifferent to them and their lives. These are moral and religious propositions. And "not inherently indifferent" is just another way of saying "essential." Of course, there are numerous ways of being indifferent to the epistemic status of such a proposition. One is simply not caring—the way of the psychopath or the wholly immature. But one is taking things for granted, for instance, taking for granted the truth of one's own moral principles, the rightness of one's decisions. To do this is to suppose that one knows the epistemic status of such propositions; but this assumption is, on Johannes's theory, mistaken and delusory.

When, in what conditions, can the fact that a proposition is objectively uncertain "repel," cause an individual concern or offence? When can the proposition's objective uncertainty arouse his *passion*? If he is not objectively mad, if and only if the question of the proposition's truth-value is a question of how the individual should act and live. For of indifferent truths, the fact of objective uncertainty need not and should not arouse tension and passion. If such a proposition is very probably true, one will naturally tend to believe it very strongly; if less certainly true, to believe it with a certain relaxation. The tension and passion which are aroused by a proposition's epistemic uncertainty are a function not just of that uncertainty but of the individual's being faced with real, important decisions just in virtue of being face to face with this proposition. Now, it is argued in an earlier work (*PS*) that what is at work is the passion of reason, of thinking. But it is precisely not just a passion of *thinking* that is at work when an ethical proposition's objective uncertainty arouses the individual to concern or offence.

It is not the fact of objective uncertainty alone that is properly a cause of tension, a source of passion. It is the fact that a proposition is objectively uncertain *together* with the fact that it is seen as relevant to some decision—as a prima facie major premiss in moral reasoning. The passion which Johannes is talking about is essentially the individual's natural and proper response to recognizing that all possible major premisses in moral reasoning are objectively uncertain, undecidable.

Let me illustrate. The individual finds himself in a situation, which he can grasp adequately and which presents itself to him as requiring a moral decision. He wants to do what in this situation is right. (He who wills the end wills the means; and the end here is the right action to be found and done—*eupraxia telos*.) Now, the right act, whatever it is, is in principle discoverable by a derivation from the minor premiss (which I suppose the individual has got) and the correct major premiss. So the individual knows that in order to make the right decision he must discover the correct major premiss. So he wills to discover this; but at the same time he knows that he cannot, since all potential major premisses are undecidable.

The passion (*Inderlighedens Lidenskab*) which Johannes talks of is essentially a passion concerned with one's actions, one's decisions. It is *a passion about rightness* or—and this is not distinct—a passion about truth in connection with action (*alétheia praktiké*). So it is a kind of passion which is quite sharply different from the passions of aesthetics, the imaginary, the imagination. Later in *AE*, Johannes introduces the term "existential pathos." When writing about pathos he is writing about passion. For "pathos" is simply a direct transliteration of the Greek, and Aristotelian, word for passion. Johannes makes it plain that existential pathos, whether or not including "passion" in the ordinary sense, also and essentially means action. "Ethical pathos is in action" (*AE*, 349); the pathos of the religious too, neither being adequately indicated by aesthetic productions.

There are many ways of being passionately concerned about the rightness of one's decisions and actions, about the correctness of the major premisses one is going to use. We can narrow down Johannes's meaning by once again considering the idea of an essential truth. For we must now recognize that whether or not there are any truths which are in themselves—objectively—essential to human life, there are at any rate propositions which individuals take to be essential to their own lives. What Johannes is really talking about, therefore, is a passion that is generated by concern for the rightness of one's actions, where rightness of action is seen by the individual as essential; or, where the truth of the major premiss is seen by the individual as of essential concern.

A scholar or a business man can, for example, be concerned about the rightness of his decisions and actions and about the correctness of his principles (of scholarship or financial activity). At first sight, we may want to say that Johannes is not talking about this kind of passion at all. But why not? This is certainly an "existential" pathos, a concern with action rather than merely imagination. We want to say, perhaps, that at any rate such a passion cannot be generated by the individual's feeling that the rightness of his decisions is essential. This may well be so. But not necessarily. Johannes explicitly recognizes that people can work up a concern of the absolute or essential type about objects (scholarship, business, etc.) which are not in themselves worthy of such concern. Still, in the measure in which the individual does have such a concern, I think we should say that his concern is an ethical concern, or very like a true ethical concern. For, whatever the actual object of his concern and his pursuit, his concern (his passion) is of a kind which justifies our ascribing to him a genuine concept of *ethical* rightness. (It is a central principle in SK's ethics, as it is in Aristotle's and much traditional Christian moral theology, that it is not the actual object of a man's pursuit which counts morally but the intentional object. For this necessarily has, for the individual, the form of "the good" or "the right." And it is manifested in what SK calls the "how" of his actions, that is, the way in which he pursues his goals; e.g. his worshipping a false god in truth and humility and purity.)

So Johannes's phrases "subjectivity, inwardness, is the truth" and "this passion is precisely the truth" refer to a situation of the following general sort. The individual is in a situation which he sees as presenting him with a decision. The situation is such that he believes that there is a right decision and a wrong one (or several) and that rightness of decision is here *moral* and *essential*. But at the same time he recognizes that the rightness of his decision will depend on the *correctness* of the major premiss from which he acts, *but* that whatever this major premiss is, it is of a kind whose truth-value is *undecidable* by him.

The phrases "subjectivity, inwardness, is the truth" and "this passion is precisely the truth" do not represent the individual's own mind. On the contrary, it is part of the account Johannes presents that the individual continues to operate with a standard concept of truth, indeed a realist concept. Johannes's phrases represent his—an observer's—assessment of the individual and his actual epistemic predicament. But assessment of what?

Like the individual, the observer wants to be able to say that the individual's decision was right or wrong. (These judgments are a normal part of our ordinary apparatus of everyday practical and moral activity.) But in what terms can the observer make this assessment, seeing that, like the individual, he already accepts the undecidability of principles apparently essential to the assessment? He does so, according to Johannes, by considering the way in which the individual makes his decision, that is, by considering the depth and strength of the individual's existential pathos, his passion. For this reveals to the observer in what measure the individual, in making his decision, is doing so *before* a conception of right and wrong, a conception of the *essential* nature of getting things right and acting rightly. The individual's existential pathos, passion, is simply another measure for his concept of the Good. And the individual who acts with the deepest passion is doing all that any human being can possibly do, namely, to pursue what he takes to be the Good (even if mistakenly) as wholly and single-mindedly as he can.

This brings me as far as I can go in this chapter. "Right decision" means primarily, of course, "correct decision," "decision according to true major premises." In *this* sense, observers as much as agents are unable to decide whether particular decisions were or are right or wrong. But Johannes's argument does not, whatever it does, force us to abandon the realist conception of truth for moral principles and decisions. It forces us to push that conception back, so to speak, until it becomes a transcendental concept. Then operationally the right decision is the decision made with the deepest passion, the maximum existential pathos. For it is the decision made according to the individual's best conception of the Good, and no more can be asked of human beings than that.

Still, part of the force of retaining the notion of truth, as Johannes does, is to emphasize the unavoidability in morality of a realist conception of truth. It is to emphasize that for us, as individuals who cannot escape having to make decisions and act, although there is no way of knowing whether our conceptions of the Good and the Right actually coincide with the Good and the Right themselves, there is the possibility of seeing the moral life as a continual striving to bring our conceptions closer to the actual Good and Right themselves. *Truth* of our principles and decisions would be a function of *adequacy* of our conceptions of Good to the moral ideals themselves and is therefore to be held constantly before us as an ideal that is intelligible and pursuable. *The right decision may later be rightly repented*; and the repentance does not show that the decision was not right.

IV

The Assumption of Love

BASIC FRAMES FOR BELIEFS

SK is going to argue that love (*agapé*) is a possible basis for belief; and that it is the right basis. What do I mean "basis for belief"?

According to SK, a man's beliefs are not just a product of his epistemic powers (sensation, reason). Beliefs are also grounded in certain general a priori frames. These frames will no doubt be partly epistemic (conceptual schemes, theories, very general presuppositions). But they are also a matter of feelings, desires, hopes. That is why they can also be called "basic attitudes." We are used to the idea of an attitude to people, even the idea of an attitude to life (optimism, pessimism, despair). SK argues, in effect, that we must extend this idea so that it includes the function of providing an a priori frame for all a man's beliefs.

I

I shall begin by examining the list of basic attitudes and then proceed to the general points of epistemology.

Frivolity, inexperience, simplicity believe everything that is said; vanity, conceit, self-satisfaction believe everything flattering that is said; envy, spite, corruption believe everything evil that is said, mistrust believes nothing at all. Experience will teach that one acts most prudently by not believing everything—but love believes all things. (*KG*, 215)

A. "Frivolity, inexperience, simplicity believe everything that is said." These are the different forms of naivety. They are ways of taking at face

value what people say or do, of not considering the possible divergence of
outer and inner. They ignore the possibility of deception or misreading.
Simplicity is unaware of the manifold possibilities and so reads action in
just one or a few ways. Inexperience is unaware of lying and hypocrisy
and so reads action as the doer projects it. Frivolity does not bother. All
are frames which ignore the possibility that the inner may not match the
outer. More generally, they ignore the possibility that the evidence may
not match the facts. This possibility is necessarily ever-present in all experience.

Importantly, in all these frames credulity is unbiased. In other frames
we shall find biased credulities and incredulities; not here. Naive frames
prevent a man's reading good-looking acts as concealed evil, but they also
prevent his reading evil-looking acts as good. Moreover, when he meets a
good-looking act, he cannot help reading it as good. His reading is not
his deliberate choice and so not to his credit. SK marks the distinction by
calling these frames "an understanding, a foolish understanding" (*KG*,
221).

B. "Vanity, conceit, self-satisfaction believe everything flattering that
is said." These are forms of self-love—not, of course, the right self-love
SK talks about earlier (*KG*, 39), but the self-love that is selfishness. Here,
then, we have bias. It is mainly bias about yourself. Your evil-looking acts
are either overlooked or read charitably. This reading is doubly biased.
First, it goes against probabilities. Second, it is kept for your own evil-
looking acts, not other people's. Conversely, your own good-looking acts
are read charitably, this time with the probabilities. Again, this is for
yourself only.

I emphasize this point, because for SK self-love must be comparative.
The selfish man does not just biasedly read good in his acts and himself;
he reads good in comparison with other people. So, SK says that it is also
typical of self-love to believe ill of others (*KG*, 219). You fool selectively
with evidence in your own case, but not for other people.

C. "Envy, spite, corruption believe everything evil that is said." This
time about other people, not yourself. This frame is the mirror image of
the preceding one. Each involves biased credulity and scepticism. If self-
love is mainly credulity about yourself, these frames of malice are mainly
scepticism about others.

The malicious man either ignores other people's good-looking acts or
reads them, against the probabilities, for evil. Their evil-looking acts,
however, he reads with the probabilities. So, the malicious man postulates
deceit and hypocrisy in others. But selectively. He refuses to allow the

possibility of that kind of deceit SK often talks of—the deceit of not looking as good as you actually are (the deception of a saint or of the love-praiser who pretends to be the most selfish man in town) (*KG*, 342).

Although SK does not say so, it is plain that the frames of self-love must be essentially self-deceiving. The selfish man necessarily deceives himself about himself, but also about others. The same holds for the frames of malice.

D. "Mistrust believes nothing at all." Here we have an apparently unbiased and total scepticism. The frame of mistrust involves a general a priori choice. It is the choice to make *no* reading from acts, whether good-looking or evil-looking. Neither readings with the probabilities, whether for good or evil, nor readings against the probabilities. This frame may look epistemologically viable, even prudent. But SK singles it out, curiously, as the particular object of his attack in this chapter (*KG*, pt. 2, p. 2) and the particular opposite of love.

E. "Experience will teach that one acts most prudently by not believing everything." SK is using "experience" here in its Aristotelian sense, not its empiricist one. He does not mean the bare having of experience (implying of sense-data). He means the power of learning, and the acquisition of having learned, from your experiences. This distinction matters, because it shows why "experience" names a general a priori frame—for the reading of experiences.

The connection between the experience and prudence is internal and essential. This frame just is the frame of reading all acts with the probabilities. It is the frame of probabilities, that is, of prudence. So it is not epistemologically neutral. SK remarks later, "what men call experience is really a mixture of mistrust and love" (*KG*, 216).

F. "But love believes all things." The lover reads other people's good-looking acts charitably, with the probabilities; their ill-looking acts, against the probabilities, he also reads charitably.

Unlike the naive frames, the frame of love is fully aware of the ever-present possibility of deception. In this it is like mistrust and experience. It also knows about probabilities. Again unlike naivety, the lover reads evil-looking acts for good. Self-love reads the evil-looking for good; but it is only the self-lover's acts that he so reads, whereas the lover reads others' so. In this respect, love is the contrary of self-love. In another, it is the contrary of malice; where malice reads all the acts of others for evil, love reads them all for good.

Let me return briefly to the frame of experience. Experience resembles naivety in accepting probable readings just because they are probable. But it is the opposite of naivety in an important respect, that it includes the awareness of every-present possible deception. So the readings of experience are always conscious, made against that background; and we can therefore say that the man of experience *chooses* his readings, where the naive man does not. If naivety is a form of your understanding, experience is not. In this respect it is like mistrust and love, which also embody fundamental choices. Unlike naivety, however, experience does not automatically select the probable readings. Some probable readings it will, presumably, reject, because of "experience." You learn to tell a con-man when you meet one.

Experience is like mistrust in its awareness that deception is always possible. For this reason it is like mistrust in a fundamental and important way. It embodies a refusal to make any full commitments to its beliefs, unless the probability of a belief's truth is 100 per cent. But this failing is important. For it means that the man of experience forms and holds and ranks his beliefs strictly by their probabilities. He takes a belief's (objective) probability as the sole and sufficient ground for his believing. "Probability" here includes the higher-order prudential probabilities conferred by experience, which may override the immediate probability a belief appears to have. But this is to say that the frame of experience does not really *choose*. It pretends that the question, What should I believe about this? can be answered simply by calculating relative probabilities, in the light of experience. That is to suppose that the "choice" by which our beliefs should be chosen are (objectively) laid down for us by logic, probability-theory, scientific theory, and so on.

Then how can experience be a mixture of mistrust *and love*? Partly, no doubt, because the reading of experience will often be the same as the reading of love. Experience, unlike vanity and malice, is willing to allow the possibility of good in other people and often reads their good-looking acts for good. Moreover, it may well sometimes, through experience, read evil-looking acts for good, or at least refuse an immediate evil reading.

But, more deeply, because, unlike mistrust, experience does give you *beliefs* about others. And this is like love. Also, unlike the frames of vanity and malice, which urge you to belief in the evil within others, experience can urge you to believe in the good within others. So does naivety. Except that the naive man has never faced the possibility of deception, and the prudent man has. So the prudent man sometimes believes in the good within others, though aware that he may be deceived. This is like the lover.

Perhaps SK implies, in his phrase "a mixture of mistrust and love," that there is something arbitrary and random in the choices of belief that experience makes. Each of the other frames has a *single* clear criterion for readings, for beliefs (appearances, favouring yourself, disfavouring others, favouring others, or the negative criterion of total scepticism). The frame of experience tries to use probabilities as criterion. But there are many different kinds and levels of probability involved in reading any concrete situation. In the end, it seems that the man of experience has to choose, arbitrarily, where to draw the line between mistrust and love, between not believing and believing. But for this particular choice he has no guide.

2

SK's attack on objectivity is a familiar story. But what exactly is he attacking? It is not, as he makes plain, the idea of objective truth, or objective knowledge. It is not the utility and value, in their own spheres, of the various branches of objective knowledge: science, history, and so on. What he attacks is the attempt to make "objectivity" into your basic epistemological attitude. He attacks thinkers who want to include objectivity among the possible basic attitudes. He does so on the grounds that objectivity is not a possible basic attitude. By extension, he attacks people who try to adopt it as their basic attitude. I shall call "objectivity," when paraded as an alleged basic epistemological attitude, *indifference*. And I now want to consider the three ideas of knowledge, belief, and indifference.

SK states a fundamental principle of epistemology in these words: "Knowledge *per se* is impersonal and must be communicated impersonally. Knowledge places everything in the category of possibility, and to the extent that it is in possibility it is outside the reality of existence" (*KG*, 218). He adds, "Knowledge is infinitely detached, the infinite indifference in equilibrium."

Here again SK assumes a sceptical thesis. We can put it in two ways: no knowledge of any particular matter of fact can (in logic) be certain; no proposition about any particular matter of fact can (in logic) be necessarily true. So, all propositions about particular matters of fact are possibly true and possibly false, too; all claims to knowledge of any particular matter of fact are possibly right and possibly wrong, too. This is a thesis in logic and so is indifferent to the objective probability of any particular factual claim.

When SK says, "To the extent that it (sc. knowledge) is in possibility it is outside the reality of existence," he is not denying that some matters of fact are real or exist, others not. He is not denying that truths about particular matters of fact are truths about "the reality of existence." His underlying point is that there is no such thing as just "existence" or "the reality of existence." There is existence for me and for you, and generally for each living individual. And there is a "reality of existence" for each of us, again taken individually and separately. SK does not deny that the idea of existence—the reality of the totality of existing entities—is intelligible. But it is so only as the idea of the world as it is for God. *Sub specie aeterni*, we may gloss this claim, adding that for SK no living human being can occupy the frame of eternity. The attempt to adopt "objectivity" as one's basic frame is, in fact, just the attempt to adopt eternity as frame. But that would be a possibility only if we could remove ourselves from time and place, which we cannot.

When SK says that knowledge "is outside the reality of existence," he is making the sceptical point. Individuals, each existing in his or her own reality, can have only beliefs about this reality. Some beliefs are, of course, true; no sceptic would deny that. But, in spite of the fact that we tend to call true beliefs (given certain added conditions) "knowledge," SK distinguishes true beliefs from knowledge.

Why? Here we meet another fundamental principle of epistemology. A belief is not just a proposition, an entity with a truth-value. It is, and is essentially, what some particular individual believes. Even if, as we often say, two people believe the same proposition, or have "the same belief," there are two beliefs, not one, in the case; what there is one of is a proposition. And this is an item of knowledge. This principle identifies beliefs as mental entities. And since there are no group minds, and no minds recognizable to us except human minds, all beliefs belong to particular human minds, the minds of particular individual human beings.

A third fundamental epistemological principle helps to identify beliefs among mental entities. Any belief must be the product of assent. SK regards assent as a genuine action. To give one's assent to a proposition is quite literally to do something. So if one has not done this, whatever it is, one cannot have assented to and so cannot now assent to a proposition, and therefore cannot now properly *believe* it. SK uses this principle in distinguishing beliefs proper from the various kinds of imagination (poetizing, hypothesizing, day-dreaming, wishful thinking, and so on). It also distinguishes beliefs proper from the rest of the stuff that floats about in our minds, without our knowing how it got there. So it is quite possible that, though I believe that I believe *P*, and others believe that I believe *P*, I do not in fact believe *P*, because I have not done what is necessary to make *P* into a *belief* of mine.

Whatever exactly assent is, SK is clear that it is a kind of decision or choice: "In judging you *choose*" (*KG*, 215). So whenever we can properly say that someone believes anything, we may add that he must have made a choice. He must have made a choice to believe what he believes. This claim links up with SK's sceptical position. If any proposition about a particular matter of fact may (in logic) be either true or false, whatever the probabilities, then it is not possible to weaken the thesis that all beliefs (about matters of fact) involve choice by saying that some such choices are "determined" by the weight of the evidence. Even if the evidence is, so to speak, practically 100 per cent one way—as, for instance, is the evidence that I am now typing on a typewriter—still, evidence is only evidence and is not a choice, an act. To get from that evidence to my belief that I am now typing on a typewriter I must still make that choice. This conceptual point would still hold even if the probability of the latter proposition was, contrary to all logic, 100 per cent. Presumably it holds, for instance, of "beliefs" in arithmetic.

But since the probability of any proposition about a particular matter of fact is necessarily less than 100 per cent, the probability of its contradictory always more than zero per cent, it is always a choice whether to believe it or its contradictory, in a quite straightforward sense of "choice." If you are aware of the epistemic situation, you know that even if a proposition's probability is 99.99 per cent, it does not follow that it is true. It may be false. So you know that in choosing to believe it you are taking a risk; you may be choosing to believe a false proposition. It does not help to say that in making this choice you are very probably right. For you are still possibly wrong.

Empirical evidence grounds possible inferences to belief (to assent to a proposition or to its contradictory). Between evidence and belief there must be a choice. Now, a man's choices of belief might be arbitrary, random. But this is unlikely. And if his choices of belief are not arbitrary, he must have some general principles of choice for beliefs. These are precisely what I earlier called "basic attitudes." So the epistemological sequence runs, in SK's account, as follows: evidence (knowledge of possibilities), basic attitude, choice (assent), belief.

A fourth fundamental epistemological principle goes closely with the third. SK states it thus: "One does not believe on the basis of knowledge" (*KG*, 215). He is here contradicting a familiar, but confused, picture of a rational belief. The picture is this. Observing the world, we gather certain objective data. These data serve as evidence for and against the truth of certain propositions about the way the world actually is. We form our beliefs about the world by considering the data, deciding which particular propositions they support, and then adopting (if rational) well-supported propositions as our beliefs.

But "knowledge" is knowledge only of possibilities. SK is not denying that we can have objective knowledge of the data. He would not, however, express the matter in this way. It is, let us suppose, a matter of fact that a man has behaved towards me in a particular way. This is, to use SK's own words, "as knowledge... entirely true" (*KG*, 214). The point is that, however true this proposition, it does not entail the truth of any proposition about the man's inner states. Generally, the truth of a proposition about data does not entail the truth of any proposition about what the data are data for—the real state of things.

SK puts the point like this. "It (sc. existence) presents you with truth and deception as two equal possibilities in contrast to each other..." (*KG*, 215). Appearances may be "truthful" or "deceptive." Things may be as the evidence suggests, or they may not be. The point of saying that the possibilities are "equal" is not to say that the probabilities are equal, too. Of course, they are usually unequal; usually one piece of evidence makes one proposition more probable than the other. But it makes no sense to say that the latter is "less possible" than the former.

It is for this reason that SK calls knowledge "the infinite indifference in equilibrium" (*KG*, 218). The equilibrium is between two opposite possibilities. Knowledge is always knowledge that either P or *not-P*. Either the man loves me or he does not love me. Thus, "in knowledge there is no decision. . . . Knowledge is the infinite art of equivocation" (*KG*, 218). Understanding what knowledge really is, what the idea of knowledge of the real state of affairs or a man's inner state comes to, is being able "with the infinite art of equivocation to grasp the possibilities and get them in equilibrium, or to reach the bottom in transparency" (*KG*, 218). Most men, by contrast, "have a supine or passionate predilection for a certain kind of possibility" (*KG*, 218). This precisely describes the frames of naivety, experience, self-love, and malice. Each is an a priori predilection for a certain sort of (range of) possibilities, relative to given evidence, a predilection thus for making certain sorts of inference.

Now a word about the frame of objectivity, or indifference. Trying to live within the frame of objective truth or knowledge means trying to live with only the equilibrium of possibilities. But as a matter of fact this would be impossible. As SK remarks, "the individual first of all begins his life with *ergo*, with *faith*. But most men do not even faintly notice that in one way or another at every moment of their lives they live by virtue or an *ergo*, by a faith—so carelessly do they live" (*KG*, 218). In particular, each of us lives within a frame—which is "a faith," in the sense that it is a priori relative to experience—even the frame of experience itself. In general, each of us lives and acts continually as if giving assent to various propositions about reality. We do not live as consistent sceptics; we do not question the reality of chairs. But the reality of a chair is, of course, not entailed by any evidence we actually have. So, in acting as if the chair was real, we are implicitly acting upon "a faith": the implicit choice to believe a proposition suggested by the evidence.

I want to conclude this part of the argument by stating a fifth fundamental epistemological principle. This is not stated explicitly, so far as I know, by SK. None the less, it plainly functions within his thought. Every basic frame is a priori relative to experience. So the frames cannot be "conclusions" or "deductions" from the evidence that experience (allegedly) offers. This is because all beliefs are grounded on evidence *and* use of a particular frame. All inferences require and embody the use of some particular frame. Therefore, there cannot be a frame-neutral way of reasoning from the evidence of experience to any frame. Certainly there can be ways of reasoning from experience to this or that frame. The trouble is that each already involves use of the frame it is supposed to lead to neutrally and objectively. Thus, a man who has already adopted the frame of experience will naturally find that experience provides sufficient grounds for adopting the frame of experience and rejecting the other alternative frames as foolish or irrational. And so on. But this game can be played with any of the frames.

The conclusion is that, while we cannot avoid choosing a particular frame within which to assess experience, and indeed to live, we cannot rely on any neutral way to make this choice. But different frames often determine different judgments on particular actions or situations. To decide which of the possible judgments on any situation is "correct" (or most reasonable to adopt), we would need some criterion for deciding which frame yielded (or was most likely to yield) the correct or reasonable judgment. But, as there is no neutral criterion, there is no way, apparently, of deciding this. So it appears impossible to decide, objectively, what is the correct judgment, or the most reasonable one, in any situation. If so, the question really faces us: What criterion, *what kind of criterion*, can we use to decide which judgments are (most likely to be) correct?

In *KG*, SK is not concerned with general problems of epistemology except in so far as they illuminate the specific problems of knowledge of "other minds." So we can reduce that question to a narrower one: What kind of criterion can we use to decide which judgments about other people—their natures, their inner states, their moral qualities—are (most likely to be) correct?

But even this formulation is strange. It is strange because we are still hung up on the concept of correctness. This is not necessarily, however, the real issue. The real issue is more general: Which judgments *ought* we to make? Certainly the correct judgments, *if* there were any criterion here for correctness. So our question becomes this: What kind of criterion should we be looking for that will enable us to answer the question, which judgments about other people *ought* we to make?

POSSIBILITIES OF DECEPTION AND SELF-DECEPTION

"In every expression of truth or of true love there exists the possibility of deception which corresponds to it exactly" (*KG*, 215). If we want a criterion for selecting the right, or the best, frame of judgment, it seems reasonable that the criterion is minimizing the probability of deception, that is, minimizing the probability of making mistaken judgments in particular cases.

Frivolity, inexperience, and simplicity—the frames of naivety—are ruled out a priori by this criterion. Being naive is, among other things, being liable to deception, to making mistakes of judgment about people. SK is quite clear that this is simply foolish (see *KG*, 221). It is simply foolish not to provide yourself with the knowledge of the world which will protect you against that kind of elementary deception. It is simply foolish to remain in a frame in which you are a priori unlikely to make any correct judgments except by accident. That has nothing to do with wisdom or with love.

Although SK does not discuss other cases, it seems plain that similar objections fall heavily on the frames of self-love and malice. This is because each frame is a biased form of scepticism. And each is liable to err in judgments, not only in cases where one is biasedly unsceptical, but also in cases where one is biasedly sceptical. The self-lover, for instance, is just as likely to make mistakes of judgment about himself (through his biased unscepticism about himself) as about other people (through his biased scepticism about others). So we can say a priori that these frames fail the test of minimizing probable mistakes of judgment. By this simple epistemic test alone, whatever its final validity, we can say at once that the right frame of judgment must be one in which you neither love yourself (vanity, conceit, self-satisfaction) nor hate others (envy, spite, corruption).

This leaves the frames of experience, mistrust, and love. How can we now decide between them? On the face of it, the frame of experience is analytically the most reasonable to adopt. For is not the criterion minimizing the probability of deception? And the judgments that experience dictates are precisely those judgments that are most probably true, those judgments about people's inner states that are most probable in the light of the appearances. All this is undeniable. The criterion we are so far suggesting is not minimizing deception. It is minimizing the probability of deception. The point of making this distinction is plain. We cannot *know* that we have or have not been deceived in any particular case. So "minimising deception" is not a criterion that we can use.

Yet even here we may wonder. For if we cannot *know* in any particular case whether a judgment is correct or mistaken, that is, whether we have been deceived or not, then how can we tell that it is (was) probably correct? We need some *grounds* for saying this, for distinguishing "probably correct," "probably mistaken," and so on. But, lacking the external check of comparison with the actual success or failure of the judgment, what grounds can we have?

Generally, what sense can it make to say that a frame of judgment, a theory, does or does not minimize the probability of mistaken judgments (maximize the probability of correct judgments) if we have no way of knowing that any particular judgment is correct? How can we apply that alleged criterion to frames if not by considering the particular judgments each frame generates and by considering the success- and failure-rates of the frames?

In other words, how do we—how can we—*know* that the frame of experience minimizes the probability of error and deception? How can we know that the probability of making mistakes in judgment will be minimized if we adopt the policy of making just those judgments which the evidence makes probable, in proportion somehow with this probability? At first sight, this looks like a silly question. To say that the evidence makes a certain judgment probable is simply to say that you are more likely to be right if you make that judgment rather than its contrary. So adopting the policy of making just such judgments is adopting the policy such that the judgments it generates are more likely to be right than are their contraries. The problem, though, remains. How do we arrive, in the first place, at the knowledge that a judgment is probable, that is, probably correct? How do we know that someone who makes this judgment is more likely to be right, less likely to be deceived, than someone who makes the contrary judgment? Only if we have some way of telling which judgment *is* correct, which mistaken. But just this we do not have.

An obvious move at this point is to suggest a weaker, but genuinely useable, sense for the required criterion. That is, people's patterns of behaviour, their words and actions. Is not this what we do in our everyday lives, too? We say that our judgments about people are born out or not by what they subsequently do. My judgment that you are speaking truthfully can be born out or not by what you subsequently do; my judgment that you are honest can be born out or not by what you are discovered doing later (or, of course, earlier or at the time).

But the same difficulty still faces us. For now we have just made the correctness or incorrectness of a judgment depend on observing behaviour. We test the judgment that a certain man is truthful by seeing whether he proceeds to act truthfully. But how are we now supposed to see things? Exactly the same problem of testing faces us in respect to the man's later acts and words that faced us with his earlier ones.

There are two likely responses to this circularity. One is to think of inner states as some kind of theoretical construct, judgments about people's inner states as essentially hypothesis-using and -making. The other is to think of inner states as reducible to observable words and actions; more precisely, to identify judgments about inner states as some kind of hypothetical judgment (for instance, prediction) about observable behaviour.

SK never considers a response of the latter kind; he never for a moment considered any kind of behaviourism as having the slightest plausibility. Since he always wrote within the frameworks of morality or religion, we can easily see why. For a behaviourist reinterpretation of the central concepts of morality—still more, religion—seems quite absurd.

If, though, we think of inner states—honesty, truthfulness, love, and so on—as condensed hypotheses, then we appear to be able to suggest a genuine sense for the criterion of minimizing the probability of error and deception. To judge that a man is, say, loving is to postulate that he has certain inner properties which tend to cause or to express themselves in typical words and actions. So, if he proceeds to say and do the kinds of things that I have imagined, my judgment is confirmed; the contrary judgment, that he is unloving and deceitful, disconfirmed. This does not require a behaviourist interpretation. The judgment that a man is loving need not be interpreted as *meaning* that he will do and say those kinds of things. We can, for instance, think of the relation as causal; inner states can be postulated as causes of behaviour.

Anyway, the demand that a frame of judgment minimize the probability of error and deception can now be interpreted as the demand that (whatever the precise nature of the theory) to use that frame is to be maximally liable to make predictions of behaviour which turn out true. It is the demand that use of that frame enforces postulation of inner states (with their attached predictive implications) which subsequent behaviour most often confirms.

So the obvious, and perhaps analytical, preferability of the frame of experience over all other frames is just this: it gives us a frame generating judgments about people's inner states, which (given the usual ideas about what kind of behaviour each inner state tends to cause) their subsequent behaviour confirms, more often and better than is the case with judgments generated by any alternative frame.

Still, if the criterion for choosing between frames is supposed to be minimizing the probability of being deceived, we shall plainly have to choose the frame of mistrust even over experience. For the man of experience, even though making the most probable judgments, can be and no doubt sometimes is mistaken. Against this the mistrustful man is protected in advance, simply by never making any judgment in other people's favour. (Recall that this is what SK means by "believes nothing at all.")

The mistrustful man cannot, then, make a mistake that the experienced man can make. He cannot make the mistake of "believing too well of a person" (*KG*, 219). The experienced man does sometimes make this mistake. On the other hand, the mistrustful man may make mistakes of a kind the man of experience does not necessarily make. He may commit "the error of believing too ill of a person" (*KG*, 219). Sometimes the man of experience will genuinely give other people credit for their good intentions.

So, it is not clear, in the end, whether you gain more a priori security against deception by being mistrustful or by relying on experience. The mistrustful man is safe from being taken in by people who look better than they are. But he is liable to be wrong about people who are better than they look. The man who relies on experience, on the contrary, may be taken in by the frauds and deceivers; but he may well sometimes see through black appearances undeceived. The decision must, at this point, be made on the grounds of the difference between these kinds of mistake.

SK points out a curious bias in our implicit attitudes towards these two opposed kinds of error. The bias is embedded even in our language, showing that it goes deep in our unconscious thinking, too. To believe too well of someone, mistakenly, is thought to be foolish, stupid. It is to have been "deceived" by that person. But to believe ill of someone, mistakenly, is not thought foolish, stupid in itself. It is not thought of as a failure in one's cleverness. Nor do we say that the person who turned out better than we judged has "deceived" us, that we have been "deceived." (This point will reappear later in connection with the idea of self-deception.) So we seem to be naturally biased towards regarding deception by good appearances as more to be avoided than deception by black appearances. If so, we shall be naturally biased in favour of mistrustfulness over reliance on experience.

We can now see why SK writes that experience "is really a mixture of mistrust and love" (*KG*, 216). From the point of view of mistrust, the man who relies on experience is simply too trusting. On the other hand, from the standpoint of love (which I have not yet assessed), he is too mistrustful of black appearances.

I

"What, then, is the deep secret of mistrust? It is a misuse of knowledge, a misuse which straightway wishes in one breath to link its conclusion and interpretation to something which as knowledge is entirely true. . . . What mistrust says or presents is really only knowledge, the secret or the falsity lies in this that it straightway converts this knowledge into a belief, making belief appear to be nothing at all, making it appear as if it were something requiring no attention, since surely everyone who has the same knowledge 'must *necessarily* come to the same conclusion'." (*KG*, 214–15)

Unlike the frame of indifference, mistrust is a frame for beliefs. It is the frame for believing nothing. By this, SK means believing nothing good. Believing nothing good about others is not the same as believing evil of them, which is malice. It is refusing to believe good about others, even where the evidence speaks strongly. The mistrustful person is using the familiar sceptical thesis: "there is no unconditional criterion of truth or of honesty and integrity" (*KG*, 215). SK emphasizes that there is nothing wrong with this thesis. Indeed, the loving person knows it as well as the mistrustful one. The frame of love, once distinguished from mere naivety, "is initiated in the same knowledge" (*KG*, 216); the same knowledge as mistrust. Still, to know this is not itself necessarily to be mistrustful and does not entail mistrust as its only rational expression. Even if you accept the sceptical thesis, you are still faced inescapably with a *choice* about what you are going to believe of any particular person in any situation. To love is to believe that, whatever the appearances, this person is not deceiving you, is good; to have mistrust is to believe that, whatever the appearances, he may be deceiving you, may not be good. To believe that is not, once again, to believe that he is deceiving you: that is malice, not mistrust. It is, however, to refuse to believe positively that he *is not* deceiving you.

However, there is a plain connection between mistrust and malice. "To believe nothing is right on the border where believing evil begins" (*KG*, 220). For there is an intrinsic bias in mistrust. Mistrust is an inclination to look sceptically on good-looking acts but not on ill-looking ones. So it is being sceptical about evidence that people are not deceivers, unsceptical about evidence that they are deceivers. In fact, the mistrustful person plainly *wants* to discover that people are deceivers, are not to be trusted. He is not neutral about this. Mistrust "has a penchant for evil" (*KG*, 220). If so, mistrust is after all the contrary of love. For love includes a scepticism biased in the contrary way. To have love as one's a priori frame is to be sceptical when the evidence points to someone's being a deceiver but to refuse scepticism when it points to his not being a deceiver.

Moreover, in logic—and certainly in ethics—you may be as clever in your selective scepticism in favour of others as in that of mistrust or malice. In a later chapter SK writes: "O, if men would rightly understand what splendid use they could make of their imaginative powers, their acuteness, their inventiveness, and their ability to relate by using them to find if possible a mitigating explanation—then they would gain more and more a taste for one of the most beautiful joys of life" (*KG*, 271). Any power that can be used to detect deceit and evil can also be used to detect the good and the true. So, using one's cleverness to detect the false and evil is intrinsically no more reasonable than using it to detect the good and true. But there is an inherent link between cleverness and the "penchant for evil." Cleverness can be a trap (see *KG*, 24). It has become a trap if it is used to make discoveries about the false and evil.

Why? Because in order to be capable of using cleverness to make discoveries about other people's falsity and evil, you must have a mind filled with possibilities of deceit and evil. "What the world admires as shrewdness is really an understanding of evil" (*KG*, 265–66). But you cannot have an understanding *of* evil without having an "understanding *with* evil" (*KG*, 266). (See *T3*, 70, and the whole of this section of the discourse, pp. 67–71.)

Here SK uses the image of the child. We have earlier heard about childishness as a simple defect: naivety. But now SK is talking about a very different frame: childlikeness. If a child is witness to evil or corruption, though he may be able to recount everything that was done or said, he will be unable to recount just that which reveals the evil or corruption within. "What has the child left out? What has the child not discovered? It is the evil" (*KG*, 266). Henry James's late novel *What Maisie Knew* is a profound example of this truth; Richard Hughes's *High Wind in Jamaica*, another. So it is impossible to detect evil unless you have the concepts of evil within your mind. But it is not possible to have the concepts of evil within your mind without your mind being itself tainted. There is no such thing as "a pure understanding of evil" (*KG*, 266). So, the ability to cleverly detect falsity and evil is itself a product of corruption, not just cleverness.

Sometimes SK seems to speak out against cleverness in itself. For instance, he remarks that "if a man is clever, in a certain sense he cannot help it; nor should he be ashamed of developing his cleverness—but should be all the more ashamed of acting cleverly" (*KG*, 243). And he adds that "cleverness has really become something to be conquered by the help of Christianity, just as savagery and brutishness at other times." None the less, it is really the misuse of cleverness, not the thing itself, that SK is attacking. For we are to become clever in the detection of possible good, cleverer than those who make it their business to be clever in detecting possible falsity.

Here SK introduces the concept of *wisdom*. Wisdom is the cleverness of the child who "cannot see with open eyes what takes place right in front of him" when it is evil (*KG*, 267). (This is one of several places in *KG* where SK refers to Socrates and Plato.) It is not, once again, that one who loves is naive. "In a certain sense he himself sees that humanly speaking he is deceived" (*KG*, 229). He sees what is being done before him and understands it quite well, understands what it may signify. It is just that he has chosen not to use the concepts of falsity and evil in his reading of other people's words and acts.

This claim goes very deep. For it means that the frame of love is distinguished from the alternative frames of mistrust, malice, self-love, and experience by the exclusion of a certain range of concepts: the concepts of deceit, falsity, hidden evil in men's words and acts. The child's frame simply lacks these concepts, and so does the frame of naivety. But we cannot be children, and we are required not to be naive, that is, foolish.

But *what* one can see (interpret) is dependent on the conceptual scheme by which one interprets the evidence before one. It is not that the loving person lacks, as do the child and the naive person, the concepts of evil. "Love knows better than anyone else everything that mistrust knows, yet without being mistrustful; love knows what experience knows..." (*KG*, 216). The loving person does not lack the concepts of evil. He knows as well as anyone what the possibilities of deceit and falsity and evil are. It is just that he refuses to use this part of his knowledge in reading the words and deeds of other people. For him it is indeed "knowledge," in SK's sense of the word: it remains "possibility." The loving person knows that deceit and so on are possible. He just will not ever allow himself to suppose that he is confronting *actual* deceit. The mistrustful person does not deny that the act he sees *might* be good; he simply will never decisively choose to assert that it *is* good.

2

SK's argument, in a nutshell, is this. On epistemic grounds alone, nothing positively requires us to adopt the frame of experience (or mistrust) over the frame of love. But experience and mistrust turn out to reveal a mind which is inescapably infected by its habitual use of concepts of evil. Of this sort of man SK writes: "His eyes are sharpened and equipped, alas, not in the understanding of truth, rather of untruth, consequently his vision is narrowed more and more so that infected he sees evil in everything..." (*KG*, 267).

Notice how SK says "not in the understanding of truth, rather of untruth": not just "of the good, rather of the evil." If there were no real good, if all were actually evil and deceit, then such a habit of mind would presumably be conducive to accurate vision and thus required of us on epistemic grounds. But if there is real good, then not only is this habit of mind condemnable on intrinsic grounds; it is also epistemically defective. For it makes us unable to see the real good that is before us. It narrows our vision; it fails to sharpen our eyes in the understanding of truth. So SK's *epistemic* objection to the habit of mind that is most plainly expressed in worldly cleverness and scandal-mongering is that it makes us increasingly more unable to see, and so to judge correctly, the good that is around us.

But this habit of mind is also condemnable on intrinsic grounds, that is, morally. This is a theme SK introduces right at the beginning of *KG*: "To cheat oneself out of love is the most terrible deception; it is an eternal loss for which there is no reparation, either in time or in eternity" (*KG*, 23–24). At the simplest level, not to live within the frame of love is—not to love. It is to lack the kind of vision, the kind of belief and hope, the kind of life, that is given within that frame. And that is, even on the simplest level, to be without a great good.

"To believe the good is itself a blessing," writes SK (*KG*, 221). And he goes on to refer to "the blessedness of devotedness, the blessedness of love." Throughout *KG* he speaks of the joys of loving, the joy that loving brings with it. For instance: "Is, then, the life of the lover wasted...? Answer: is not seeking one's own the wasting of one's life? No, in truth, this life is not wasted. This the lover knows in blessed joy in himself and with God" (*KG*, 260). And on an earlier page: "to will to love men, to will to serve the good, to serve truth for truth's sake, the only thing which could...give him the joy of life for eternity" (*KG*, 126). And so on.

So there is, in a quite ordinary straightforward sense, a happiness intrinsic to the life of the person who lives by the frame of love. SK allows, however, that this may well seem impossible or unintelligible to you, if you do not share that frame. "The world can quite clearly understand what his resolution is about but not his resolution, no more than the *mistrustful* world can understand the blessedness which the true lover has within himself" (*KG*, 229).

On the simplest level, therefore, living within any frame except love is cheating oneself out of this kind of happiness. There is a happiness peculiar to frivolity, to inexperience, to simplicity. But the happiness of frivolity is mostly a consequence of being unable to care about others. And the happiness of inexperience or simplicity is a consequence of ignorance. These kinds of happiness are, like Candide's, possible only if you are blind to certain things about human existence. The lover is not blind, certainly not frivolous. He sees, he cares, and he is *still* happy: happy in his loving, happy in that he loves. (No doubt he will very often also be unhappy—on behalf of other people.) So already, even on this simple level, SK faces us with a choice: Would you rather have the intrinsically happy life of one who loves or the kind of life that either the mistrustful person or the semi-mistrustful one (the man of experience) can have?

But his real point is made by means of the concept of eternity, the eternal. "The person who has deceived himself has prevented himself from winning the eternal" (*KG*, 24). "In eternity he cannot dispense with love and cannot escape discovering that he has lost everything." I cannot discuss SK's concept of the eternal in adequate detail. I will just consider one central feature of this concept. For SK, "the eternal" is not, or not just, the designation of something outside time. It also describes something that can be within a person, something that can be characteristic of a person, of a person's way of living and thinking and seeing. In *KG*, SK uses the idea of the "heart" in this sense. Thus he writes: "Love, to be sure, proceeds from the heart, but let us not in our haste about this forget the eternal truth that love forms the heart" (p. 29). And he adds that "to have a heart in this natural sense is infinitely different from forming a heart in the eternal sense."

These words refer us to a conception of the human being, a conception of what it is to be an individual. In SK's view, individuality is something that we are not born with, and indeed could not be born with; it is something that can only be achieved. Individuality is also called "spirit." SK makes it quite plain in *KG* that by "spirit" he does not mean some kind of entity, over and above the body and the mind and distinct from them. "Spirit" refers rather to the way in which a person lives and exists. Now, to describe this, we must use the language we already have. But this language is designed for speaking about what is natural, that is, the body and the mind, what SK usually calls "psyche." So its use to speak about the spiritual must be transferred. On the other hand, it does not follow that what is said about spirit and the spiritual is not true. This follows only if we assume that what is said about the natural is literal and that only what is literally so can be true. It is therefore only from the point of view of the naturalist that talk about spirit cannot be true. But why beg this question?

Spirit, or true individuality, is something that each of us has to acquire. And its acquisition is called by SK "edification," or "upbuilding." When one is upbuilt, precisely what is built up? SK's answer is love. "But spiritually understood, what are the ground and foundation of the life of the spirit which are to bear the building? In very fact it is love; love is the deepest ground of the life of the spirit. Spiritually understood, the foundation is laid in every person in whom there is love. And the edifice which, spiritually understood, is to be constructed, is again love: and it is love which edifies" (*KG*, 204–5).

Of course, it is unhelpful to be told that if you do not choose the frame and life of love, you thereby forfeit your chance of winning a kind of selfhood that is essentially loving. That is a mere tautology. It is not a tautology, however, that choosing a frame is also, whether or not we are aware, choosing a certain sort of personality. Even if SK's whole argument reduced to a narrow circle, it would still at least have shock value. It would remind us that the choice of frames is not simply a choice that is open to *me*—that is, to a given individual—to whom it will make no essential difference which frame is chosen. It is a choice which affects me radically. It is more radical, for instance, than the choice of vocations, which already is liable to affect the whole course of one's life and growth and personality. Choosing the frame of love is choosing implicitly to become a certain kind of person, a loving person. Choosing the frame of mistrust is by contrast choosing to become a mistrustful person; choosing the frame of experience is choosing to become a shrewd, clever, worldly-wise, calculating, probability-dependent person.

There is a curious passage in *KG* where SK argues that a child can never deceive its parents. This is on the natural assumption that "the parents have such a superiority in wisdom and insight and therefore also such a superiority in true love for the child, who quite poorly understands how to love himself" (*KG*, 222). SK is not saying that children cannot pull the wool over their parents' eyes. Just so, the person who is loved can often easily pull the wool over the eyes of someone who truly loves him or her. Children can, and do, contrive to deceive their parents. But this is only deceiving "in a *childish and foolish* understanding." Puzzlingly, SK adds: "*consequently* it is not in fact true" (*KG*, 222).

What can he mean? Well, what does deceiving consist in? It requires that the alleged deceiver know the truth about what he is doing, the deceived person be made to believe something false about it. Now, in one sense that is happening when the child "deceives" its parents. The child knows, in ordinary terms, what is has been doing; its parents do not. But there is something the child does not know about what it has been doing. It believes, we may suppose, that what it has been doing is good for it. But it is by hypothesis mistaken. Its parents, in contrast, know what is good for it; and they would therefore know, if rightly apprised, that what it was doing was not good for it. So, in respect of the question whether the child's doings have been for its good, the child has not deceived its parents. Nor could it. It could not do so unless it knew what was for its good—better than its parents knew. So, in deceiving its parents in the ordinary sense, the child is in fact merely deceiving itself in a much more important way.

SK generalizes from this example. "In relationship to everything which is not love, therefore in relationship to every deception, true love is unconditionally superior; consequently it can never be deceived . . ." (*KG*, 222). The assumption is plainly that true love for someone necessarily involves knowing what is for that person's good—at least knowing it better than he or she can. On that assumption, the lover can never be deceived, in the sense that nothing the other person says or does can give the lover a mistaken idea of the former's good, an idea farther from the truth than the latter's idea. To deceive, in the childish sense, the man who truly loves is to deceive oneself in the much more important sense that one strays from one's true good.

Is that suppressed assumption plausible? Yes, but only on one further assumption: that it is precisely love itself, loving truly, which is for one's true good—that and that alone. For the lover certainly believes this. And, presumably, the person who has chosen another life than love disbelieves it. If you have chosen to live within the alternative frames, what are you likely to believe concerning your true good, the true good for human beings? For SK, there are only two possible ways of conceiving the good. One is the lover's: that the good is something eternal, namely, an eternal blessedness. The other is everyone else's: that the good is something of and in this world, something we can win within this life, and lose within it, too. SK identifies belief in the eternal, God, with the frame of love. Love is rightly grasped only from the perspective of God-belief; God is genuinely believed in only within the frame and life of love. Thus, SK writes, "only in self-renunciation can one effectually praise love, for God is love, and only in self-renunciation can a human being hold God fast" (*KG*, 334).

Here, we are almost at rock bottom. SK has argued that, like the child, "one cannot deceive the true lover, who believes all things, for *to deceive him is to deceive* oneself" (*KG*, 225). The deceiver has deceived himself by deceiving himself out of love. His self-deception lies just in the fact that he does not love. SK can call this *self*-deception, because each of us has a choice between the life of love and one of its alternatives, experience or mistrust. And he can call it self-*deception*, because this choice involves a basic frame for beliefs.

What kind of argument does all this provide? It is not, strictly speaking, an argument at all. SK does not start from assumptions and work with concepts that he and his worldly opponents share. On all important assumptions they differ, and to all important concepts they give radically distinct senses. To his opponents what he says must sound like nonsense.

Moreover, SK cannot even argue that—whatever the epistemic facts—the man who does not choose love *loses* something which the lover has or gains, unless he can show independently that there is some such good to be lost. And he plainly cannot, and does not suppose that he can, show independently that there exists a good of that kind. He never supposes that he can *prove*, in a way acceptable to the man who operates within the naturalistic frame of experience, that there is an eternal blessedness to be won—or lost. At most he can draw our attention to the inevitable fact of despair. "One who is self-deceived thinks, of course, that he is able to console himself, yes, to have more than conquered; a fool's conceit hides for him how inconsolable his life is" (*KG*, 24).

But these words present no argument, and SK does not imagine that they do. In *KG*, in fact, he takes full account of the absolute impossibility of presenting anything like an argument for the basic assumptions of the standpoint of love. He does so by emphasizing that this standpoint—which he identifies with the Christian—is essentially an offence, when considered from the standpoint of the empirical, the natural, the worldly. See, for instance, *KG* 70–71 and 191–94: "Christianity is, *divinely* understood, the highest good, and therefore also, humanly understood, an extremely dangerous good, because understood in a purely human way it is so far from being a rare flower that it is an offence and foolishness, now as in the beginning and as long as the world endures."

Certainly we can distinguish between a kind of consolation that the lover (the Christian) alone can have, and all other kinds of consolation.

First comes pain and suffering and the loss of joy, and then afterwards, alas, sometimes long afterward, comes consolation. But Christian consolation can never be said to come afterward, for since it is the consolation of the eternal, it is older than all temporal joy. As soon as this consolation comes, it comes with the head-start of the eternal and swallows up, as it were, pain, for pain and the loss of joy are momentary—even if the moment were a year—and the momentary is drowned in the eternal. Neither is Christian consolation a substitute for lost joy, since it is joy itself. All other joy is essentially disconsolateness in comparison with Christianity's consolation. (*KG*, 76)

These words recall that to love is blessedness in itself, regardless of what comes before or after. And they introduce the idea of hope. One of SK's early edifying discourses is called "The Expectation of an Eternal Blessedness is Man's Highest Good"; and this theme is central to *KG*, too. Thus, for instance, the lover "hopes for the forgiveness of sins and of some day becoming blessed," and so on (*KG*, 245). All such hopes plainly are impossible and meaningless to anyone who lives outside the frame which gives them sense. Moreover, one might very well say, with SK, that to live in the expectation of an eternal blessedness must be in itself a joy quite different in kind from any joy that can be felt by someone who does not share that expectation—for whom this life is all, and death the end of everything. None the less, this is still not an argument. From the stand-point of experience, one can simply reply yes, but that it is a joy grounded on a nonsensical belief, and that moreover there are very real joys which I can experience here and now, and do.

THE POSSIBILITY OF HOPE

I

"Without the eternal one lives by the help of habit, prudence, conformity, experience, custom, and usage," SK observes. "In fact, take them all, put them all together, prepare the mixture over the smouldering or merely earthly ignited fire of passions, and you will discover that you can get all kinds of things out of it: variously concocted tough slime which men call a realistic view of life—but one never gets possibility out of this . . ." (*KG*, 235). "In truth, everyone who does not understand that the whole of his life shall be a time of hope is in despair" (*KG*, 236); and he adds that "everyone who lives without possibility is in despair." These observations are not, or are not merely, psychological. For a man may, according to SK, be in despair without being conscious of the fact. Now, in the pas-sages I am discussing, "possibility" means something stronger than bare logical, even bare physical, possibility. For a realistic view of life does not deny that there are real possibilities ahead, and around. The fact or event whose probability is 0.01 per cent is a real possibility. Only the realist will not bet on it. On the other hand, if he is a thoroughgoing realist, he will bet 0.01 per cent of his total stake on it; for he will not deny that this possibility may in fact be the truth or come to pass. So how can SK say that the realist "lives without possibility"?

Possibility is always ambivalent or multivalent, except where there is only one possibility. But this is no longer "possibility"; it is "necessity." However, SK denies that there are in fact any necessities, that is, any necessary consequences or sequences, within the world. Here again is a familiar sceptical principle. No causal relations are logically necessary relations. All that exists comes to exist, and all that comes to exist does so without necessity; for that which is necessary cannot come to exist. That which is necessary is, in one of its many uses, the "eternal"; and it is a very basic theorem of SK's that the eternal does not and cannot exist. (There is one exception to this generalization, but as such it is the absolutely para-doxical, and so can be an exception only for faith.)

So "possibility," at first sight, covers the possibility of evil as well as the possibility of good. Living with the possibility of evil, living in the expectation of evil, is fear (see *KG*, 234). Hope is the contrary: living in the expectation of good. It is what George MacDonald expresses at the end of *Phantastes*, in the words "A great good is coming—is coming—is coming to thee, Anodos." When SK writes "living without possibility," he means living without the expectant hope of the good.

It is precisely this that the realist lacks. We have a proverb which runs, "The triumph of hope over experience." That antithesis is just SK's. The realist does not lack all hopes—but neither does he lack all fears. If he is strongly realistic, a true man of experience, presumably he hopes for the probable or reasonably probable good. Perhaps at the back of his mind he still hopes for relatively improbable goods, like winning the lottery. But he will certainly not expect to win the lottery. His actual expectations will be governed by probabilities. But it is what he expects that is operative in his life. Hopes which are not expectations are like day-dreams. The realist will keep them at the back of his mind, and they will not affect his life and actions. But it is precisely this that SK is talking about. For if a man's hopes do not affect his action, then we have good grounds for saying that they are not genuine hopes; they are more like day-dreams. A normal and intelligible criterion for real hoping is whether your hopes affect your action. In the case of the realist, neither his hopes nor his fears do so, unless they are for relatively probable occurrences. But in that case it is judgments of probability, not the hoping or fearing, which are decisive for his actions.

"Living with possibility," therefore, means living in such a way that your hopes, or fears, genuinely affect your actions and life. Whatever general frames these two ways of living involve, they cannot be the frame of "experience." They must entail sometimes going against experience, the probabilities. Hope and fear must be able to survive the crushing weight of the years; as SK remarks, "For most men possibility and hope, or the sense of the possible, dwindle away with the years" (*KG*, 234). They dwindle because they are matched to a sense of probabilities, and in most people the sense of probabilities grows stronger and more dominating with the years. It is only hope and fear of an essentially different kind that can survive the growth of experience unthreatened. That is the hope, and fear, that Anodos possessed.

Then it is a way of living within which one's hopes and fears, except as themselves determined by one's experience of probabilities, do not affect one's decisions and actions—a way of living which in fact is marked by the absence of genuine hope or genuine fear—that SK says is "in despair." It is plainly not by lacking genuine *fear* that a man might plausibly be in despair; on the contrary. So a minor puzzle is created by SK's remark that even in hope there lies a concealed fear. To expect an eternal blessedness is also to be aware of the possibility of the opposite. Therefore, it must be simply in virtue of lacking genuine hope that a human life, in SK's view, is in despair. There is an either-or: either a frame involving hope or one involving despair. This recapitulates the opposition between the frames of love and mistrust.

Why should a frame lacking hope be essentially one of despair? Because in lacking hope, you lack expectation of good. And "the possibility of the good is the eternal" (*KG*, 234). So in lacking hope, you lack the eternal; the idea of the eternal will be lacking from your epistemological frame, from your basic attitude—from all that aids you in deciding how to judge and how to act.

Now, to introduce the concept of the eternal is to involve oneself in profound complexities. I want to take up only one issue, albeit a central one. The concept of the eternal, put together with the concept of a possible good, yields the concept of eternal blessedness. It is this that is the essential and proper object of hope. "In ordinary speech one often calls something hope which is not hope at all, but desire, longing, long-ing-filled expectancy, now of one thing, now of another..." (*KG*, 234). Such a frame is not one of hope proper. Hope of this kind is perfectly available to the man who lives in the frame of experience. He will cer-tainly hope for things he desires. But hope of this ordinary kind is also available within other frames. Naivety is characterized by hope, even though the naive person's hopes are often unrealistic. The self-loving person will no doubt often hope for good things for himself; why not the malicious person, too?

So in most people's lives a kind of hope plays a perfectly intelligible role. Hope comes and goes. You hope when something you see as good appears as a possible acquisition, but not at other times. You do not hope constantly. And whether you happen, at any particular time, to be in hope or in fear depends wholly on what appears to be on the horizons of your life. So hope is determined by external and contingent conditions. It is, then, a matter of accident that, within any such frame, a man ever hopes for anything. As far as the frame governing his beliefs and attitudes is concerned, hope is a wholly accidental matter.

However, SK distinguishes such a kind of hope, and the frames it characterizes, from a kind of hope which is not contingent on external conditions, and a frame within which hope of this kind is essential. Hope that is not determined by and contingent on external conditions must be grounded in something other than a sense of probabilities. This is precisely "the sense of the possible." And here SK is using "the possible" in a rather strong sense. It is almost to say: the possible, although improbable, and indeed almost paradoxical. The contrast with probability is essential. To have hope of this kind, to hope in this sense, is to hope and keep on hoping in spite of experience and probability. It is to believe in the possibility of the good.

I was not using the word "paradox" loosely. In its original sense, a paradox is simply an assertion that is contrary to common belief, ordinary opinions, common sense. Such is its use, for instance, in Aristotle. The opinion of Thrasymachus, that justice is really the interest of the stronger, is an example of the paradoxical. It is not self-contradictory, nor absurd, nor even obviously wrong. But even if it were right, it would still be no less a paradox. To connect this concept of paradox with the concept of hope is to say that hoping is not just for the improbable, but for the paradoxical, for a possibility which offends common sense.

I put it this way in order to bring out the intrinsic relation between the frames of hope and experience. They are internally opposed. For it is by reference to what the frame of experience determines as belief-worthy and hope-worthy that the frame of hope is defined. To hope is precisely to hope for that which the man of experience thinks it absurd to hope for. "Hope that is seen is not hope" (Romans 8:24).

Hope is, in fact, hope for an eternal blessedness. But not just for oneself. Such a hope would be selfish (self-love or malice) and so self-defeating. For a man capable of hoping for eternal blessedness for himself but not for other people would not in fact have any conception of eternal blessedness. Having this concept guarantees hoping for others as well as for oneself. SK remarks that "no one can hope unless he also loves: he cannot *hope for himself* without loving, for they are eternally inseparable; but if he loves, he also hopes for others" (*KG*, 239). The frame of hope is identical, then, with the frame of love. Again, this distinguishes hope from hope-within-experience. "Worldly comprehension considers that a man can very well hope for himself without hoping for others, and that one does not need love to hope for oneself, although one certainly needs love in order to hope for others . . ." (*KG*, 243).

The reason why one cannot hope for oneself without loving is, I think, that to hope for oneself is to hope for one's eternal blessedness. But that cannot be conceived apart from belief in God. And it is impossible to believe in God—even to conceive of God—apart from loving. The frame which is essentially one of hoping is a frame to which the concept of the eternal is essential: "To hope is itself instruction, *is the relationship to the eternal*" (*KG*, 237; my emphasis). If hoping without the concept of the eternal is only pseudo-hoping, accidental hoping, then use of the concept of the eternal without genuine hope is impossible.

Now I want to consider briefly the idea of expecting. Chapter 5 of part 2 of *KG* is called "Love Abides." This means that love is constant, constant in faith (belief) and hope as well as in itself. There are connections between these three features of love. "Believing all things" involves believing good of other persons. And this includes believing in the possibility of good for them and in them—even against the appearances and probabilities. Here is one reference to the future. Hoping all things means hoping for good for and in others.

Now, SK argues that what is needed to believe in such possibilities is a certain act—an act of believing. This is a deliberate choice: a decision to assent to a certain possible though improbable future. He describes it thus: "O, the powers of the eternal are needed at the decisive moment straightway to transform the past into the future!" (*KG*, 284).

What is it to "transform the past into the future"? SK is writing here about a particular kind of situation, the breach of a relationship. So "the past" he means is the relationship of love as it used to be: the fact that the other formerly loved the lover. "The future" means a possible future in which once again the other proves to love the lover. The act of believing or hoping is called "transforming" because it consists in giving the future the exact form of the past. As it was, so it shall be.

All of this implies also a thesis about love in the present. On the surface, the present situation is the contrary of the actual past and the possible hoped-for future. However, the act of transforming the future is also an act of transforming the present. In choosing to believe in a possible future in which he is loved as he was, the lover also chooses to believe in a present in which he is loved. In each case, his choice goes against probabilities. In his reading of the phrase "love abides," SK means not just that the lover's love abides, but that it involves the belief that the other person's love also abides—despite appearances.

The parallel between expectation and belief is stressed by SK "If love's expectation is able to make a man, essentially understood, weak, it must be because his expectation stands in a dependent relationship to time; so that time has the power to decide whether or not the expectation becomes fulfilled or not" (*KG*, 289). Just as there are two kinds of hope, so too for expectation. In both cases, SK singles out a choice that has made itself independent of evidence, in contrast with the ordinary attitude for which actual events are of paramount relevance.

Plainly, a hope for someone's eternal blessedness is not capable of support or refutation by anything that actually happens in this world. Just so, I think, SK wants to say that the expectation characteristic of the lover is not refutable by any experience. Nothing that happens "has the power to decide" whether the other person loves you again. The epistemological point is the same as the point concerning the present. If it is possible, within the frame of love, to believe despite appearances and probabilities that someone loves you, or is essentially loving, this implies that nothing that happens "has the power to decide" for you that your belief is false—or true either. Only you have that power.

2

There is a clear parallel in SK's thought between the logic of "believe" and the logic of "hope." That is why his analysis of hope illuminates his concept of belief not only by analogy but also directly. Believing, in SK's sense, involves hoping, and vice versa. Just as it is the person who "believes all" who is "never deceived," so it is the person who "hopes all" who is "never put to shame."

Now, although SK does not work out the parallels, it is plain that the different possible attitudes towards belief are also different possible attitudes towards, or frames for, hope. So there will be a style of hoping typical of the naive man: frivolous, inexperienced, or simple-minded hoping. Another for the self-lover: vain, conceited, self-satisfied hoping for oneself. Another for the malicious person: envious, spiteful, corrupted hopes concerning others. There will be the kind of hope that is available from the standpoint of experience and probability: realistic, rationally grounded, hoping. That I have already discussed. There will be a kind of hoping typical of the mistrustful person, which I have not discussed.

The mistrustful man's hoping is really a kind of despair. It is despairing about other people. Where the lover is always hopeful of good for others, and the man of experience sometimes, the mistrustful person is never hopeful of good for them. That is, he has always given people up for lost. Naive hopes are often revealed as void. That brings, I suppose, the shame of naivety; although it is never any shame, from SK's point of view, to be caught hoping better for others than in fact arrives. The hopes of the self-loving and malicious, too, will often be dashed. Here the shame is, or should be, genuine. Even the man of experience will sometimes hope in vain. People on whom he pins his bets will sometimes go wrong, let him down, turn out unredeemable. From such shame only the mistrustful man is completely protected. Since he "hopes nothing at all," that is, nothing good for others, his hopes for them can never be disappointed. For he has no hopes for others at all. "For to hope is to expect the possibility of good" (*KG*, 234); not just anything, and definitely not the possibility of ill. So mistrust is despairing about others.

Now, as the lover cannot be deceived, so he can never be put to shame. Why is this? Can his hopes for others not be revealed as void? I argued earlier that it is central to SK's position that there are kinds of hope which can never, in logic, be revealed as dashed. For there are kinds of belief about other people which can never be revealed as false. These are beliefs which cannot be falsified by observable evidence.

The paradigm of such a belief is exposed in the chapter on hope. It is the belief in the possibility of an eternal blessedness. It is to believe in the possibility of "more and more glorious advancement in the good from perfection to perfection or resurrection from downfall or salvation from lostness and thus beyond" (*KG*, 237). This possibility is the proper object of hoping. But the proper object of believing, that is, believing all things, corresponds to this possibility. It is believing good. And that means, among other things, believing, of other people, that they are *in themselves* on the way to that possibility.

I stress "in themselves." For if loving involves believing that others are, *whatever the appearances*, on the way to their eternal blessedness, then it requires us to believe that we have real essential selves, which are not necessarily manifested—still less wholly embodied—in our visible words and actions. The choice of love involves also choosing a certain general conception of the individual.

SK himself indicates the nucleus of this concept when he writes that "love to one's neighbour is love between two individual beings, each eternally qualified as spirit" (*KG*, 68). As these words imply, it is not necessary to suppose, for instance, that individuals—the essential person— are disembodied or detachable from their bodies. (These kinds of view are, anyway, contrary to the pictures we get in the New Testament.) Nor do we need any particular metaphysical theory of eternity and time. We do, however, need some conception to give content to the idea of "neighbour." For a neighbour is essentially a person *to* whom I have duties and *from* whom I may expect correlative duties. All that we really need is to think of human beings as essentially capable of an eternal blessedness. SK expresses the same thought also in these words: *"the lover presupposes that love is in the other person's heart"* (*KG*, 206; SK's emphasis). He adds a few pages later that believing all things means precisely presupposing that love is fundamentally present. So, the loving person conceives of human beings, it seems, as fundamentally and essentially loving beings.

SK emphasizes, however, that this is not just a conception of the essential self. It carries over into one's conception of individuals as speakers and doers in this life. It is a mark of love, and love alone, that it *"loves each human being according to the other's individuality"* (*KG*, 252; SK's emphasis). This is because to love is to have authentic individuality, and "to have individuality is to believe in the individuality of every other person" (*KG*, 253). The connection between love and this strong concept of individuality is, however, still closer than just thinking of people as individuals. For loving simply is "to aid one or another human being to become his own" (*KG*, 260). And this is explained also as "to become one's self, free, independent, his own" (*KG*, 255). "This is the greatest benefaction," adds SK.

These are not distinct conceptions. For to become one's self is to become loving. And this is "the highest good and the greatest blessedness" (*KG*, 225). Believing and hoping the good for someone is simply believing and hoping that he or she will become (what he or she already essentially is) truly loving—loving in truth.

For SK, love and the eternal are internally related concepts. "What is it that really binds the temporal and the eternal? What is it other than love..." (*KG*, 24). "To cheat oneself out of love is the most terrible deception; it is an eternal loss..." (*KG*, 23). Similarly: "If there is less love in him, there is also less of the eternal in him, but if there is less of the eternal in him, there is also less possibility, less awareness of possibility..." (*KG*, 241). True love "is eternal, relates itself to the eternal, rests in the eternal" (*KG*, 289).

Therefore, it follows that to love, because it means presupposing love in the person one loves, means believing that he is essentially related to the eternal (eternal blessedness), has the eternal within him as a possibility. This conceptual relation is central in SK. It is impossible to break it without shattering his whole theory, and it is equally impossible to pretend that it is not there at all. Why? Because either one thinks of human beings in terms of the concept of the eternal or one does not. But to lack the concept of the eternal is precisely to be in despair (see *KG*, 55).

I return briefly to the claim that hope can never be put to shame. Why not? Because what he hopes has an essential relation to the eternal. His hope, and his belief, involves conceiving people as individuals, each of whom has a possibility of gaining the eternal through and in loving. But this conception of human beings is clearly not falsifiable by anything that anyone can observe. Nothing that happens could possibly count against this conception nor for it. But, by parity of reasoning, nothing that happens—that we can observe or experience—can possibly count for or against the contrary conception of human beings. That is, in outline, one of the structures of concepts which lies behind the paradoxical claim that the man who hopes all, that is, the possibility of the good, can never be put to shame. But SK has another consideration, too, a simpler one.

Just as he listed the frames of belief which do not "believe all," so he lists a number of attitudes which do not involve "hoping all." These include shrewdness, anger and bitterness, the "evil eye," envy, small-mindedness (which is fearful), and vain worldliness. From each of these stances it is easy to see how one might give up hoping for others—give up hoping for good for and in them, give them up as hopeless. So they are all at root forms of despair. For it is a mark of despair "to *suppose* the impossibility of the good" (*KG*, 237). And there is no third choice between supposing that the good is possible for someone and supposing that it is not, which is just supposing that it is impossible.

SK's list of ways of failing in hope makes something clear which has for a long time been obscurely waiting on the horizon of this argument. It is the moral unneutrality of all these stances: just as self-love and malice are, plainly, morally unneutral and condemnable frames of belief. If so, some kinds of hope are morally condemnable in themselves. Hoping for evil for others, hoping that they will fail to achieve the good, are plainly evil hopes. They are things "for which it is a shame to hope" (*KG*, 244). Here the shame is already within the hope, within the hoping. A man who hopes for these kinds of things is hoping for something *shameful*. His hope is in itself shameful, whatever the outcome of events. Whether his hope is fulfilled or not makes no difference. It is, and always will have been, shameful to have had such a hope. So the man who adopts one or another of these attitudes is already, whatever happens, "put to shame."

It makes absolutely no difference whether such a man recognizes his shame or not. Probably he will not. He is just the kind of person we should expect to find laughing at the people who still hope for good, especially when their hopes appear to be going unfulfilled. In SK's view, it is far worse for a man *not* to feel shame when he ought to than to feel shame. For shame is one of the most powerful instruments in the service of the good.

Hoping for someone's evil or failure, therefore, betrays a petty or corrupted mind. (One thing it certainly betrays: the absence of love.) This thought introduces an idea that SK uses prominently in the chapter on belief. It is the idea of the "world of pettiness."

Let me cite some representative remarks. "Alas, if vanity could gain power over the true lover, he would certainly be deceived, for vanity draws him down out of love into the lower world of mean-mindedness and wrangling, where one fools others and is fooled" (*KG*, 225). Again: "so that the lover falls away from love and sinks down into the illusory world of childish squabbling with the deceiver..." (*KG*, 228). Here is another: "But now suppose that in eternity it became clear that the lover really had been deceived... The true lover will therefore not even be able to understand the objection. Alas, but the rest of us, I regret, are able to understand it all too easily, for *the lower level of conception and the pact between earthly passions and illusion* are very difficult to shake loose" (*KG*, 229).

This "pettiness" operates especially in relation to hope. For the failure to hope for good for others "must be because there is something which weighs him (sc. the non-hoper) down and gives him a tendency to expect the other person's discouragement, downfall, perdition. This down-drag is worldliness, the earthly passions of the unloving mind, for in itself worldliness is heavy, ponderous, sluggish, slack, dispirited, dejected..." (*KG*, 240).

A central feature of the worldly standpoint (one I have already mentioned) is its readiness to use the concepts of evil in interpreting what is going on. It is to this tendency that SK counterposes the childlikeness of love, like wisdom. "What the world admires as shrewdness is really an understanding of evil—wisdom is an understanding of the good" (*KG*, 265–66).

In a passage of astonishing bitterness, SK applies the distinction between worldliness and love (wisdom) to the ways in which we talk about each other. Gossiping, talking about the faults of our neighbours, "is therefore a sign of corruption" (*KG*, 269). It is no mitigation that the evil told is true, that is, what the world of experience would hold true. "It is inconceivable that one with the earnestness of the eternal could be rigorous in taking care that the evil he told was unconditionally factual and then be able to use his life in this nauseous service of factuality: the reporting of evil" (*KG*, 270). SK compares gossip to "setting fire to a whole community" (*KG*, 271). Why? Because of its effects: to embitter, injure, besmirch, mislead, corrupt, destroy.

This attack takes us back to the attack on cleverness. In each case, SK is saying that there is a frame of mind which it is shameful to have. And they are at bottom the same. Moreover, this frame of mind is not strange or uncommon. It is simply possessing, and being ready to use, the concepts of falsity, deceit, evil, and sin in judging what goes on around you. And who does not do this? Perhaps not SK's naive individual: not the child. But doubtless the self-lover, for others; the malicious individual; the man of experience, wise in the ways of the world; certainly the mistrustful man.

3

As I have reconstructed it, SK's argument goes something like this. There are several possible frames for belief. Which are we to adopt? On the face of it, that frame which minimizes the probability of our being deceived, maximizes the probability that our judgments will be right. Recall that we are concerned with understanding other people. SK then argues, however, that the criterion of deception cannot be used without begging crucial questions of epistemology. Worse, the frames which pass the test of deception turn out to have features which are morally and psychologically disastrous. To adopt such a frame is to condemn oneself to despair. It is to choose a life characterized by lack of hope, loss of any conception of an absolute good, and a fundamentally petty and calculating worldliness. So, while passing the test of deception (set, however, only in their own terms), these frames fail the much deeper and broader test of self-deception, of deceiving oneself out of the possibility of a great good.

But there is an argument in *KG* which undercuts the whole discussion of the different kinds of deception. For that discussion takes something important for granted. It assumes that, however else we can assess frames of belief, we cannot escape assessing them by reference to the judgments they yield. The assumption is that we judge each other, that we want to and need to judge each other, and that therefore what matters is that our judgments should be right as often as possible. SK also questions, and then denies, this assumption. That he does so should not, perhaps, be a very great surprise. For SK is always, strikingly so in *KG*, leaning heavily on the New Testament. And the passages in Matthew and Luke in which Jesus speaks of love also speak of judging: "Judge not, that ye be not judged"; or, "and ye shall not be judged."

This note is sounded in the very first chapter of *KG*: "For one is not to work in order that love becomes known by its fruits but to work to make love capable of being recognised by its fruits" (*KG*, 31). This is expanded on the next page: "In truth, love shall be recognisable by its fruits, but still it does not follow from this that you are to take it upon yourself to be the man who knows." The tree's job is to bear fruit itself, not to judge the fruit of other trees. Why not? Because judging is not itself a fruit of love, not itself one of the works of love. In saying this, SK is not saying that the loving person must be blind, ignorant, self-deceiving, or merely naive. He is distinguishing judging from the proper works of love: having faith in people, hoping for the best, not interpreting behaviour for ill, having mercy, forgiving, being reconciled with others, and so on.

One reason is this. "Precisely because existence will test *you*, test *your* love or whether there is love in you, for this very reason with the help of the understanding it presents you with truth and deception as two equal possibilities in contrast to each other, so that there must be a revelation of what is in you since *you* judge, that is, since in judging you choose" (*KG*, 215). To judge ill of someone is to reveal mistrust, pure or mixed in experience; to judge well is to reveal love. To judge that someone else is loving is to reveal only one's own love.

Another, and more catastrophic reason, is, "one who judges that the other person lacks love takes the groundwork away—and he cannot build up..." (*KG*, 208). SK gives a powerful example of what "removing the groundwork" can mean. Judging that someone has done wrong, not forgiving the deed in the manner of love, cannot diminish but actually tends to strengthen and increase the wrongdoing (see *KG*, 275–76).

On the other hand, SK is not trying to argue that the loving person must pretend not to understand when evil has been visibly done if that is ever the case. Love is not complaisance or collusion. It is an important part of loving someone to want to bring that person to the truth and to bring the truth to that person. And this must include the truth about his or her own deeds and self. But this is to be done *not by judging* but by loving. "No, it is of especial importance, and implicit in the work of love, that through the help of love the unloving person becomes clearly aware of his irresponsibility he has acted so that he deeply feels his wrong doing. This the lover has to do, and then he will also win the vanquished..." (*KG*, 312). By loving, not by judging.

"Judge not, that ye be not judged." In the conclusion of *KG*, SK speaks of "*the Christian like-for-like, the like-for-like of the eternal*" (p. 345). He explains this principle in two subsequent remarks. (*A*) "For, Christianly understood, to love human beings is to love God and to love God is to love human beings; what you do unto men you do unto God, and therefore what you do unto men God does unto you" (pp. 351–52). (*B*) "For God is himself really the pure like-for-like, the pure rendition of the infinitising at every moment of that which at every moment is in a man" (p. 352). In these words, again, we catch an echo of the gospel passages. "Therefore all things whatsoever ye would that men should do to you, do

you even so to them" (Matt. 7:12). Even for the stronger claim there is a
clear textual precedent: "And the King shall answer and say unto them,
Verily I say unto you, Inasmuch as ye have done it unto one of the least of
these my brethren, ye have done it unto me" (Matt. 25:40). Separating
the sheep and the goats.

Thus, too, even for judging, loving, and forgiving. *"To accuse another
person before God is to accuse oneself, like-for-like"* (*KG*, 349). Similarly for
judging. If you want God to judge someone else, "it does not then help
any that you intend that he shall judge someone else, for you yourself
have made him your judge, and he is, *like-for-like*, simultaneously your
judge, that is, he judges you also. If, on the other hand, you do not
engage in accusing someone before God or in making God into a judge,
God is then a merciful God" (*KG*, 349–50). Is God, then, not love? Yes,
certainly: but only for the person who loves. For such a person, God is
the "infinitizing" of the love within. Judging there must no doubt be; but
it is self-judgment, in self-knowledge and confession. And here one is
before a God who judges. "For what is conscience? In the conscience it is
God who looks upon a human being so that the human being now must
look to him in all things. In this way God educates" (*KG*, 346). But the
conscience is speaking only to oneself. To understand oneself suddenly as
a "Thou" to whom the eternal "I" is speaking (see *KG*, 98) is to understand the absolute separation between oneself and all other human individuals. "The direction is inwards; essentially you have only to do with
yourself before God. This world of inwardness, the new version of what
other men call reality, this is reality. In this world of inwardness the
Christian like-for-like is at home. It wants to turn you away from the
external (but without taking you out of the world), upwards or inwards"
(*KG*, 351). These themes remind us how closely *KG* follows upon *OTA*,
how closely it is followed by *CT*.

V

Edifying Beliefs and the Self

THE THEORY of subjective truth is central to SK's thought. It is central to his theory of belief, to his understanding of Christianity and of the relation between reason and Christian faith, and to his entire literary production. Yet it still remains obscure. So, therefore, does the essence of SK's thought. Why? Because the theory contains a number of positions which appear partially intelligible on their own, but which when synthesized appear to generate paradoxes.

I begin by setting down four passages from different works. I shall then consider some problems that they appear to raise, both singly and together.

A. When the question of the truth is raised subjectively, reflection is directed subjectively to the nature of the individual's relationship; if only the mode of this relationship is in the truth, the individual is in the truth even if he should happen to be thus related to what is not true. (*AE*, 178)

B. Only the truth which *edifies* is truth *for you*. This is an essential predicate relating to the truth as inwardness; its decisive characteristic as edifying *for you*, i.e. for the subject, constitutes its essential difference from all objective knowledge. (*AE*, 226)

C. The curious thing is that there is a "how" which has this quality, that if *it* is truly given, then the "what" is also given.... Here, quite certainly, we have inwardness at its maximum proving to be objectivity once again. (*JSK*, 355)

D. It is a confused use of language if one speaks about the curtain being rolled up on the stage of the eternal at the time of death, because the eternal is no stage—it is truth. (*KG*, 95)

The first and second passages each present what will be readily recognized as the idea of truth as subjectivity. But each requires deep consideration. For it is not plain what justifies SK in using the idea of truth in either context. It is not plain why subjectivity, a mode of relationship, or inwardness may be called "truth."

Apparently quite different ideas are presented in passages C and D, ideas of truth as objectivity. C is puzzling, because it states SK's central thesis in a way which appears to stress its paradoxicality. D is puzzling simply because the sense of identifying the idea of truth and the idea of the eternal is not in the least plain.

Any plausible account of SK's theory of subjective truth must satisfy two requirements. It must explain his application of the idea of truth to the realm of inwardness. And it must explain his thesis that, if we really grasp the first account, we may then be able to grasp how reintroduction of the idea of the objective is justified.

Passage B presents, I believe, the crucial idea. This is the idea of edification, upbuilding. This idea is a key which unlocks the heart of SK's theory; and neglect of this idea has contributed largely to the theory's continuing obscurity.

I

What is edification? We must think not in pedagogical and pastoral terms but in plastic and metaphysical ones. Edification is a process of transformation. It is the transformation of a foundation into a complete structure. It is the creation of a complete structure on and out of its foundation.

The structure which edification creates is the self. SK refers to this in various ways: for instance, as the "inner self," the "ideal self," the "second self," and often just the "spirit." And he contrasts it with the actual self, the aesthetical in a man, the contingent phenomenal ego.

Edification is not a natural and spontaneous process, like accumulating experience, memories, or knowledge. It is a process which is the outcome of a conscious and willed action, or resolution. "But the intelligibility of the talk and the listener's understanding of it, are still not the talk's true aim. This by no means gives the meditation its proper emphasis. For in order to achieve its proper emphasis the talk must unequivocally demand something of the listener ... ; the talk must unconditionally demand the reader's own decisive activity and all depends upon this" (*OTA1*, 178). He adds that the "thou" of an edifying talk is addressed to a particular individual only if that individual makes it addressed to him. SK's general name for this kind of activity is "appropriation."

Therefore, it is quite wrong to suppose that "edifying" is a predicate which can be attached objectively to certain thoughts or discourses as distinct from others. A thought or discourse becomes "edifying" just if some individual allows himself to be edified by it. It is even better to say, just if some individual edifies himself by means of it. Edification is an activity that individuals can perform only on themselves. It is the individual's activity of transforming himself. As Johannes Climacus says: "The truth is the subject's transformation in himself" (*AE*, 38).

What is appropriated by the individual is called by SK "essential knowledge" (*AE*, 176). And he defines this as "only such knowledge as has an essential relationship to existence" (*AE*, 176). There are obvious peculiarities about the idea of knowledge. One may easily wonder if "belief," or even "choice," would not be a more accurate term to use. Both suggestions are in fact apt. In *EE2*, SK permits Judge William to explain that his phrase "to choose oneself" is intended to express the sense of the standard phrase "to know oneself" but also to reveal an implication of this idea of knowledge which the latter phrase conceals. SK calls essential knowledge "knowledge" only because he is speaking of what is standardly referred to as "self-knowledge."

We can say with equal truth that what the individual appropriates in the activity of edification is some set of spiritual qualities, "goods of the spirit" (see *CT*, 121ff.). To appropriate spiritual qualities is to appropriate—more precisely, to become—spirit.

One more general point: the activity of edification is quite unlike, say, the activity of memorizing or the process of being emotionally moved. It is an activity of questioning, the questioning of oneself. Such questioning is concerned with a particular range of features of one's life and deals with these in terms of a particular species of categories. It is a moral self-questioning concerning one's activities, regarded as acts of will or choices.

But such a questioner is far from doubting in the Cartesian (or sceptical) sense. His questions express not doubt but guilt. Guilt is primarily awareness of one's own disposition to evil.

2

According to SK, only the true self is capable of being edified; the external, aesthetic, phenomenal self is incapable. This is, I believe, a logical or conceptual truth: at any rate, a necessary truth. SK does not wish to deny that many processes can occur to, and within, a man's phenomenal ego. The ego can be transformed in many kinds of ways. But no transformation of the ego can possibly be of the kind that the idea of edification picks out.

The kind of self-transformation that SK has in mind must necessarily show in one's activity. However, we must go carefully at this point. It is quite wrong to suppose that SK is saying that moral transformation must show in one's actions. Such a transformation need by no means be externally visible. For it is primarily the transformation of "resignation." SK describes this also as the awareness that one is as nothing, that one can do nothing. And resignation, although an activity, is an inner activity. It consists simply in "relegating to the status of what may have to be renounced" everything of this world (*AE*, 350). The "may have to be" is crucial and distinguishes SK's idea of resignation decisively from any idea of external and visible asceticism.

Now, we might well wonder what logical connection exists between a self-questioning prompted by awareness of one's disposition to evil and a relegation of everything worldly to the status of the renounceable, or conditional. The connection is that both activities spring immediately out of one and the same source. This is the adoption of a moral point of view, of moral categories for the allocation of values and the justification of activities. For SK, to think in moral terms is to become immediately aware of one's own essential moral guilt—that is, unless one proceeds directly to self-deception. And it is at the same time to become aware that no worldly thing can have in itself a value which is a moral value. For moral value can attach only to activities, and only in so far as they are acts of will.

In *SD*, SK gives a famous definition of the idea of spirit. However obscure the details, SK's negative point at least is plain. He wishes to stress that by "spirit" he does not mean any kind of substance or any kind of quality; and the qualification he adds to his first account implies also that he does not mean any kind of relation either. It would be closer to the truth, if we are going to speak in Aristotelian terms, to say that "spirit" refers to a way of activity. It is exactly thus, I believe, that SK also categorizes the Kantian idea of the moral subject or agent. To be a moral subject is to be active in certain characteristic ways.

The idea of a spiritual quality, therefore, must be taken in a rather Pickwickian sense. In *CT*, SK makes it plain that it is impossible to possess a spiritual quality, at least one of the more perfect kind, without communicating it. This is another conceptual thesis.

The true, or inner, self can be defined as that about an individual which can be related to itself in the characteristic way that is active moral self-transformation. Alternatively, it may be defined as the individual himself, in so far as he relates to himself as a moral self-transformer. If we look at SK's claims in this way, I believe, we shall cease to feel impelled to criticize him for introducing an unexplained psychological dualism in his idea of man. There is indeed a dualism, but it is neither unnecessary nor paradoxical. It is simply an expression of the fundamental fact that individuals can form moral points of view and conceptions of themselves and can proceed to act upon themselves in the light of these general and particular ideas. An existence of that kind is plainly possible, and plainly different from an existence which is free of moral conceptions or self-consciousness or both.

SK's position is not, however, merely banal. Much of his work is given to exploring the genuine metaphysical presuppositions of that fundamental fact. Thus, for instance, the whole discussion of the idea of the subjective existing thinker in the opening pages of *AE*. But even here the metaphysical theses are deductions from common moral data—more precisely, from the possibility of such moral data—not their logical premisses.

3

It is a corollary of SK's idea of edification that no thought or discourse can be objectively edifying, since its being edifying rests in some individual's act of appropriating it for his own inner edification. No proposition can be called edifying. Beliefs, however, may be edifying. For a belief, in SK's theory, is the product of an act of assent to some proposition. So a belief is edifying if its believer's act of assent was also an act of edifying appropriation.

An edifying belief is a belief which an individual holds as his answer to an act of moral self-questioning. The most plausible interpretation of this general idea is that an edifying belief is a moral commitment. Also an edifying belief is, by definition, a belief by appropriation of which, and holding in his active existence, an individual is spiritually upbuilt. By and in the continuous activity of guiding his existence by reference to such a belief the individual builds himself up as the kind of self-reflective being we call a moral agent.

Now, we may well ask what aspects of a man's being or existence can, logically, be built up by such an act; namely, by an act of appropriating a belief about oneself, as true of oneself and for oneself, as a principle for the inner transformation of one's whole life into moral categories. There are several plain answers. A man may build up his moral conscience thus, his habit of moral reflection. He may build up what SK calls his "inward-ness," including his habit of thinking about himself in moral terms. He may build up his sincerity or "purity of heart," his will to truth concern-ing himself and his life. He may build up his sense of moral guilt and resignation and the attached habits of self-examination and self-renuncia-tion. Yet there is one potential item on this list that I have not yet men-tioned. It is self-knowledge. And it is central to SK's thought that the edifying produces, or increases, self-knowledge. I shall take up this point later.

Why should an edifying belief build up the self? Because it transforms the self; because the individual proceeds to transform himself by means of the belief. He transforms himself by means of it just because it is the answer to a question about himself of a characteristic kind, namely, a question about his transformability. For the general form of the question that precedes edification is, What is the right shape for my life to take? Even to ask such a question is to presuppose that I have the ability and responsibility to transform my life.

Further, it is impossible for an individual to pose himself such a ques-tion without immediately becoming aware that he is, and has always been, in essential ignorance. This is the ignorance which SK describes as fol-lows: "There is an ignorance about one's own life that is equally tragic for the learned and for the simple, for both are bound by the same responsi-bility. This ignorance is called self-deceit" (*OTA1*, 52). That is to say, it cannot be a mere contingency that a man is unconscious of his moral self. We may reply that it can, since children are certainly not conscious that they have moral selves until and unless they have been given moral train-ing. But this reply misses the point. The point is that at the time when an individual comes to be aware that he has so far missed his essential moral nature, he must in the same act see himself as having failed in his moral responsibilities. The guilt of which SK speaks centrally is not, primarily, guilt over recognized misdeeds. It is primarily and fundamentally a sense of irrevocably missed opportunities for moral action and moral good.

In the same passage that I cited just above, SK goes on to say that the only thing that can remove self-deceit is purity of heart. This remark implies a theory of self-deceit. It implies that whatever self-deceit is, it is essentially a product of an act of an impure heart, an impure will. Self-deceit is the product of a will to obscure one's own existence to oneself. Recognition of one's essential ignorance about oneself is, therefore, recognition that one has been engaged in obscuring one's own existence to oneself. The self-ignorance is seen to be willed and thus culpable. Conversely, the effort towards self-knowledge is an effort to achieve purity; SK sometimes calls this "transparency."

4

But edifying beliefs do not just operate as means to, or causes of, the upbuilding of one's true self. They function as essential constituents of the upbuilt self. The true self is a self to which such beliefs are essential.

It may seem puzzling how this can be so. But it is puzzling only if we try to conceive the self as some kind of entity, or substance. If the self were a spiritual substance, it would certainly not be plain that criteria for identifying the self can involve specification of certain kinds of belief. But if we recall that SK conceives the self as, so to speak, a man's power of moral self-reflection, the matter ceases to be so puzzling. If one's self is defined by the way in which one holds beliefs about oneself, then plainly a transformation of the kind of beliefs one holds about oneself is also a transformation of one's self.

Extra difficulty may be produced by thinking of beliefs as mental objects or contents, as thoughts or propositions held assentingly in the mind. It may then seem natural to separate the ideas of the mind or self and its objects or contents. However, the relation between a man (or his mind) and his moral principles is not an instance of the subject-predicate or substance-attribute relation. I make no pretence to have a decent analysis of moral principles; but I do claim that a man's moral principles are not attributes that attach to him, for instance, in the way that his intelligence or his historical knowledge attach to him as attributes.

An edifying belief is not an edifying *proposition*. For SK there cannot possibly be any such thing as an edifying proposition. It is precisely what distinguishes a belief from a proposition that makes it conceivable that edifying beliefs, but not edifying propositions, may be constituents of the true self. The distinguishing feature is the individual's act of assent.

But this act of assent, although often a once-for-all turning of the will in a particular direction ("way"), must be more than a single resolution. If that were all that a man's assent consisted in, then we could not credit him with genuine assent at all. What is required is his continual re-enactment of assent. SK sometimes refers to this by the term "repetition." Again, he refers to the same requirement by the term "continuity," or "inner history." Fidelity to a principle of action—more precisely, a moral principle—is the only way in which a man's life can acquire genuine continuity. It is the only way in which he himself can acquire continuity, sameness. We might put SK's point thus: Although the idea of a man's remaining the same, or being the same now that he was formerly, has very many senses, depending on what kind of characteristic is being referred to, this idea can have only one sense when we are referring to what is essential to his being the individual he is, in contrast with all that is accidental to this.

It follows that the self-transformation which all edification requires is not instantaneous. There may indeed be an instantaneous self-transformation. But self-transformation is essentially a continuous work; moreover, a lifelong one. In *AE*, SK remarks that the life of the "subjective existing thinker" is a striving without an external *telos*, which does not imply that it has no internal *telos*. In *EE2*, he writes: "The individual is not fighting with external foes but fights with himself, fights out love from within him. And they (sc. these virtues) have reference to time, for their truth does not consist in being once for all but in being constantly what they are. And by these virtues nothing else is acquired, only they themselves are acquired" (p. 142).

5

There is a crucially important section of *SD* in which SK proposes a conception of the self. He says, "Each thing is qualitatively that by which it is measured, and that which is qualitatively its measure is ethically its goal; and the measure and goal are qualitatively that which something is" (p. 210). Also, "the measure for the self is always that in the face of which it is a self."

We can say immediately that to be a moral subject is to exist in the face of the ethical. That means to exist in the constant conscious light of ethical values, demands, goals. These are the ideas by which such an individual measures not only his deeds but also his inner self, his thoughts and wishes and motives and feelings; and even that innermost self with which he obscurely identifies himself.

SK usually refers to the ethical as "the eternal." This is sometimes capitalized. Sometimes the relevant term is simply "God." "Only the Eternal is always appropriate and always present, is always true. Only the Eternal applies to each human being, whatever his age may be" (*OTA1*,

33). The voice of the eternal is conscience. In the same work, SK says that "it must be heard by the individual, for the individual has become the eternal echo of this voice. It must be heard. There is no place to flee from it. For in the infinite there is no place, the individual is himself the place" (*OTA1*, 186). Again, in *CT*, he writes:

There is only One who knows what He Himself is, that is God; and He knows also what every man in himself is, for it is precisely by being before God that every man is. The man who is not before God is not before himself, for this a man can be only by being before Him who is in and for himself. If one is oneself by being in Him who is in and for Himself, one can be in others or before others, but one cannot by being merely before others be oneself. (P. 43)

This is a major theme of *OTA1*. Unfortunately, it has gone too often unremarked, as that work's characteristic use of the ideas of doublemindedness and singlemindedness has led to its being read in psychological terms. Yet to "singlemindedness" we should add that work's idea of "being at one with oneself." "It is indeed like a changing of raiment to lay off manyness, in order rightly to center down upon one thing; to interrupt the busy course of activity, in order to put on the quiet of contemplation and be at one with oneself" (*OTA1*, 47). SK adds, "But he that in truth becomes at one with himself, he is in the silence." In this work SK identifies a large number of interests or goals which impose radical doublemindedness on the man or woman who pursues them. By contrast, he argues, only the ethical in itself allows, indeed imposes, a radical singlemindedness. However, the conception of the measure requires us to give the work a parallel reading; the pursuit of such interests and goals imposes, and springs from, a radical disunity in the individual's own self. Ethical subjecthood alone allows for a unity of the self. Moreover, it is a unity that exists, so to speak, both synchronically and diachronically. Not only are the various elements of the self at any given time comprehended within an overall unity; also identifications of the self at different times fall under a unity that SK calls "continuity" and "sameness."

The process of edification is the process of coming to exist before the eternal. This explains why it is inept to interpret what SK says about self-knowledge and subjectivity in anything like an existentialist way. (It is irrelevant that he often uses the word "existential" in connection with these ideas. For what he says is utterly unlike and incompatible with anything in Heidegger or Sartre.) Interest in and knowledge of the phenomenal self is as far distant as possible from the kind of self-inquiry that edification requires. In one of the early edifying discourses, SK discusses the view that the need of God constitutes man's highest perfection. "Through this view of life," he writes, *"a man learns to know himself"* (*T*, 156). He proceeds at once, however, to distinguish knowledge of a man's self in its relation to something else from knowledge of a man's self in its relation to himself (*T*, 157). Edification, and ethics, involves the latter, not the former.

In the same discourse, SK refers to the truth that "in relation to external things a man can do absolutely nothing" (*T*, 162). This is the same belief that I referred to earlier as "resignation." Acceptance of this belief is the first step to true self-knowledge. We might equally well say that it is the first step in knowledge of the true self. An essential part of the identification of a man's first, phenomenal, self is some conception of this self's phenomenal powers, some conception of this self as having phenomenal powers. Of course, SK does not wish to deny that individuals have phenomenal powers and can perform phenomenal deeds. He only wants us to notice that since there is essentially a contingent link between any desire or intention and its fulfilment in this world, it is logically impossible to build a description of any phenomenal object or situation, regarded as the fulfilment of an act of will, into the identification of a man's *essential* self. (Wittgenstein has a very similar argument in his *Notebooks, 1914–1916*.)

Coming to believe that in relation to external things a man can do absolutely nothing need not, of course, be accompanied by adopting a moral point of view. But SK did not overlook this. He only points out that in such a case the belief will produce some kind of despair, and quite logically so. For values will still be located in the external; only their achievement will now be seen as impossible, except by pure chance.

However, the same belief may well accompany adoption of a moral point of view. For then it expresses the moral "revaluation of all values." Even so, SK insists, this belief is only the first step towards acquiring and knowing one's true self. A second step is required. And the second step is again a discovery. It is the discovery of inward opposition to one's own self and will. "The man who fails to discover the existence of this inward struggle is involved in a misunderstanding, and his life is consequently imperfect. But if he does discover this struggle, he will here again be made to understand that he can do nothing of himself" (*T*, 164). The discovery of the inner struggle is the discovery that we create our own temptations for ourselves. It is the discovery that temptations do not come from outside, from the external.

But this is the discovery, so to speak, of an ethical standard which is absolute and independent of one's own will. It might be described as the recognition that one is essentially guilty; that moral failure and success are not simply dependent on accidental circumstances, so that I just happen to have acquired moral guilt, due to unfortunate accidents, and might easily have remained guiltless had circumstances favoured my character.

This experience, I believe, is what SK describes as coming to experience the existence of God. For a man who comes to believe that he can do absolutely nothing either phenomenally or ethically, except by accident, it begins to become possible to speak of his existing "before God." Thus SK writes: "Whoever can do nothing of himself, cannot undertake the least enterprise without God's help, or without coming to notice that there is a God.... Whoever knows in himself that he can do nothing, has each day and each moment the desired and indubitable occasion to experience the living God" (*T*, 168).

But we might also describe this experience as coming to have a conception of one's own perfection; that is, a conception of man's perfection. It is a conception of man as perfectible according to an absolute and independent moral standard. But once again, it is possible to arrive at this general conception either with or without faith. And if a man arrives at it without a faith that his perfectibility is achievable, he must necessarily be in despair. Yet he must know that he cannot achieve his perfection by himself, since he already identifies himself as essentially a tempter, hence morally guilty, before himself. So the only alternative to despair is that faith which SK describes as experience of "the living God." (It is worth a mention in passing that SK constantly attaches the ideas of comfort, hope, and joy to this experience. This balances his familiar stress on suffering.)

6

The process of edification is a process of constant deepening. It can also be described as a process of increasing self-transparency, of making oneself increasingly transparent to oneself. In a beautiful image, SK writes: "*Purity of heart*: it is a figure of speech that compares the heart to the sea, and why just to this? Simply for the reason that the depth of the sea determines its purity, and its purity determines its transparency.... As the sea mirrors the elevation of heaven in its pure depths, so may the heart when it is calm and deeply transparent mirror the divine elevation of the Good in its pure depths" (*OTA1*, 176–77).

In this passage SK is saying that the transparency of the individual to himself exactly mirrors the depth of his conception of the good. We might equally well say that it mirrors his conception of the truth. This is the central thesis in the epistemological theory that revolves around the idea of edification. We can have differing conceptions of the truth; and our conceptions and understandings of ourselves necessarily match our conceptions of the truth. In particular, the process of self-questioning is one that constantly alters by deepening. We can question ourselves more or less deeply. Our self-questioning can be directed by deeper or more superficial ideas of the truth, and so also of our selves. But it is in the natural logic, and so also the natural psychology, of a true self-questioning that the individual's idea of the truth constantly deepens, the more deeply he questions himself. Our initial conceptions of the truth, and of ourselves, are extremely superficial. The questions we pose ourselves at this stage are likely to be matchingly superficial, their answers too. The deeper questions, like the deeper moral and religious difficulties, can reveal themselves only as a result of a process of constantly self-deepening questioning. This process is, among other things, a process of fighting one's way through a series of obscurities which the self erects around itself. There is, of course, no guarantee that self-questioning will proceed constantly more deeply. The process may come to a halt; a man may more or less consciously decide to halt it. The questioner may decide to rest content with one or another relatively superficial and obscure conception of himself. He may, so to speak, allow himself to be taken in by one of the obscurities that the self temptingly casts up to protect itself. Nor, again, does there appear to be any determinate finite limit to the process. This, I believe, is also central to SK's argument.

On the other hand, in one important sense there is for SK a limit to the process of deepening transparency. The limit is reached when a man, to speak figuratively, achieves a conception of himself—his real self—that is so transparent that he sees clear through it, it vanishes as an object and obstacle to his vision, and he sees only the absolute truth. He sees God. If I may quote again from an earlier passage in *OTA1*: "But he that in truth becomes at one with himself, he is in the silence. And this is indeed like a changing of raiment; to strip oneself of all that is as full of noise as it is empty, in order to be hidden in the silence, to become open. This silence is the simple festivity of the holy act of confession" (*OTA1*, 47–48). The process of deepening transparency is a process of increasing "silence," simply because what the individual fights his way through is a series of selves which are constantly chattering. Their chatter is a mark of the superficiality of their conceptions of the true and the good. Human language, as SK often remarks, is not well contrived to speak of the deep, but is instead essentially worldly and selfish. "It speaks only about their own affairs, little about God's" (*T*, 109). The deeper a man's conception of the true and the good, on the other hand, the less significance he will find in phenomenal things, external and internal, and so the less to talk about or think about. As his conception of the true and the good grows deeper, its significance in relation to his existence constantly increases, so as to swallow up everything else. At the ideal limit, only the true and the good can appear to have any significance at all. (This is not to say, obviously, that the individual has then become oblivious of the world. SK does not confuse a centering of significance with a contraction of consciousness.) And this is precisely the beginning of a true conception of God.

I have already stressed that SK is no kind of existentialist. "God" does not simply refer to the individual's final conception of the true and the good. It names a personal being whom SK, along with all Christians, acknowledged and worshipped. So it is very likely that SK would have agreed that, in a sense, his account fits the traditional idea that God's existence can be experimentally verified. He would merely have added that it is quite useless, indeed stupid, to tell a man that if he tries the way of constantly deepening self-questioning, he will finally discover God. It is stupid for the very simple reason that the proposition can make no sense to a man who is not already on his own way of self-questioning, indeed who is not already at the point where his conception of the true and the good has become absolute. Certainly experience can verify that "inwardness at its maximum" proves to be objectivity. But this truth cannot even be understood except in the experience itself.

Let us recall SK's claim "only the truth which *edifies* is *truth for you*" (*AE*, 226). The only way by which an individual can arrive at a true conception of God, that is, at the belief that God exists, is his own particular way: the way of his own self-questioning. In *OTA1*, SK writes that "the place and the path are within a man and just as the place is the blessed state of the striving soul, so the path is the striving soul's continual transformation" (pp. 84–85). Similarly in *OTA3*: "For each person the way first exists, or comes into existence, when he goes on it, for the way is *the manner* of our going" (p. 93).

Still, at the limit there is a "place," distinct from the individual's path, a "what" that he discovers by reaching the limit of his "how." This is God. At this point we can therefore say, speaking literally, that the way becomes God. We might also say that at this point the individual is not just "in the truth" but "in the Truth." At this point, he is in the truth in such a manner that he is necessarily thus related to what is true—the absolute truth.

7

Edification is not merely a formal process but a particular process with a determinate content. This content is love. "Love is the ground; love is the building; love builds up. To build up is to build up love, and it is love which builds up" (*KG*, 205). Similarly, he says: "Spiritually understood, love is the deepest ground of the life of the spirit." But love is not just the characteristic attitude or activity of the individual who is being edified. It is also, so to speak, his very substance, his true self. Recall for a moment SK's thesis that the self is defined by its qualitative measure. In proportion as an individual approaches the absolute conception of the true and the good, his self approaches a metaphysically absolute status. This is what is commonly called "immortality," or eternity. Finally, the individual who exists in the face of the eternal must have achieved changelessness, eternal life. This is the same as love. "What is it that gives a human being immortality, what else but the love which abides?" (*KG*, 289).

This position presupposes a deeper identification, that the absolutely true and good is to be identified with love. This position is indeed SK's. The more deeply a man conceives of the good, the closer he comes to identifying it with love. "What is the highest good and the greatest blessedness? Certainly it is to love in truth" (*KG*, 225). But in what sense can we identify the *true* with love? How can love be the standard or criterion of truth?

To be able to answer that question satisfactorily would be to grasp the heart of SK's whole thought. I cannot even begin to approach an answer here. But the answer can be described by considering the idea that SK expresses in the following words: "To cheat oneself out of love is the most terrible deception; it is an eternal loss for which there is no reparation, either in time or in eternity" (*KG*, 23). The more deeply a man understands himself, the more clearly he will see that every fundamental position of his will except one necessarily involves self-deception, and thus a willed rejection of truth. That one fundamental position is love. As a man approaches truth, he sees more and more clearly that every fundamental criterion for truth except one—love—is in fact a criterion for willed obscurity. He discovers that it is only in love that it is possible to genuinely will the truth—and so to discover it. The pursuit of true love and the pursuit of absolute truth are identical. Each ends in the discovery of God.

8

A Note. In his edifying and Christian works, SK is not concerned with metaphysics. Still, metaphysical issues are raised, and metaphysical theories implied, by what he says. This is particularly true for *KG* and *SD*. The two crucial terms in SK's metaphysics are "eternity" and "spirit." Now, it is of the highest importance to distinguish SK's own metaphysics—whatever it may be—from the metaphysical theories and analyses in the pseudonymous works. SK's edifying-Christian use of "eternity" and "the eternal" has nothing whatever in common with the discussions in *BA* and *PS*, and these are irrelevant in trying to grasp what "eternity" means in *OTA*, or *KG*, or *CT*. Analogously for "spirit." The edifying-Christian is not in the least concerned, for instance, with the classical problems of mind and body, or the material and the immaterial, or survival after death, or immortality, or heaven and hell. And "eternity" and "spirit" in these works are used in ways which are quite unrelated to the classical problems.

Take "eternity," "the eternal." In the edifying-Christian works, the right conceptual context for understanding this idea is given by *truth, the ethical*, and *love*. The eternal is the truth, the necessary truth, the necessary. It is conscience in the individual; it is the distinction between right and wrong, the separation between the just and the unjust, "the Judgement." It is the Good, the only categorical and single object of the will. It is love, Christian love, to gain which is to win the eternal, to lose which is an eternal loss. It is love, for only love abides and does not alter. For, at bottom, love is God, and God is unchanging and unchangeable; God's love is unchangeable. It is the upholder of all existence, and the source of our very being. These kinds of claims, all taken from *OTA*, *KG*, *CT*, and *SD*, give the conceptual context for SK's own idea of eternity.

Or take "spirit." Here, the right framework is given by ideas like *transparency, continuity, consistency, self-reflection, renunciation, dying to*. It is given by the analysis of *transferred language*, the logic of analogy and negation, in *KG*, part 2, chapter 1. As he does with "eternity," SK consciously uses "spirit" as an abbreviated name for a category of discourse: that is, a way of formulating propositions, making arguments, and relating concepts, which is specific to a particular subject regarded from a particular perspective. This is roughly what Wittgenstein calls a "language-game." For SK, as a believing and practising Christian, the categories of "eternity" and "spirit" are not just *games*, ways of arranging words. They **mean** something, they *point to* something, and what they mean is quite real, and indeed ultimately the only reality there is. But it cannot be got at in speech (description, argument, analysis) or thought except in and through the characteristic uses of language which define its language-game, its category. So there can be no question of an autonomous metaphysics, detached from the contexts SK assigns. The edifying-Christian concepts of "eternity" and "spirit" cannot be theorized in terms (contexts) other than those SK assigns in his acknowledged works. So, for example, if we asked SK for a clear *metaphysical* statement about the relation of eternity to time, he could only give us what we already have in, say, *KG*: reflections about ways in which the true Christian lover detaches his loving from considering the future, the past, outcomes, and so on. "Eternity" and "spirit" simply cannot even be discussed outside the context of a Christian ethics; no discussion outside that context bears on SK's own understanding of those concepts.

VI

Self-knowledge as Transparency

IN THIS and the next two chapters I shall discuss the idea of self-knowledge. Self-knowledge is a constant theme in SK's writings, together with its conceptual kin: self-examination, self-deceit, self-ignorance, and so forth. It is discussed in early pseudonymous books (*EE, PS, AE*), in the early edifying discourses (*T, TTLI*), in the edifying literature proper (*OTAI, KG, CT*), and in many of the central later works (*SD, GU, TS, DS*). This width of context implies a corresponding width of analyses. And indeed this is just what we find. For as these works have different purposes and presuppositions and are addressed to different readers, so the analyses and discussions of self-knowledge they contain differ in systematic ways. Very roughly, the earlier treatments are ethical, the later religious and specifically Christian.

But there is absolutely nothing "relativist" about SK's cast of mind or his thinking. The mere fact that there are different ways of looking at and understanding the idea of self-knowledge does not in the least entail that all these ways have equal—or indeed any—validity. On the contrary. For SK, it is plain that however appealing and plausible the earlier accounts, they are at best first steps, at best superficial—and at worst dangerously misleading and corrupting. However, they are the first steps. There is no way into the deeper self-knowledge except through the primitive and shallow. That is moral self-knowledge: the self-knowledge pictured so movingly and lovingly in Plato's *Apology*. So this is where we must begin. And we must begin, without the pretence of foreknowledge, by working ourselves into that conception.

Here are three passages which may help us to work our way into SK's thought.

Let us now for once compare an ethical and an aesthetical individual. The principal difference, and one on which everything hinges, is that the ethical individual is transparent to himself and does not live *ins Blaue hinein* as does the aesthetical individual. This difference states the whole case. He who lives ethically has seen himself, knows himself, penetrates with his consciousness his whole concretion.... (*EE2*, 262)

The ethical individual knows himself, but this knowledge is not a mere contemplation (for with that the individual is determined by his necessity), it is a reflection upon himself which itself is an action, and therefore I have deliberately preferred to use the expression "choose oneself" instead of know oneself. (*EE2*, 263)

I should like to say that in making a choice it is not so much a question of choosing the right as of the energy, the earnestness, the pathos with which one chooses. (*EE2*, 171)

The image of transparency is not unique to *EE2*. It is used also at crucial points in *AE*, *OTA1*, *KG*, *SD*, and *GU* and so represents a constant and deep feature in SK's thinking about self-knowledge. The image is not, of course, unique to and original with SK. It is a commonplace of devotional and mystical writings. Nor is the image independent. It is rooted in the ancient comparison of knowledge to vision and also in the tradition which speaks of God (or the Good) as "light." Ultimately SK aims to put these two analogies together, to suggest that true self-knowledge is the clear vision of oneself in the light of the vision of God.

But here we must go slowly. If being transparent to myself is knowing myself, if knowing myself is choosing or having chosen myself, and if choice is essentially an expression of energy, pathos, passion, then it must follow that SK identifies being self-transparent with having or exercising a certain sort of energy or passion. What is the sense of this identification?

I want to sharpen the question by suggesting that we recall at this point the original meanings of the crucial terms used in the identification (see the third quotation in the list above). These are "energy" and "pathos." Each is a Greek word transliterated into English, as into Danish also. In its original sense, each word is closely connected with the idea of action. *Pathos* is a spring of action; *energeia* is a being's proper mode of activity. If we follow out this loose hint, it becomes plausible that SK is really identifying self-transparency, self-knowledge, with a certain mode of activity or a certain action. Does the hint help?

I

Whatever self-knowledge is, it seems that it must be connected with the idea of being able to give a true or correct account of myself: of my past history, my present situation, my feelings and reflections, my character and characteristics, and so on. It is tempting to say that the ability to give a correct account of myself must be the criterion for self-knowledge. For surely a man who gives, in all sincerity, an incorrect account of himself cannot be said to possess self-knowledge.

However, this claim may well be too strong. For not everyone has the perfect photographic memory needed for recalling fully and accurately everything in his life. And not everyone has the linguistic resources and skill needed to recount everything that he has experienced.

Thus, Socrates spent his later life in the pursuit of self-knowledge. But he seems to have been quite uninterested in autobiography and little interested in the past. Certainly he set great store by being able to give a true account of himself. But this account is what Plato's Socratic dialogues contain and indicate. In the *Apology*, Socrates is concerned to give a general explanation of his characteristic way of life, by explaining his general aims. These include discovering what wisdom is, what "Know thyself!" means, and the sense in which reason is the principle of everything. In the *Crito*, Socrates wants simply to explain to his friend what he is doing, why he is remaining in prison facing his death. And this includes explaining his attitudes towards the laws of Athens. In the *Phaedo*, his discussion of death and of the soul's immortality is simultaneously a piece of objective philosophizing, a rational-moral account of his own understanding of his situation, and an exemplification by Plato of the character of a man who was capable of such a discussion in such a situation.

At the end of *EE2*, Judge William makes a remark about the *extraordinarius*, the man who honestly finds that the universal demands of morality are beyond him. "He will not be in any obscurity with regard to this step, he possesses a deposition which he can produce any moment; no alarm can confuse it for him, no absence of mind; though he were to wake up in the middle of the night, he will instantly be able to render an account of everything" (p. 336). The same can be said about the ordinary ethical individual. And it is just this that could have been said about Socrates. SK is not saying that such a man can instantly reel off an autobiography or *curriculum vitae*. He may not be able to remember, either instantly or at all, what he was doing on the night of the twenty-third. (On the other hand, we should expect him to be able to remember when suitably re-minded.) What he can instantly produce is an account of the kind we can call a "deposition" (*Forklaring*). And what is this? What is it that the individual cannot become confused about or forget, once he has become clearly aware of it? In a nutshell, his moral principles and aims. What Socrates could produce in an instant, without confusion or absence of mind, was the kind of account of his activity and existence that he gives in the Assembly and in the prison.

Earlier in *EE2*, SK connects the idea of transparency with the idea of time. "The reason why the man who lives aesthetically can in a higher sense explain nothing, is that he constantly lives in the moment. . . . Be-neath this, you are constantly only in the moment, and therefore your life dissolves, and it is impossible for you to explain it" (p. 183). The contrary term is "continuity." This is elucidated in the preceding essay: "The healthy individual lives at once both in hope and in recollection, and only thereby does his life acquire true and substantial continuity" (pp. 144–45). The ideas of hope and recollection need clarifying. Once more, it is not that the ethical individual has the whole of his past constantly before him, the whole of his future constantly in his mind. The "recollection" that SK means is not his recalling what he was doing on the night of the twenty-third, nor is the "hope" an ability to say what he intends to be doing on the night of the twenty-sixth. Socrates may still be our para-digm. Roughly, the *Apology* and the *Crito* show in what sense Socrates recollects and how this recollection bears on his present activity; the *Phaedo* shows what kind of hope he has and how this too helps to explain his present attitudes. And all three works together display a coherent picture of a life of "true and substantial continuity." Moral searching, moral decisions, and moral faith all connect together.

2

In *EE2*, Judge William writes as follows: "Ethics says that it is the significance of life and of reality that every man become revealed. So if he is not, the revelation will appear as a punishment" (p. 327). To have self-knowledge is to have become revealed to oneself. Transparency is self-revelation.

What is it to become revealed to oneself? In *AE*, Johannes Climacus speaks of "an ethical pathos, which with a quiet, incorruptible, and yet infinite passion of resolve embraces the modest ethical task, and edified thereby stands self-revealed before God and man" (pp. 227–28). And in the next paragraph occur the words "existence makes the understanding of the simplest truth for the common man in existential transparency very difficult and very strenuous" (p. 228). Once again, these passages identify a sense of "self-revelation" which has little to do with the autobiographical, everything with the Socratic.

The essential point is implied in the word "existential." Transparency is essentially existential, although SK does not always attach this qualification. But "existence" in SK always means "existing," that is, an individual's actual life and activity. Existential transparency, then, means transparency of the individual's actual life and activities to himself. So self-revelation is revelation of one's life and activities to oneself.

How can my life and activities *not* be revealed to myself—assuming that I am conscious? How can I *not* know what I am doing, what I am trying to do, what I have been trying to do? We have to bear in mind yet once more that SK is talking not about the autobiographical capacity but about the capacity to give a deposition about oneself. "Self-revelation" means the kind of way in which I must be visible, intelligible, to myself if I am to be capable of making a Socratic deposition about myself. And SK's position implies the claim that even if there are senses in which any conscious agent must be self-revealed, must know what he is doing, there is also a profoundly important sense in which the universal capacity for self-knowledge implied in normal intentionality does not by itself guarantee that the agent has yet become revealed to himself, a sense in which this universal capacity for self-knowledge can coexist with radical self-concealment. So what is that sense?

At the end of *OTA1*, SK describes his own discourse:

The talk assumes, then, that you will the Good and asks you now, *what kind of life you live, whether or not you truthfully will only one thing.* . . . It asks you above all else, it asks you first and foremost, whether you really live in such a way that you are capable of answering that question, in such a way that the question truthfully exists for you. Because in order to be able earnestly to answer that serious question, a man must already have made a choice in life . . . so that his life can win the transparency that is a condition for being able to put the question to himself and for being able to answer it. (P. 183)

The Socratic deposition is a man's answer, in moral terms, to that serious question.

So, SK is saying that a man can become capable of making a Socratic deposition about himself only if he is capable of asking the serious question about himself. And his claim is that the ordinary capacity for self-knowledge does not guarantee that a man is capable of asking the serious question. He cannot mean that extra conditions are required if I am to be able to put to myself any question of the form, What kind of life am I living? For I can certainly put that question to myself in its simple auto-biographical sense without any extra conditions. We must, then, stress the idea of seriousness. This is to stress the idea of that question's "truthfully" existing for a man. If the question exists for me only as a request for autobiographical research, it does not yet exist for me "truthfully." It is not yet a "serious question." Self-revelation will be the kind of knowledge a man has about himself that he wins as a result of putting seriously to himself the question, What kind of life am I living?

The contrary of self-revelation is self-concealment. The two main forms of self-concealment are being confused about myself and having forgotten about myself. Each corresponds to a way in which the serious question either has not yet arisen for me or has arisen only unseriously. The individual who is self-concealed is the one who can give only a confused or forgetful answer to the question, What kind of life are you living? put suddenly to him in the middle of the night. He might give an inadequate answer because he has never seriously considered that question before.

In *OTA1*, just as in *AE* and *EE2*, SK argues that the sense of "seriously" is "ethically." It is tempting to suppose that he is trading on our ordinary, though vague, ideas about what the ethical is and using these ideas to identify a special sense for the idea of seriousness. I believe that this reading is wrong. Rather, SK is trying to use the idea of seriousness, together with related ideas like the idea of choice, to give sense to the idea of the ethical (the ideas of good and evil, right and wrong). So, though it may be temporarily illuminating to explain SK's claim about self-knowledge as a claim that self-revelation is the outcome of answering the question, What kind of life am I living? in ethical terms, this will not do as an explication of SK's own position or of his arguments. We have to go round his way.

To become revealed to oneself is to have become able to answer "the serious question." SK does not say that transparency, self-revelation, is what a man achieves in answering the question; still less does he say that it is what one achieves only in answering the question correctly. On the contrary, he explicitly writes in *OTA1* that transparency is "a condition for being able to put the question to" himself and being able to answer it. It is not one's answer that confers, or indicates, transparency. It is the mere fact of one's putting the question to oneself. Transparency, self-revelation, is not the knowing of the question's answer; it is the question's arising for one. So the clarity and power of recollection that we are discussing go not with being able to answer the question well but with just being able to ask the question. The logic of Socratic depositions is once again visibly distinct from the logic of autobiography. For it is certainly a condition of ascribing clarity and memory in the ordinary senses that a man not only be able to ask himself the autobiographical question, What kind of life have I been leading? but that he also be able to answer it in a way which satisfies some reasonably objective criteria of clarity and completeness. This is precisely not so for Socratic depositions. Here, if we can speak of criteria at all, we must say that the criteria for clarity and recollection are given in the Socratic question's seriously arising for a man. Conversely, the question's not arising, or not arising seriously, signifies in itself confusion and absence of recollection—of a certain deep sort.

Even so, why should the individual who has seriously considered this question be able to give a Socratic deposition that is clear and unforgetful? Why should merely trying to answer the question about myself guarantee that I shall not give a confused and forgetful answer if suddenly awoken? SK's argument, I believe, is that seriously answering the question is necessarily answering it clearly and unforgetfully. For the imperative to answer the question contains within itself an imperative to answer it clearly and unforgetfully. The individual who understands the seriousness of the question also therein understands that he is required to examine himself as clearly and completely as possible.

Here we come back once more to the difference between a Socratic deposition and an autobiography. Part of the difference is exhibited in a difference between the ways in which the ideas (or ideals) of clarity and completeness of recollection fit depositions and autobiographies respectively. For autobiographies, it seems likely that these ideals are relatively objective. An autobiography's clarity or lack of it can be established relatively objectively, just by looking at the writer's use of language to express his thoughts. Its completeness or forgetfulness can be established just by comparing what the autobiography contains with the writer's actual life. But this is not how the ideas of clarity and completeness fit Socratic depositions. The confessional writings of Rousseau and Tolstoy are much fuller and more detailed than Socrates' apologetic remarks. But they are also arguably much more confused, and arguably even much more essentially forgetful—forgetful of something essential. So, at least, SK need not be read as claiming that pondering the serious question about one's life guarantees by itself the ability to write a clear and complete autobiography. It guarantees a different sort of clarity and recollection.

3

Let us look back briefly at SK's use of the idea of significance. He writes that "it is the significance of life and of reality that every man become revealed" (*EE2*, 327). So it is, for instance, the significance of my life that I become revealed. But revealed to whom? First of all, I suppose most of us would immediately answer, to myself; only secondarily to other people. This claim does not mean that I must conceive the significance of my life to be revelation to myself. I may and probably should conceive it, or conceive it also, in different and concrete terms: to found and administer a leper colony, to teach and write moral philosophy, to raise a family, and so on. The idea of my life's having a significance attaches in virtue of my having a definite kind of life.

Consider the question, What kind of life am I living? The serious answer to this question takes the form of action, of a life of decisions and choices. Implicit in this answer lies a Socratic deposition. I may never work out such a deposition about myself, and I may never be called upon to make one. Still, in my giving the serious answer which consists in a decisive way of life is implicitly contained the fact that if suddenly called upon, I could make a Socratic deposition. I could make a statement whose force was "I am living a life of the following kind: . . ." Filling the gap would be an account of my own life. This account need not contain reference to the idea of my life's having a significance. But it must be an account of such a nature that a sympathetic observer could justifiably comment, "He has described a way of life whose significance is that . . ."

Self-revelation is different from revelation to others. I do not only mean the obvious, that I am not the others. I mean that in being revealed to myself, I may stand in a relation to myself different from that in which you stand to me when I am revealed to you. Socratic depositions are revealing to others. My account of my life reveals me to you; that is, assuming that you can see that it is truthful. So, too, does my way of life itself; assuming that you can grasp it. But either way I cannot be revealed to you unless you can observe my life and words, and unless you reflect on what you observe. It is not in this way that I am revealed to myself. My being revealed to myself is not a consequence but a condition of my being able to live as I do, to make the kind of deposition I make.

To say that I am revealed to you is to say that you see the significance of my life. To say that I am revealed to myself is to say that my life has significance. Now, my life cannot have significance, in the sense SK is speaking about, unless it has significance for me. Still, whereas the significance of my life has to be revealed to you, it does not have to be revealed to me in order to exist for me. On the contrary. For in the same passage in which SK speaks about the significance of life and reality, he also says that self-revelation can be punishment. If the significance, such as it is, of my life comes to exist for me only in being revealed to me, SK seems to be saying, its being revealed to me will strike me as punishment. My life's significance avoids being a punishment for me only if it exists for me in a way other than in being revealed to me. But how can my life have significance for me in any way other than in coming to appear significant to me? SK's answer, I believe, would be if and only if my life has significance through my decision to give it a particular kind of significance.

Just as SK's idea of living in the present (the aesthetic existence) needs elucidation through his ideas of decision and action, so too does his idea of life's significance. It is his view that a life which is lived in the present cannot have significance. More precisely, though there may well be senses in which we can allow that a man's life has significance even though it is lived wholly in the present, there must necessarily be a crucial sense in which such a life cannot be seen as significant—either by others, or by the man himself.

4

Let us go back to the idea of the question's arising seriously. So far, I have said only that "seriously" goes with the ability to make a Socratic deposition in contrast with writing one's autobiography. But of course this is not enough. SK certainly does not believe that a man's having achieved the ethical stance is indicated by his being able to ask himself questions and to paint pictures of his life in moral terms. Many of us are quite capable of making depositions about our lives that sound like Socratic apologies. But our depositions are not Socratic unless our lives as well as our speeches have a certain pattern.

It is a criterion of the question's arising seriously for a man that its arising is connected by him not only with self-description or the feelings but with action. A man understands the question in its non-serious auto-biographical sense if he knows that to answer it he must describe his life clearly and completely. A man understands the question seriously only if he grasps that to answer it he must necessarily engage himself in some course of action. More simply, the question's arising seriously for him is its arising as a request to himself to engage in deciding about some course of action—not just words. What made Socrates' apology a Socratic, and not an idle or hypocritical, deposition was that it was a secondary response to a question whose primary response was Socrates' actual life. And this is evident within the secondary, verbal, response itself. The deposition interprets a life part of which is the very making of the deposition itself.

It is in this, still very general and vague, light that we should take SK's remarks about time. "Hope," "recollection," and "continuity" must all refer to ways of grasping one's life in connection with making decisions, engaging in activity. Hoping, in the relevant sense, is not merely forming rose-coloured pictures of a possible future; recollecting is not merely summoning up pictures of one's past. These are things that everybody can do, serious question or no serious question. They are the substance of the would-be autobiographer's reflections. So too for "continuity." Most of us, and all of us qua autobiographers, assume with no difficulty that we have a continuity as persons, lasting and persistent identities. And these self-ascribed and other-ascribed identities are what autobiographies, biographies, and all person-indexed talk, are about. But none of this hits SK's "continuity." This, too, has to be grasped in essential connection with decisions and actions.

I want to repeat here a puzzling remark Judge William makes early in *EE2*: "The reason why the man who lives aesthetically can in a higher sense explain nothing, is that he constantly lives in the moment.... You are constantly only in the moment, and therefore your life dissolves, and it is impossible for you to explain it" (p. 183).

This is puzzling because it seems to represent an argument whose intermediate steps are all left out. It is not self-evident that a man who lives in the moment—whatever exactly that means—cannot explain himself, his life, the significance of his life. SK implies that such a man cannot make a Socratic deposition about himself. But it is not evident why. SK implies that such a man cannot answer, and cannot seriously have asked, the question, What kind of life am I living? But again it is not evident why. In a nutshell, SK's whole position is that a man who lives in the moment cannot have an ethical viewpoint. But this position is at best acceptable only as the conclusion of some argument.

Living in the moment is a way of living that lacks hope and recollection in their essential connection with decisive activity and that therefore also lacks the kind of continuity that is essentially expressed in terms of decision and action. SK is obviously not saying that the man who lives in the moment is incapable of thinking ahead into the possible future or of remembering what he has been doing; still less, that neither he nor we can identify him as an individual persisting over time. He is saying that merely being able to think ahead does not guarantee being able to "hope" in the sense that is essentially connected with decision, just as merely being able to remember does not guarantee being able to "recollect" in that sense.

The crucial ideas of hope and recollection must be connected with the ideas of choice and action. The connection is established by SK in the idea of resolution. In the first essay in *EE2*, Judge William contrasts the love which exists within marriage with the romantic idea of marriage. He writes that "in the ethical and religious purpose marital love possesses the possibility of an inner history..." (p. 96). His first point is that the making of a resolution creates a point to which the individual can always thereafter refer back in interpreting his existence and deliberating his future. Thus, "Conjugal love shows itself to be historical by the fact that it represents a process of assimilation which deals with the experience and refers back the experience to itself" (*EE2*, 99). The resolution is both "the power in the constancy" and "the law of motion" within marriage. It is the principle of the marriage's persistence through time and the principle which explains the ways in which the marriage changes from time to time.

This inner historicity of marriage is expressed, in particular, in two essential features of a true marriage. First, "it lies in the historical character of marriage that this understanding is reached by a continuous process, not simply once for all. It is just as in the individual life: when one has attained clarity about oneself, when one has had courage to will to see oneself, it by no means follows that now the history is finished, for now it begins, now for the first time it acquires real significance for the fact that every individual moment experienced leads on to this total view" (*EE2*, 120). Second, "the second kind of history begins with possession, and history is the development through which one acquires possession" (*EE2*, 136). Judge William illustrates this remark a little later, speaking of conjugal love: "It is faithful, constant, humble, patient, long-suffering, indulgent, sincere, contented, vigilant, willing, joyful. All these virtues have the characteristic that they are inward qualifications of the individual. The individual is not fighting with external foes but fights with himself, fights out love from within him. And they have reference to time, for their truth does not consist in being once for all but in being constantly what they are. And by these virtues nothing else is acquired, only they themselves are acquired" (*EE2*, 142).

The hope and recollection which SK connects with continuity are identified by their inner relation with resolution. "Recollection" essentially means comparing my present situation with my resolution in the past. Now, there are comparisons and comparisons. To "recollect" is not merely to indulge in reminiscing. It is not merely to look at present and past side by side. It is to look back to the resolution made in the past as a guide to what to make of my present situation and what to decide and to do. Analogously for "hope"; SK's "hope" does not just mean looking forward optimistically into a possible and desirable future. It means looking forward to the fulfilment or the constant carrying out of my resolution. In this sense, hope plainly requires recollection. I cannot look forward to carrying out a resolution unless I am simultaneously looking back at the resolution itself. But just as plainly, recollection in the required sense entails the presence of hope. It is through the way in which both hope and recollection necessarily accompany each other that we can see how SK naturally calls a life based on a resolution "continuous." It has within it a constantly relevant principle, which can serve both as the individual's own principle for living his life and, if necessary, explaining it in a Socratic deposition, and as the principle by which others can understand his life and its significance.

We can now see part of what SK means when he says that only by making "a choice in life" can a man "win the transparency that is a condition for being able to put the question to himself and for being able to answer it" (*OTA1*, 183). The kind of choice he means is a resolution, a resolution of the kind that is the basis of marriage. So, making a resolution of that kind is a condition for becoming transparent, becoming self-revealed. But why? What can the man who has made such a resolution see about himself that cannot be seen otherwise?

The first part of the answer to this question is fairly easy. He can see that he is living a life *sensu eminenti*. For his making his resolution is itself an implicit response to the serious question, What kind of life am I living? It represents a decision, say, to live a married life. Whatever the biographical details of his subsequent life, whatever his powers of intellect and memory, it is this general principle that he will be able to state if he is woken in the middle of the night. This will be the content of his deposition, the explanation "in a higher sense" of his life.

A Socratic deposition is essentially the account of a man's inner history. Autobiography, by contrast, is the account of outer history. "Inner" here does not mean "mental" or "psychological." For much of our mental activity belongs, in SK's view, to the realm of the "outer," not the "inner." So a man writing his autobiography may well describe his thoughts, feelings, wishes, regrets, and so on. But this will not necessarily identify his inner life; and in SK's sense it is quite possible that he may have had no inner life at all. The true inner life is the life of genuine resolution or action *sensu eminenti*, the life whose content and significance is the individual's striving to make and uphold his commitments. So the true account of my inner history can only be my account of my strivings to constantly acquire something that I began by taking into my possession.

It is this kind of life that I am asking about if I seriously ask the question, What kind of life am I living? I am really asking, What is the possession towards whose constant acquisition I am striving? So of course I cannot even begin to ask this question until I have some idea of there being such a thing as a possession that has to be constantly acquired by striving.

Here I want to draw attention once more to the fact that SK says that transparency is a condition for being able to put the question to himself and for being able to answer it (*OTA1*, 183)—a condition, and not just a consequence. Whatever "transparency" means, it cannot mean a condition that necessarily follows asking oneself the serious question. Self-knowledge is not a condition that we can reach only as the result of answering a certain kind of question about ourselves. It is, rather, a pre-condition for being able to ask ourselves the question. Further, from SK's claim that only by resolving can a man win transparency, it appears that in his view self-knowledge is the immediate result of resolving. Resolution seems to be not just a necessary condition but a sufficient condition for self-knowledge.

But this suggestion faces us with a second problem. What is it about resolution, choice, that guarantees a certain kind of self-knowledge to the chooser? Here there is a plausible line. We can distinguish between genuine actions, which are the outcomes of acts of choice, and actions in the everyday sense, which may well be the outcomes just of impulse, desire, fear, social pressure, conventionality, habit, and so on. This distinction is vague, of course, until we specify precisely what makes an act one of choice; it may also be notional, in that it may prove impossible in practice to be certain that any particular action is done out of choice rather than out of any of the other possible sources. It is, then, arguable that acts done out of choice have a peculiar feature: that the agent can know, with respect to such an act, precisely why he did it. He can know this in virtue of knowing that he did it out of his own free resolution and knowing what this resolution was. I cannot answer the question, What were you doing? unless I can answer the question, Why did you do what you were doing? But I cannot answer that question with any certainty except on the condition that I was doing what I did for my own self-chosen reasons. And because my reasons were self-chosen, they are necessarily clear to me. It makes no sense to say that I did not clearly know what my reasons were.

In so far as my actions, and thus my life, are the product of my choices, I can know what I have been doing and so be in a position to give a clear account of my life. Otherwise, I cannot. For I cannot know with clarity or certainty the conditions and movements of my physical and psychological apparatus. There is an inescapable obscurity about the psychophysical apparatus from which spring our actions, like our thoughts and wishes and desires. If "self-knowledge" means knowledge of this psychophysical apparatus as it exists and operates within me, then although I can no doubt come to see various things about it as my life proceeds, I cannot hope ever to achieve clarity or certainty about it. The Apollonian command, "Know thyself!" cannot therefore be taken to mean "Become clear and certain about your psychophysical conditions and movements!" And, of course, Socrates did not imagine for an instant that it did mean this. He was not under the misconception that he could gain self-knowledge by, say, undergoing psychoanalysis.

I cannot achieve transparency to myself within my immediate psychophysical existence, since there is an inescapable obscurity about this kind of existence, and since actions which flow immediately out of it cannot have the "why" that attaches to them only as an outcome of choice. By contrast, so much of my existence as is lived at the level of (moral) choice can be transparent to me. Thus, I believe, for the SK of *EE2*, for Judge William. But SK's own thought by no means stops at this point.

For self-knowledge, in SK, is also the correlative of conscience. A first suggestion, then, is that self-knowledge is the examination of one's own conscience and also the result of such a self-examination. By "conscience" I do not mean a man's general moral consciousness, his moral principles and ideals. I mean, rather, what is meant in phrases like "on my conscience," "a matter of conscience," "obey my conscience," and "have a good (bad, clear) conscience." Conscience, in this sense, speaks to particular actions and situations. It speaks, moreover, of the past. My conscience does not tell me what I ought to do; it tells me what I ought to have done. So examining one's conscience means asking oneself, Did I do what I ought to have done? And it is as a generalization of this kind of question that we should take the serious question, What kind of life am I living?

This identifies more sharply SK's idea of transparency. I am transparent to myself in asking myself just these kinds of questions. I want to stress "asking." For self-transparency is not the having of clear and certain answers to the examination of my conscience. This is because there cannot be clear and certain answers to this kind of self-examination. Examination of one's conscience is necessarily carried on under the pressure of shame and remorse, as an act of confessing oneself in the light of truth and rightness. And anyone who claimed clarity and certainty here would plainly be deceiving himself. Transparency, if clarity at all, is much nearer to having a clear conscience. But this idea, too, must not be misinterpreted. Having a clear conscience does not mean knowing that what I did was right or good. For that I cannot know. It is, rather, having a pure heart, a pure will.

5

We can restate SK's claim thus: It is the significance of life and of reality that every man become transparent to himself. So if he is not, the transparency will appear as a punishment. Now, what sense can we make of this thesis?

What does SK mean by "significance" and "punishment"? He does not mean that something bad will happen to an individual who does not strive after or achieve self-knowledge. Nothing need necessarily happen to such an individual; except, of course, that he fails to achieve self-knowledge. He remains in obscurity about himself. Place him in a situation like Socrates' and he will be unable to give an account like Socrates' of his existence and activity. Wake him up suddenly in the night and ask him to explain and justify his mode of life; he will be able to give you only a confused deposition, one with gaps and holes in it. But how is this a punishment? In what sense is it an evil for such a man that he cannot give a clear correct account of himself? Not in any sense that he need necessarily think of as bad; for he may thoroughly enjoy his life and feel no distress at being unable to make a coherent moral deposition. The punishment lies just in that. And it will seem to be an evil only if you already believe the pursuit of self-knowledge to be obligatory for all.

Even this, however, is too strong. It is not in SK's mind to try to prove that self-knowledge is obligatory or is a universal good. That would be to attempt directness where directness is impossible. The punishment is, rather, just that the inability to give a coherent account of myself goes with my life's lacking significance. (Once again, I may not feel this to be an evil.) The relevant sense of "significance" is this: a coherent account of my life is possible only if my life has significance; and conversely, if my life has significance, then I can give a coherent account of it. For the significance of my life just is the coherence of my account of my life.

The latter claim needs qualification. We need to be able to recognize the possibility that the significance I give to my life is different from the significance everybody else sees in it. In particular, we need to be able to recognize the possibility of radical self-deceit or illusion. My account of my life must be, in some reasonable sense, correct as well as coherent if we are going to use "depositions" as criteria for self-knowledge and its absence.

The idea of revelation as "punishment" has, then, a second sense as well as the first. If an individual has contrived to avoid achieving self-knowledge, then, supposing that it were possible for somebody to give him an accurate account of his existence, that account would be felt as a punishment. More precisely, if the individual is able and willing to recognize that account of his own life as accurate, he will feel it as a punishment. For he will recognize that this account is radically discrepant from his own account, such as it is; and in accepting the former as accurate he necessarily sees the latter as radically inaccurate and incoherent. That is, he sees himself as having failed to achieve significance in, or a significant conception of, his own life.

But this too, as a punishment, depends essentially on how the individual takes it. It is quite possible that such a man might remain undistressed at the discrepancy. So in his case the revelation cannot operate as a punishment by causing him moral distress. It is punishment in the extreme case just in that it causes him no moral distress. Plainly SK is using a non-standard conception of punishment in these arguments. It is one which seems, in fact, to match one standard use of the idea of a judgment. For we might say that the fact that he feels no shame is itself a judgment on him. And so it is—although not from the man's own point of view.

SK's view, then, is that the question arises seriously for a man only if he is in a certain condition. So, he argues, if we can imagine the question's arising by itself, so to speak, for a man who has never himself asked the question, that very arising of the question will appear as a punishment to the man. But again, why?

SK's position rests on supposing that the question arises spontaneously within the man's mind, rather than being put to him, so to speak, from outside—by God or by a recording angel. For certainly, even if God Himself displays the picture of my life to me and puts to me the question, What kind of life are you, have you been, living? I need not necessarily feel the question as a punishment. I need not feel shame or remorse. It is true that we can perfectly straightforwardly say that if this happened, my *not* feeling shame would itself be a judgment on me. But SK has a further point. The question cannot arise within a man's mind, cannot arise seriously, unless it is accompanied by certain feelings. These feelings have, in general, to do with actions and omissions. Shame is one such; SK's own preferred term is "repentance."

So, if the question, What kind of life am I living? is necessarily accompanied by shame whenever it arises seriously for a man, it will be accompanied by shame if it arises spontaneously for a man who has never yet asked it of himself. Perhaps we can go further. The question's arising seriously is marked precisely by the presence of shame, repentance. If we read SK in this way, his thesis that self-revelation will appear as a punishment to the man who has not become self-revealed is construed as expressing a conceptual truth.

An analogous point applies also to the idea of my life's having significance for you. There is a straightforward sense in which the fact that my life's significance becomes revealed to you may appear to you as a punishment for me. A man whose deposition is confused and absent-minded or whose words entirely fail to make up a deposition at all may well be said to be "condemned out of his own mouth." He is judged by his own words, by his own failure. Thus, whether or not I feel shame, whether or not I even acknowledge the facts, visible incoherence in my life or visible discrepancy between my life and my self-reports may be seen as a kind of punishment in itself.

6

I now want to introduce an idea that is foreign to the ethical discussion. This will point the analysis of self-knowledge forward. Consider this remark from one of the Christian edifying works.

... so that what neither a man's burning wish nor his determined resolution may attain to, may be granted unto him in the sorrowing of repentance; to will only one thing. (*OTA1*, 32)

Now, "willing one thing" is identified, in this work, with the kind of self-knowledge that SK calls "transparency." Hence a man who does not will one thing is not self-transparent. So repentance is a condition for transparency; its absence entails ignorance and obscurity about oneself. It is not the only such condition. Remorse is the other.

The one beckons forward to the Good, the other calls man back from evil ...; in order to make the journey secure, they must look both forward and backward.... Because these two calls designate the place and show the way. (*OTA1*, 39–40)

The first of these passages is unambiguous. The transparency of self-knowledge can be acquired only through repentance, not through "determined resolution." So, the account given in *EE2* does not finally stand up, after all.

This does not entail that the whole of the structure of ideas I have been elucidating also collapses. It does not, for instance, entail that the idea of a deposition must be abandoned as irrelevant. This idea may and indeed must be reinterpreted. For as introduced above, it is essentially connected with the idea of resolution or choice and the idea of the ethical. And we are now, in *OTA1*, using ideas of a different kind. It is no accident that Judge William centres his account of self-knowledge in the idea of a deposition (*Forklaring*). For he is a man of the law, as well as a secret admirer of Socrates. His letters are themselves depositions, examples of the very kind of writing he discusses. Things could hardly be otherwise. For it is a central theme of his letters that he himself is trying to lead an ethical life, that his life is based on resolution. If so, it follows from his own account of the ethical life that his knowledge of himself is not primarily autobiographical but ethical.

The corresponding idea within *OTA1* is confession. Just as *EE2*, being about Socratic deposition and its conditions, is itself an example of deposition, so *OTA1* is not only about confession and the conditions a man must fulfil to be capable of confessing but is also related to the idea of confession in a second way as well. The text is itself a "spiritual preparation for the office of confession": a book whose reading is meant to help the reader put himself into the right condition for confessing.

SK explicitly connects the idea of confession with self-knowledge. "The all-knowing One does not get to know something about the maker of the confession, rather the maker of the confession gets to know about himself" (*OTA1*, 50–51). He adds below: "Much that you are able to keep hidden in darkness, you first get to know by your opening it to the knowledge of the all-knowing One" (*OTA1*, 51). It is on the next page, and in what is plainly meant to be the same argument, that SK contrasts self-deceit with purity of heart. Confession and self-deceit cannot co-exist.

Now, as these passages show, the idea of confession goes necessarily with the idea of God—the idea of God as omniscient and as moral judge. In this respect, confession differs from Socratic deposition. A man cannot confess, in SK's view, without having a conception of a god before whom, in whose sight, he is confessing. Confession is necessarily engaged in as a god-directed act, an act of communication, an act of self-revelation before another. Socratic deposition, and the corresponding kind of self-examination, lacks this logical feature. We can at best say that to examine oneself in a Socratic manner requires conceiving of an ethical absolute, say, unconditional moral laws or standards; for it is in the light of my conception of the moral standard as unconditional that I examine my conscience, and in the same light that I explain my life to others. But even this claim requires argument.

There is a second difference between confession and Socratic deposition. A man can have the kind of self-knowledge that Socrates or Judge William had, without ever actually making a deposition. But a man cannot achieve the kind of self-understanding that goes with confession unless he actually goes through an act of confessing. If I do not actually open my deed in an act of confession, I may be able to keep it hidden even from myself in darkness.

There is a kind of self-knowledge that can be gained only through an actual act of intentionally revealing one's actions before some being conceived of as omniscient and at the same time the absolute moral standard. It is possible to put part of this claim less demandingly. A man cannot confess, cannot go through a performance worthy to be called "confessing" unless he has a concept of truth as absolute and an accompanying concept of moral standards as absolute. If a man has such a conception of truth and morality, and if in the light of this conception he engages in an act of self-examination and deposition, then his performance will be an act of confession. And it is only such an act that can confer genuine self-knowledge.

As the idea of deposition is replaced by the idea of confession, so the accompanying ideas of recollection and shame are replaced by the idea of remorse. Shame is a constant feature of the Socratic stance. "Yes, there is a sense of shame, that is favourable to the Good. Woe to the man who casts it off! This sense of shame is a saving companion through life. Woe to the man that breaks with it!" (*OTA1*, 89). Just so, on an earlier page, SK writes: "So wonderful a power is remorse, so sincere is its friendship that to escape it entirely is the most terrible thing of all" (*OTA1*, 39).

VII

The Discovery of Radical Self-deceit

I SHALL BEGIN by sketching in summary outline the argument that is to follow. We are to start by considering the idea of self-knowledge. This idea is reasonably familiar. But it is very vague. In SK it is analysed not as a state or an achievement but as an activity or a project. So we start by considering the idea of a project of self-knowledge. (In SK's works the paradigm for this idea is Socrates' life, as explained by himself in the *Apology*.)

The project of self-knowledge at first appears as a project of acquisition. It appears to an individual who embarks on it as a project of acquiring truths, that is, true beliefs, about oneself.

Self-inquiry of the sort involved in the project of self-knowledge leads immediately and of itself to the individual's discovering within himself barriers to self-knowledge. These are forces that of themselves resist the acquisition of self-knowledge, that essentially resist one's efforts to be truthful with oneself about oneself. They are not contingent barriers to self-knowledge, like ignorance, imperceptivity, and slowness of mind.

To discover that there are things within one that are essentially hostile to truthfulness about oneself is to discover that one is essentially self-deceiving. The first important outcome of the project of self-knowledge is the knowledge that one is essentially opposed to the whole project. Here, if the whole project is not abandoned in despair or metamorphosed into psychotherapy, it must be radically rethought and reconstructed. The self-inquirer must now commit himself to a project of trying to understand and destroy the forces within him that essentially oppose truthfulness.

To adopt this new project is at the same time to change one's general conception of the nature of the self. The self is now seen to contain forces—conflicting forces. We recognize ourselves to be deeply split, and split below the level of our normal awareness. Such a change in the conception of the self involves also changing one's conception of self-examination and self-knowledge. And it involves a change in the conception of a truth about the self.

2

What is self-knowledge? SK's paradigm is the account of his own life that Socrates is shown as giving to his jurors in Plato's *Apology*. But just how does this Socratic self-knowledge differ from autobiographical self-knowledge? It seems unlikely that Socratic self-knowledge consists of items radically different from ordinary self-knowledge. What could these extra and radically different items, facts, be? Surely an ideally complete objective autobiography would include every truth about its subject. If any truths were left over, that would simply entail that the autobiography was incomplete. Now if this is the case, it follows also that Socratic self-knowledge cannot be distinguished from ordinary self-knowledge by a peculiar logical relation that its items might hold to actions or decisions. Socratic self-knowledge cannot be logically connected with decision in a way different from the ordinary way unless its items are themselves logically different in type from the items of ordinary self-knowledge.

The *Apology* apparently cannot be taken as a statement of Socratic self-knowledge. If it is this, it is so only indirectly and by implication. For it is a statement that is essentially given for others. It is given for definite others; for the people of Athens acting as Socrates' jury and judge. It is therefore, among other things, a defence. In the same general way, the account of himself that an individual gives is not just a statement. It is a confession. A straightforward statement of Socratic self-knowledge must presumably be the confession about his own life that the individual gives to himself. It remains an important but difficult question how far this confession can be given to others.

Still, the use of the *Apology* as a paradigm may be intended by SK to bring out not a difference but a similarity between Socrates' speech of self-defence and the kind of statement that expresses self-knowledge. SK may wish to stress that the proper form for the expression of such self-knowledge, even to the individual's own inner self, is not the form of assertion but the form of defence or confession. Whatever the linguistic form of the statement of self-knowledge, it carries the pragmatic force of an act of self-defence or confession. Self-defences and acts of confession have a peculiar feature that suggests that they must be closely linked with self-knowledge. Such acts can be performed only by the individual whom they are about. Although someone else may be able to apologize on my behalf, he cannot confess on my behalf, however hard he tries. Nor can I elect or delegate a representative for myself whom I empower to make my confessions for me; although I can easily, for instance, empower someone else to make my promises, and these will then be binding on me just as much as the promises that emerge from my own lips. Confession is essentially my own act. Nothing that anyone else does or says can possibly begin to count as my confession, since it cannot be identified as my action, which my confession has to be.

Now, why might an individual come to ask himself the Socratic question, What kind of life am I living? No doubt there are a million different possible sources for such self-questioning. SK has no particular theories about the sources in our lives of self-questioning, except that he suggests in some of the pseudonymous works that it may often develop naturally out of a certain general kind of dissatisfaction with one's ordinary life. But he is interested not so much in the genesis of such self-inquiry as in what it means to the self-inquirer.

The reasons which might explain why a man pursues Socratic self-knowledge will be quite different from the reasons why one might (rationally) aim at acquiring self-knowledge in the ordinary "objective" sense. There are several kinds of reason why objective self-knowledge might be thought desirable. Self-knowledge is likely to be useful at all levels of pragmatism and prudence. And it is likely to be interesting out of vanity, however this motive is dressed up. But reasons of these kinds do not explain why Socratic self-knowledge could be found desirable or obligatory.

If a man pursues Socratic self-knowledge, it is because he is aiming to be able to give a certain kind of account of his life. This account essentially has the form of an explanation of his life that he can offer in self-defence or self-justification or as no more than a confession to himself. So, reasons for pursuing self-knowledge in this way must be reasons for being able to defend or justify one's own life or for being able to make a genuine confession about it. So a man would not in reason adopt the Socratic project unless his life had come to appear to him as something that might well need defence or justification or as something about which a genuine confession might well be required of him. This is apparently true even of Socrates: "Because of his ethical insight, accordingly, he discovered in himself a disposition to all sorts of evils" (*AE*, 144). Up to the point when a man sees his life in these terms, the project of Socratic self-knowledge must appear to be unsupported by reason. The idea of justifying my life must seem pointless if it has never occurred to me that my life may need justifying. It is not necessary that I should believe that my life may require explanation to someone else, still less to a definite someone else. It may just come to seem to demand a kind of explanatory understanding from me myself. That is, I must just come to demand of myself justification for my own life.

The kind of account a man aims at being able to give if he adopts the Socratic project is an account of his life in terms of the reasons which led him to do the things he has done and to live the kind of life he has been living. For it is in terms of these reasons that he hopes to be able to defend and justify his actions, and with reference to them that he comes to confess his errors. Self-inquiry, then, is mainly inquiry into one's intentions, plans, hopes, desires, motives, and so on.

A man can, of course, aim to give an account of his life in terms not of its inner features but of its external features, for instance, the results of his acts. And an external account of one's life might naturally be given, and understood, as a defence or a justification. A politician, for instance, might defend or justify his life by describing the results of his activities, the benefits that they have brought to people. But such an external account is understood as a defence or justification only if we are able to supply a missing element. This missing element is precisely the man's intentions and purposes. I can pretend to justify a deed of mine by pointing to its beneficial consequences only if I imply, or say, that in acting so I intended those beneficial consequences or others of the same kind. Without the intention the act does not stand to its agent's credit. Equally, an external account of a man's life that appears at first sight to stand to his discredit can be explained away by supplying an internal account that points in the opposite direction.

3

The Socratic project, though so far described only vaguely, is familiar. But in SK's view it is optimistic and unrealistic. For it rests on a superficial idea of human nature, a superficial understanding of psychology. A deeper understanding of psychology will show that the Socratic project as so far conceived cannot be carried through to self-knowledge.

But this is not just an external comment on the idea of pursuing self-knowledge. It is also a truth that the self-inquirer himself can come to recognize in his own pursuit of self-knowledge. And recognize it he must if he is to progress farther towards genuine self-knowledge. To say this is plainly not to say that every self-inquirer necessarily comes to understand what is wrong with the Socratic idea. Probably many people never suspect that there is anything wrong. If so, they will never get beyond the superficial kind of self-knowledge that is all the Socratic project can yield. SK's point is just that each of us needs a deep understanding of human psychology in general and our own psychology in particular to be able to conceive of self-knowledge and pursue it in a deeper and more adequate way than the Socratic.

But the point has extra implications. For an understanding of psychology does more than clarify the conditions for acquiring self-knowledge. The understanding of one's own mind is itself part of the object of self-knowledge, part of the aim of pursuing self-knowledge. Any important change in my conception of the way my own mind operates implies not only changes in the way I conceive the requirements of genuine self-examination but also a change in my conception of what self-knowledge is.

Here are two characteristic passages by SK.

He who has but some acquaintance with himself knows well out of his own experience that it is rather true that at the bottom of his heart a man has a secret dread and mistrust of the truth, a fear of getting to know too much. Or dost thou really believe that it is every man's sincere wish to get to know effectually what self-denial is, to get it made so clear that every excuse, every evasion, every palliation, every appeal to the false but favourable opinion of others is cut off from him? (*CT*, 178)

No, instead of wishing, like the young man, to tear away the veil from divinity, I wish to tear the veil from human twaddle and from the conceited self-complacency with which men try to convince themselves and others that man really wants to know the truth. No, every man is more or less afraid of the truth; and that is what is human, for truth is related to being "spirit"—and that is very hard for flesh and blood and the physical lust for knowledge to bear. Between man and truth lies mortification—you see why we are all more or less afraid. (*JSK*, 413)

In every individual there is a deep fear of genuine self-knowledge. This is a fear of getting to know the truth about oneself. Because of this deep fear, there exist in every individual forces preventing him from genuine self-inquiry. These are forces that resist our efforts to be truthful with ourselves about ourselves. But they are also forces that positively encourage or impose untruthfulness or the avoidance of truthfulness. They are in fact those forces that we know as self-deceit. They can be called self-deceit and not just self-ignorance because at the bottom of the whole general psychological process there exists in each individual a dim suppressed awareness of certain facts about his life, his mind, and his personality. It is a suppressed awareness of profoundly disagreeable facts about himself. It is from this that the fear of self-knowledge grows.

But we do not simply fear self-knowledge. We also desire it. There is no need to deny this fact. Any project of Socratic self-inquiry presupposes a real desire for self-knowledge. If we simply feared all self-knowledge, we would never set ourselves to such a project. Perhaps the nature of the mind is such that even if a man does not set himself to self-inquiry, knowledge about himself is bound to come to him in the ordinary course of his reflections. Still, that phenomenon is not self-inquiry, not a project of self-knowledge. However minimal the self-knowledge a man really seeks, there is no need to deny that if he really seeks it, he really desires it, with a part of his mind and heart.

There is an obvious way of reconciling the genuine desire for self-knowledge with the deep fear of genuine self-knowledge. It is to go looking for an account of oneself that genuinely requires self-inquiry yet does not go deep enough. But why do even this much if one fears genuine self-knowledge? Because the individual has already come to see his life as something that requires defence or justification. To see that is to see one's life as not being visibly justified. SK does not for a moment imagine that everyone comes to see this or that everyone who thinks about his life comes to see this. It is quite possible to consider one's life and conclude that it requires no justification at all. The self-inquirer may then easily go looking for some account that satisfies his need for self-justification but no more.

Superficial self-inquiry has both uses and dangers. Its plainest use is that it may reveal to the individual at least something about himself, even at a merely superficial level. More important, it is needed to bring the individual face to face with his own desire to deceive himself. Probably this awareness is suppressed as soon as it arises, perhaps even earlier; we are here exploring the region where psychology is itself paradoxical. But superficial self-inquiry has an equally plain danger. It can be deeply misleading, a source of illusion as well as of revelation. For the individual may infer from his self-inquiry that self-knowledge is genuinely desirable to him, that the truth about himself is something that he does not fear at all but wholly desires. And this belief is a deeper illusion than any he will have so far encountered. Its danger is plain. The man who believes that he loves truth will sit down satisfied with the quasi-truth he believes he has discovered about himself. His self-inquiry will stop there.

The initial stages of any project of self-inquiry will be superficial. So the individual who is going to go deeper than most people must start in the same way as the rest of us. What makes him able to go deeper is that he is able to recognize what his self-inquiry has produced even superficially. He is able to see that he is afraid of the genuine truth. How? One sign may be that he comes directly to see his own fear. He is able to recognize that his inquiries are making him afraid; he neither misses this nor denies it. Another sign may be that he comes to recognize that accounts of himself that he has given in the past have been superficial. And then he may see that their superficiality was, so to speak, essential and deliberate. He may become aware that in accepting superficial ideas about himself he has been moved by fear. And then the immediately next question will be, Fear of what?

It is essential that the self-inquirer acknowledge that the superficiality of his own self-accounts has not been just accidental. A self-account would be accidentally superficial if, for instance, the individual happened to be ignorant of relevant things, or imperceptive by nature, or slow and confused of mind. Such defects are causes of error but not of self-deception. Self-deceiving accounts of oneself tend to share a common feature: they are flattering, or at least exculpatory. The genuine self-inquirer will come to see this common feature. And he will come to see that it is not an accidental feature but the very point of the account's failure.

But to see this is to see that one has all along been essentially self-deceiving. Earlier self-inquiries have been projects of partial self-deception. For they have been projects of self-flattery or self-justification or self-exculpation. Now it may be the case that a genuine account of oneself turns out to be exculpatory or justifying, even perhaps flattering, though this is unlikely. But there is all the difference in the world between a project of, say, self-exculpation and a project of self-knowledge whose result turns out to be self-exculpatory. It is precisely the difference between genuine truthfulness and self-deceit. That is what the true self-inquirer must come to acknowledge.

So he must in effect come to see that his projects of self-knowledge have really been projects of self-deceit. This is an instance of a commonplace about moral vision. The genuinely humble man is he who comes to see that all his efforts at humility have really been efforts to express his pride, the genuinely loving man he who sees that his acts of love have been acts of self-gratification. And so on.

These claims about self-knowledge are not meant in any technical sense. SK never appeals to esoteric information or skill in his reader. He implies that everything he says can be understood and verified by anyone who reads him. How can we do so? Simply by consulting our own hearts and consciences. So, in particular, SK's theories about self-knowledge and the deep structures of the self lean on no technical psychology. They do not anticipate or require interpretation through psychoanalytic theory. But psychoanalytic theory runs remarkably close to SK, as many people have noticed.

So his claim that all men are more or less afraid of the truth is not based on a hidden technical foundation. Its verity is meant to be apparent to anyone. The claim is not a priori. SK does not think that it is an analytical or conceptual truth that all men deceive themselves. There is no a priori structure within the human mind that entails self-deceit. (Original sin is not in this sense an a priori structure of the mind.) It is just a matter of fact that all men have good reason to want to deceive themselves. There is something deeply wrong with the life of every individual; but this is meant as a claim which each of us can verify for ourselves by looking inward. As usual, SK does not imagine that his remarks will be accepted by people who do not manage to find that anything is wrong in their lives; but he does not imagine that they will be reading him seriously.

4

If the self-inquirer comes to see that he is so deeply self-deceiving that even his former projects of self-knowledge have essentially been disguised projects of self-deceit, what is his response likely to be? On the one hand, he may simply abandon the whole project in despair. Plainly at this moment extremely deep forms of self-deceit and obscurity will come into play. But I am not going to follow these interesting byways. If the man genuinely continues to want self-knowledge, he is likely to take one of two apparently possible paths.

Consider this remark by SK.

But then, to live on, having accurate knowledge of and shrewd calculation upon one's own powers, talents, qualifications, possibilities, and in the same measure familiar with what human and worldly shrewdness teaches the initiated—is that to come to oneself? Yes, according to the opinion of the merely human view. But not according to the Christian opinion; for this is not to come to oneself, it is to come to the probable.... Knowledge of the probable, the deeper it is, does not in a deeper sense lead a man to himself, but farther and farther away from his deeper self; it is only in the sense of selfishness that it brings him nearer and nearer to himself. (*DS*, 121)

One attractive response to the discovery of one's own self-deceit is psychotherapy. I do not mean any particular technical medical discipline. I mean rather a general style of thinking about the human mind and its characteristic operations. This style is identified in outline by SK.

I earlier described the self-inquirer as someone who has a moral interest, not just an objective or pragmatic interest, in coming to know himself. He is interested in acquiring the best account of himself, which is an apology for himself. His discovery of his own self-deceit is therefore the discovery of an essential barrier within his own mind to the discovery of an account of his life that might function as an apology. It is, in effect, the discovery that the projected apology could not be successfully made, that the best account of his life would turn out to be not a defence or justification but a self-criticism, a pure confession—or that he could give no self-defence or justification which would not be self-flattering and self-deceiving. Still, it does not follow from this that the self-inquirer must recognize his self-deceit as itself a moral (and morally condemnable) performance. He may easily just think of it as a natural trick of the human mind, a natural response of thinking to the pressures of fear. If so, he will probably think of the inner forces of self-deceit as capable in principle of being dismantled or circumvented by purely technical, or rational, means. Their dismantling will appear as a mere technical preliminary to the real work of self-inquiry.

So one possible response to the discovery of one's essential self-deceit is the assumption that this too needs only to be examined and understood. It is the assumption that the forces of self-deceit are no more than an unexpected extra complicating characteristic, a characteristic that is of course complex but still, in principle, capable of being examined and known in the same kinds of ways as one's other characteristics.

At this point it may well seem reasonable to explore psychotherapies. For are they not designed as methods of examining and discovering precisely characteristics like self-deceit? And at just this point it becomes easy to lose one's way, to diverge from the Socratic path and turn aside once again onto a path of objective knowledge. This is one of the things that

SK calls getting to know "the probable." It is only probable for a reason that is standard in SK's epistemology: that empirical knowledge can never have the certainty of knowledge of logically indubitable truths. We may object that knowledge of oneself is precisely distinct in logical force from other kinds of empirical knowledge. For is not an individual's access to facts about himself of a logically distinct and peculiar kind, direct rather than mediated and inferential? SK does not apparently agree with this familiar view. There is certainly a sense of self-knowledge in which a man can know himself certainly—and that sense we shall come to later. But we are now talking about knowledge of the ordinary self, and this self is an empirical thing, built up of particular feelings, beliefs, dispositions, etc. So SK sees no particular reason why knowledge of the empirical self should have any claim to directness or certainty that other kinds of empirical knowledge lack.

But there is something very odd about the project of psychotherapeutic self-inquiry: the self-inquirer must simultaneously conceive himself as the object of his inquiry and as its subject. And on the face of it this conception of the self is untenable. For is the subject of self-inquiry itself to be also part of the object of its own inquiry? If yes, then must not the self-inquiry into the inquiring self be conducted in turn by some further inquiring self? If no, then must not the self-inquiry be radically incomplete, by leaving out what we might well assume to be one of the most important features of human existence—our capacity for self-observation and self-inquiry?

5

The alternative response to the discovery of one's essential self-deceit is not palliative but radical. It is to change one's whole general conception of the nature of the self, vague as this will probably have remained so far. For it is to take seriously the fact that the self-deceit now unmasked has been a project of the self, not some accidental characteristic that can be explored, understood, overcome and stripped away from the real self, leaving the latter pure and clear. It is to take seriously the fact that it is precisely this "real self" that has all along been the source of the project of self-deceit.

To take this kind of view is to commit oneself to two closely related theses. The first is that "the self" refers not to one but to two sets of phenomena. There is the self that is recognized to be the source of the ongoing project of self-deceit, the locus of the deep fear of self-revelation, the container of the deep lurking shame or guilt that grounds this fear. And there is the self as previously identified, the being whose empirical characteristics have been the object of one's inquiries: the "I" referred to in the question, What kind of life have I been living? The second thesis is that the former, deep self is essentially a moral self, in that its proper features have already been dimly identified as moral properties (shame, guilt) and its activity is now seen to be an essentially moral project. This is because the ongoing project of self-deceit is a project of covering up one's suspected moral failures. Self-deceit over a moral issue is not just a kind of self-exculpation. It is a parallel within a man's inner life to that outer act of self-exile that Socrates refused in the *Crito*.

Plainly there is something paradoxical and repugnant to common sense in the idea that individuals actually have more than one "self," however this is defined, except in those special conditions which seem to justify our talking about multiple selves. And these are by and large conditions where we can see that an individual is from time to time exhibiting quite radically distinct and perhaps inconsistent kinds of thinking and behaviour. It would accord with ordinary usage to say that such people had (or were) multiple persons in themselves. SK, I assume, goes along with common sense. So he is not claiming that self-inquiry reveals that we have more than one entity in us of the kind, whatever it is, that we can call a "self." Discovering one's "deeper self" must therefore not be interpreted as discovering an entity within oneself that is distinct from one's self as previously identified.

In the opening lines of *SD*, SK gives a notorious definition of the self. Whatever the precise meaning of his words, it is at least quite plain that he intends to deny that the self is an entity: to deny that "self" functions as a name, in the way that "head" certainly does and "mind" possibly does. The word "self" is an incomplete symbol. From what complete symbols, then, is the word, and idea of, self extracted? From a set of essentially reflexive ideas, including the ideas of self-criticism, self-reflection, self-centredness, self-sacrifice, and so forth. So the question, What is a self? can be intelligibly answered only if we interpret it as asking what it is that peculiarly distinguishes self-criticism from criticism, self-reflection from reflection, and so on.

If so, by "the first self" SK means to refer in an abbreviated way to what essentially characterizes the ways a man considers himself, so long as his ways of considering the world outside him have a certain character. In short, "the first self" is a way of referring to self-centredness. But for SK self-centredness has many forms. It does not mean obliviousness of or unconcern for external things. It means a certain general attitude to external things. This attitude has two primary marks. First, the self-centred individual sees external things as means to his own ends: to be used in his projects, or to serve his needs, or to increase his happiness. Second, he defines his projects, his needs, and his happiness in terms of these external things. (He is not, of course, aware of doing these things.)

I want to quote here another remark from the same discourse I have used above.

The prudential self-knowledge we have just described—what is its nature? Is it not a knowledge of a man's self in its relation to something else? But is it a knowledge of a man's self in its relation to himself? (*T*, 157)

Now these words must not be misconstrued. We might suppose that SK is saying that people have "a self," which can then be related either to external things or to itself. But he cannot be saying this. For any "self" that is capable of relating itself to itself, in the activities of self-reflection, must also now relate itself to external things in a way quite different from the way a self that is incapable of self-relation relates itself to externals. A being with self-consciousness must have consciousness of external things that is of a logical kind quite different from the consciousness of a being lacking self-consciousness. A self-conscious being's perception of X may, perhaps must, be accompanied by awareness that it is perceiving X.

We can put this point in an abbreviated form. There are two different kinds of self, one possessed by beings capable of self-reflection as well as consciousness of external things, the other possessed by beings incapable of self-reflection. The latter is not for SK a genuine self at all. Thus we can assume that all talk of a "self" implies a capacity for self-reflection, self-consciousness.

However, in the passage just quoted SK is drawing attention to a second distinction. This is at least as important as the one just mentioned. It is the distinction between two forms of self-reflection. The first is reflecting on oneself as a being that is conscious of external things. I can at this stage not only observe external things but also reflect on my observation of them, reflect that I am observing them. I can think to myself "I am looking at . . ." or "I desire an . . ." The "self" that I identify to myself as the object of my self-reflection is identified as the subject of consciousness of external things, things distinct from itself. But this way of putting it draws attention to a logical feature mentioned earlier. If I am identified in my self-reflection as the subject of awareness of things other than "I," it must also be true that I am not as such just an object for my self-reflection but its subject. And to become aware of this logical feature is to become aware that I am in conscious relation not only to other objects but also to myself, to "I."

So there is a possible transition from awareness of oneself *in* self-reflection to awareness of oneself *as* self-reflective. This transition is not inevitable. But if a man makes it, it becomes possible for him to conceive of self-knowledge in a sense quite different from that in which he earlier conceived it. For self-knowledge can now be represented as knowledge of a self that is essentially self-reflective, not just as knowledge of a self that is essentially conscious of external things. It is only at this point, I think, that SK wants us to speak of a genuine self.

A man's real self seems so distant from him that the entire world appears to him to be nearer than his self.... When man turns about, so as to confront himself in order to acquire an understanding of himself, it is as if he blocked the way for that first self of which we have been speaking. ...he calls the first self away from external things. For the purpose of inducing the first self to acquiesce in this recall, the deeper self makes the surrounding world reveal itself as it really is, namely as uncertain and precarious. (*T*, 158)

By "the first self," I suggest, SK means the self (I) that is the subject of awareness of things other than and outside itself, but no more. It is the first self that a man becomes conscious of when he begins to reflect on himself—reflects on himself as the subject of acts of consciousness. It is not, then, just an accidental feature of the first self that it is related to external things, to the surrounding world. In speaking of the self in this sense, we are essentially speaking of the capacity for and acts of awareness of external things. By "the real self," or "the deeper self," then, SK means the self that is implicitly involved in reflecting on itself (first sense); and that is explicitly the object of the deeper self-reflection, which is aware-ness that one is self-reflective.

The first self is not only epistemologically identifiable as the subject of awareness of the external world; it is somehow bound to the external world by ties of desire or value. This is implied by saying that the deeper self must "call the first self away from external things" and must "induce it to acquiesce in this recall." (Strictly speaking, a first self that is called away from the external is a no-thing. It does not change; it simply vanishes.) For if a man is conscious only of the external world, and of himself as conscious of the external world, then he will naturally form and identify his desires and values only in terms of the external things that he is aware of. It is in this sense that, whether or not he is the kind of man we ordinarily call selfish, SK claims he is self-centered. And this, too, is the essence of what he calls "prudential" knowledge.

If we look back briefly at the passage from *DS*, we can now see why SK there says that prudential self-knowledge gives a man knowledge of "the probable" but not knowledge of himself, that in fact it leads a man away from knowledge of himself. For the self that is the subject of awareness of the external world is the empirical self, the self that can be studied by empirical methods, including ordinary introspection. But empirical inquiries can give a man at best knowledge of empirical entities. "Prudential self-knowledge" or "knowledge of the probable" can at best be knowledge of the phenomena of one's mind. It follows, for SK, that it cannot be genuine knowledge of oneself, one's self. For no phenomenon could be a self, a genuine self.

6

For SK, discovery of the deeper self is not by itself enough. It is not enough for genuine self-knowledge. Although it brings one closer to genuine self-inquiry, it still lacks an essential condition. "When the first self and the deeper self thus become reconciled, and their common mind is turned away from outer things, there has as yet been realized only the first condition necessary for self-knowledge. In order that a man may really know himself, new dangers must be met and new conflicts won" (*T*, 162). The discovery that one is split, as it were, between two selves—a first self, represented in one's ordinary consciousness of and concerns about external reality, and a deeper self, represented in one's ability to reflect on oneself—is not yet a discovery of essential self-deceit. It is only the first step towards that discovery. What more is needed?

The essential discovery is that the first self, the ordinary consciousness, the reality-concerned and world-handling self, is essentially a projected mechanism employed by the deeper self in the service of its project of radical self-deception. Worldly consciousness is an essential tool in the deep project of evading truthfulness and self-knowledge. This is not to claim that ordinary worldly consciousness is simply a product of the deep project of avoiding self-knowledge. Of course human beings are born with a worldly consciousness, a mind that is externally directed and that takes its objects from among the external realities surrounding it. But this natural capacity is intrinsically liable to be put to the corrupt use of self-masking.

Consider two more passages from the same discourse.

So then a man strives with himself in inward conflict, but not now as before, when the deeper self strove with the first self to prevent it concerning itself overmuch with outward things. The man who fails to discover the existence of this inward struggle is involved in a misunderstanding, and his life is consequently imperfect. (*T*, 164)

Inwardly he creates in his mind those temptations of glory and fear and despon- dency, and those of pride and pleasure and defiance, greater than the temptations that meet him outwardly. It is because he thus creates his temptations for himself that he is engaged in a struggle with himself. (*T*, 165)

In these passages SK briefly identifies the deep reasons why we are all essentially self-deceiving. He identifies the sources of the universal fear of genuine self-knowledge and of the forces that work against the deeper self-inquiry. And these are also the sources of the deep illusion that earlier kinds of self-inquiry have been genuinely projects of self-knowledge in- stead of projects of self-deceit. We are all deeply afraid of getting to know the real truth about ourselves, because we are deeply aware that we are constantly engaged in creating temptations for ourselves. Our moral fail- ures are effects of our failures to resist temptations that are not presented to us from outside but created by ourselves. So our failures are failures in a double sense. We have not only succumbed to temptations; we have created the very temptations we succumbed to.

The new dangers and conflicts are precisely those that are concerned with the inner struggle and its recognition. The danger is primarily that the self-inquirer will not recognize that his struggle is an inner one. The conflict is not only this inner struggle but also what is involved in recog- nizing its existence.

VIII

The Discovery of One's Nothingness

I

THE SOCRATIC CONCEPTION of self-knowledge relies on a particular conception of truth and knowledge. This is explained in *PS*. Truth is conceived, within this perspective, as immanent. That is, individuals are capable of coming to know the truth by themselves, by the help of what Plato calls "anamnesis," recollection. Thus all that the individual needs to acquire self-knowledge is self-questioning. There is no truth about himself that is in principle inaccessible to this process. Other people can, of course, help him; Socrates thought of himself as helping others to come to a better knowledge of themselves, even if this was in the first instance a recognition of their own ignorance.

It is also important within this perspective that human beings are not conceived to be essentially hostile to or fearful of discovery of the truth about themselves. Plato was not, obviously, unaware that many people shrink from self-inquiry and self-discovery: this is a major theme, for instance, of the *Gorgias*. But he does not seem to imagine that we might have a will to falsity or ignorance or self-deceit.

Now, this Socratic conception is very different from the Christian conception we find in SK's later works. Johannes Climacus puts his finger on one crucial difference in *PS*. Truth, from a Christian perspective, is not immanent within the human mind. It is transcendent and can therefore be brought into the mind only by the help of something or someone outside humanity. For the human mind, seen from this perspective, is essentially corrupt in such a way as to be incapable of pursuing or grasping or accepting the deepest truths of its own will. The corruption of the intellect is for SK a consequence of the corruption of the will (see the argu-

ment against the Socratic conception of evil-doing in *SD*). It is precisely
God who acts, among other things, to bring truth to men. In this capacity, SK refers to God as "the Teacher"; and it is noteworthy that this
epithet occurs not only in *PS* but also in *TS*. Similarly, God is called "the
Communicator" (*IC*), in a long discussion that links Christian doctrines
with the concept of indirect communication. In SK's many discussions of
the Christian conception of the self, self-knowledge, and the truth, the
figure of Christ is absolutely central.

In this chapter, I want to consider a set of conceptions which appear to
me to express a perspective that is, so to speak, intermediate between the
plainly Socratic, discussed earlier, and the plainly Christian. This perspective is not clearly identified in SK's writings, although it can be seen in
various passages. But in digging out and reconstructing this perspective, I
am filling in a gap within SK's overall theory, in a way that is consistent
with the more familiar parts of that theory.

I identify a perspective which we might call "transcendentalist," "Stoic-
Kantian," or "paradox-absolute." This perspective is identified by a set of
conceptions that go decisively beyond the Socratic but stop short of the
Christian, or even the theistic. In identifying this perspective more precisely, we may get closer to the exact point at which, and reasons for
which, natural reason in SK ceases to function and Christian faith takes
over.

2

The conceptions that identify this perspective are the following: *confession*,
the self as nothing, *self-renunciation*, and *eternity*. Here are some representative passages from SK that seem to express parts of this perspective.

The all-knowing One does not get to know something about the maker of the
confession, rather the maker of the confession gets to know about himself.…
Much that you are able to keep hidden in darkness, you first get to know by your
opening it to the knowledge of the all-knowing One. (*OTA1*, 50–51)

But in eternity, conscience is the only voice that is heard. It must be heard by the
individual, for the individual has become the eternal echo of this voice. (*OTA1*,
186)

For what is eternity? It is the distinction between right and wrong. (*CT*, 215)

He who truly knows himself, knows precisely that he can do nothing of himself.
(*T*, 164)

When one thinks only one thought, one must in relationship to this thinking discover self-renunciation, and it is self-renunciation which discovers that God is. (*KG*, 333)

The essence of this perspective can be roughly indicated as follows: Genuine self-knowledge can be gained only through the act of confession. Confessing is a certain way of giving an account of oneself and one's life; it is giving testimony (*Vidnesbyrd*) concerning oneself, witnessing in one's own case. But witnessing here is essentially witnessing against oneself. Confessing is an act of recognizing and admitting one's failure. More, it implies recognizing and admitting that this failure was and is not accidental, that one is essentially incapable of doing good or being good. For in confessing one is confessing before a measure of truth and rightness that is absolute and eternal. In relation to this measure, one is nothing; the self is seen, so to speak, to dwindle to a point and vanish. So adopting a general project of self-renunciation (in the ordinary empirical sense of "self") is a logical corollary of confession.

This represents a perspective that, within SK's overall theory, decisively transcends the Socratic conceptions of the early works, without yet reaching a recognizably Christian vision. If we ask to whom, in SK's gallery of characters, this perspective belongs, I think there is no simple answer. Johannes Climacus, for all his praise of Socrates, seems to me to stand beyond the Socratic perspective; if only because he is able to imagine the possibility of a Christian perspective. There are things in *PS* and *AE* that go far beyond anything in or derivable from Plato's writings. So perhaps Johannes represents this perspective. Again, if we notice that most of the passages that express these conceptions occur in characteristically edifying works, we may suspect that the perspective belongs to someone who is trying to grasp the Christian message in purely ethical terms. It is partly in the light of this suspicion that I earlier used the name of Kant; I was thinking of *Religion within the Limits of Pure Reason*.

There is one implication of this perspective that is crucial in SK's overall theory. We can bring this implication out if we consider what general attitude to his life a man who adopts this perspective will have. He has recognized that he cannot come to know himself truthfully by his own work; he has recognized that his empirical self is essentially incapable of fulfilling the transcendent demands of the measures of truth and rightness; he has recognized the essential nullity of his empirical self in the light of this measure; and he has acknowledged an absolute demand to renounce and deny his empirical self. But he does not recognize the existence of anyone, any being, who is capable of helping him in his predicament; and he does not recognize the existence of anything that might give meaning to his fulfilling the transcendent demands of ethics. It seems to me plain that a man who sees life in this way will be in despair.

3

I quote a long passage from one of the early edifying discourses.

Through every deeper reflection, which makes a man *older* than the moment, and lets him grasp the eternal, he assures himself that he has an actual relationship to the world, and that consequently this relationship cannot consist merely in a knowledge about this world and about himself as a part of it, since such a knowledge is not a relationship, precisely because in this knowledge he himself is indifferent to this world, and this world is indifferent to his knowledge about it. Not until concern awakens in his soul as to what the world signifies to him and he to the world, what everything in him through which he belongs to the world, signifies to him, and he through it to the world, in that moment does the inner man proclaim itself in this *concern*. This concern is not quieted by a closer or more comprehensive knowledge; it demands another kind of knowledge, a knowledge which at no moment persists as knowledge, but transforms itself in the moment of possession into action; for otherwise it is not possessed. This concern also demands an explanation, a testimony, but of a different kind. If a man in his knowledge could know everything, but did not understand the relation of this knowledge to himself, then he would indeed, in striving for assurance about the relation of his knowledge to the object, demand a testimony, but he would not have understood that there was needed a quite different kind of testimony: then the concern would not even have awakened in his soul. As soon as this awakens, his knowledge will appear distressing, because all the knowledge in which a man loses himself, like every explanation which is brought about by such a knowledge, is ambiguous; it explains now this and now that, and can indicate the opposite, just as every testimony of this kind, precisely when it bears witness, is full of deceit and riddle, and only fosters anxiety. (*T*, 110–11)

What is it to have a relationship with the world? Whatever having a relationship with the world is, it is not having knowledge of the world. Knowing the world, knowing about the world, is not being related with the world. But why not?

Knowledge, in the ordinary sense of the word, is objective and universal. If it makes sense to say that my beliefs about the world differ from yours, this is precisely because beliefs are not objective and universal. It makes no sense to say that my knowledge about something, say, number theory or Roman history, differs from your knowledge of the same thing. In so far as we differ, one of us cannot have knowledge. Knowledge, then, is indifferent as to persons, possessors. But a relationship with the world, in SK's view, must necessarily be concerned. For by "having a relationship with the world" SK does not mean just being related as a matter of fact in such and such ways with things in the world. He means being related with the world in ways that mean something to me, because I am aware of them, and because in general I am their source. My relationship with the world is not something that just happens to be true of me, whether or not I am aware of it and whether or not I wish it. My relationship with the world is the sum of the ways in which I relate myself with the world. It is all the ways in which I take stances towards things and people which have meaning for me. So the relationship with the world includes (*a*) the ways in which I comport myself towards things and people, for example, my desires and aversions, loves and hates, and (*b*) the senses which these stances—my desires and aversions for various objects—have for me, what significance it has for me, for instance, that I have such and such a love for such and such a person.

So having a relationship with the world means that the world means something to me, and I to the world. Each object of my experience has a meaning for me because I have a particular comportment towards it and because my stance has a sense for me.

Having a relationship with the world necessarily involves self-reflection. For it requires me to become aware of my stance towards objects. In doing so, I become aware not only what things mean to me but also how I am concerned about things. I become aware of the ways in which I am concerned about things and people—about the world. Therefore, the kind of reflection SK is talking about in this passage is a kind of self-understanding. It is understanding what is revealed about myself in my having the relationship with the world that I do have. And this is a central element in self-knowledge. It is recognition that my ways of relating myself to the world (which is my life) are ways for which I am responsible and which have meaning in that they reveal the meanings (values) that I have projected upon objects.

It is this sort of self-knowledge for which SK uses the idea of testimony. Giving testimony about myself is describing my relationship with the world, explicating my relationship. This is plainly not a matter of merely saying what one does or what one is. It is explicating the significance, to me, of what I have done and been, what my life (actions, strivings, goals) means to me.

Understanding myself in this kind of way is plainly not just a matter of having some information about myself. That might be possessed neutrally, in indifference. But the knowledge SK is talking of cannot be possessed in indifference, since it is essentially knowledge of the ways in which I am not indifferent (concerned) about objects in the world. Concerned stances are essentially practical. Something's having a certain kind of significance for me is expressed precisely in my comportment towards that thing—my desires about it, my actions concerning it. I cannot take a neutral, indifferent stance towards my understanding of my concerned stances. Understanding one of my concerns is itself intrinsically concerned. Understanding, say, the significance for me of the ways in which I love and behave towards a certain individual itself necessarily bears on my love and my behaviour. And, of course, unless my relationship was wholly unconscious, it must already have been constructed around some conception of the object and its significance to me. So, becoming able to give myself testimony about this relationship is merely taking further something already implied in the fact of having a relationship. Relationships, because intrinsically relations of meaning, are themselves already essentially reflective. There is no difference of kind between being related to the world and gaining self-knowledge. The real difference, which SK is pointing to, is between "relationships" with the world which are not intrinsically reflective, and thus not essentially significant, and self-knowledge. A man who has all his life been living, so to speak, objectively—just relating himself immediately with objects and persons through his desires and aversions—may come to see that his way of living and acting and relating has not been such as to establish for him any significance in his life. This is just what is discovered in the hypothetical transition between the aesthetic and the ethical states. The man who is living aesthetically may have a normally clear and accurate picture of himself, his likes and dislikes, his talents, goals, etc. But he will never have asked himself what all this means. So, naturally he will be unable to answer the question that marks the ethical: What does your life mean to you? He will never have asked himself how and why *he* established just such relationships, patterns of action and desire and striving, in his life; about the ways in which he is responsible for these patterns, these relationships—this life of his. It is just this that is explicated when one gives testimony about oneself.

We can put the difference like this. The individual who has reached the point of being able to give testimony about himself is the one who has gained a certain sort of self-knowledge. For he has come to conceive his life in a particular kind of way—as his own responsibility, his own choice.

It does not matter that, he believes, his previous choices were largely or wholly unconscious or unreflective or amoral. That is, on the contrary, precisely one of the most important and revealing discoveries a man can make about the way in which he exercised his responsibilities for his own life, the way in which he made his choices. It is also why SK says that the first moment of the ethical is repentance. It is not repentance over wrong or evil choices so much as over the fact that I have spent my life in misusing my responsibility for myself. A man's not consciously taking responsibility for himself is itself the worst failure of his responsibility for himself.

4

Now let us consider the idea of confession. For SK claims that testimony about oneself is given essentially in the form of confession. Confession is itself essentially an act of the conscience. Whatever else, or whoever else, a man confesses before, he must confess before his own conscience. This is part of the notion of confession. If we want to stress that confession is confessing *to* someone, then we must here say that it is at any rate confessing to oneself.

SK writes as follows: "And yet there is no one who accuses, who would dare to accuse, where everyone is guilty! And there is no one who condemns, who would dare to condemn where everyone is intent upon his own accounting. No one accuses except the thoughts, no one condemns except that One who sees in secret and hears confession in secret. Aye, even when a voice is heard, it is you yourself speaking with yourself through the speaker's words..." (*TTL*, 1). He adds that "the all-knowing One does not get to know something about the maker of the confession, rather the maker of the confession gets to know about himself" (*OTA1*, 50). And "much that you are able to keep hidden in darkness, you first get to know by your opening it to the knowledge of the all-knowing One" (*OTA1*, 51). Confessing is essentially being with oneself. "One cannot confess without this at-oneness with oneself.... But he that in truth becomes at one with himself, he is in the silence" (*OTA1*, 47).

Testimony can be given either to oneself or to someone else. Normally, as the word itself implies, it is given to others. The legal flavour of the analogy makes it plain that we are to think of giving testimony as something like standing up in a lawcourt and offering an account of one's deeds, an account which can in principle be supported by evidence. But SK thinks of ethical testimony as given primarily to oneself. This is indeed essential. There is no particular need for a piece of legal testimony to be given by a man to himself, before or during his actual testifying before others. But it is part of SK's conception of the ethical that unless I give myself my testimony, whether or not I am testifying before others, my testifying cannot be ethical. The confession to myself is essential and primary; the confession before, or to, others is secondary.

That is why even God is secondary in SK's account. Unless I already give myself my testimony, my testimony even before God will not count as ethical. It will not count as confession. For confession before God is not simply saying things about oneself with the belief that one is saying them to God. It is saying things which one means and sincerely believes: saying things *as an act of confession.* My words could not count as a confession unless I understand myself as making a confession. And to understand that, I must believe that the things I am confessing require confessing. But in coming to see my life in this way no external being is required. All I need is the conception "should not have been done," as it applies to my own acts. If I do not have this conception, then whatever I say about myself, to whomever I say it, my words cannot possibly constitute a confession. They cannot possibly constitute an *ethical* account of my life.

To confess, I must have a certain kind of conception of my life and deeds. I must regard what I do as *confessible*, as at least potentially needing to be confessed and capable of being confessed. For that, however, I must have a certain stance towards my life. I must look on my life as something for which I bear responsibility. Without the responsibility, there could be nothing for me to confess. So the ability to make a confession presupposes the ability to give testimony about my life. In giving testimony, I explicate my conception of my responsibilities for my deeds and life and how I have born these responsibilities or failed to live up to them adequately.

All this requires that I possess conceptions of my acts which are also standards by which acts can be measured. I must at the very least possess standards of a kind which allow me to measure success and failure in assuming and carrying out my own responsibilities. Already these are beyond merely practical measures, for example, money, fame, power. Practical measures can certainly measure practical successes and failures, but that is all they can do. In giving testimony, however, I am testifying to much more than the practical successes and failures of my life. It cannot be enough, for instance, to explain that I have accumulated such and such a quantity of money. For that does not explain *why* accumulating money should appear to me to be significant or worth while, how that gives a measure of the meaning of my life to me. To explain this, I must give an account of a different and higher-order type. I must explain why I have adopted money as a measure of success and failure, that is, what significance human life has, when the measure of its success or failure is taken to be wealth. And an explanation of this new kind will be in general an ethical accounting. Traditional moralists, of course, have tended to argue that it is in principle impossible to give such an account for the example I have chosen—wealth—that there is *no* possible way in which human life can be shown to be significant in virtue of having wealth for the measure of its success.

Confession, then, is an account of my own life that I give essentially to myself. And I give it in terms of a measure that I apply to my own life regarded as my responsibility, my choice. In confessing, I confront my actual life, including my inner acts—for example, wishes and regrets—with the measure that is implicit in the kind of significance I have chosen to endow the world with.

Now, why should SK say that in the act of confession the individual gets to know about himself? On the face of it, this is impossible. For how can a man confess unless he already has an idea of what he has done in his life and a measure by which he recognizes that his life exhibits failures which require confession? How can confession precede and produce self-knowledge?

This question rests, first, on the same old misunderstanding about self-knowledge that I have tried to uncover before. If we suppose that self-knowledge is an achieved state of true beliefs about ourselves, then obviously self-knowledge must precede and cannot itself be produced by the act of stating what one has done wrong. But if we recall that, for SK, self-knowledge is essentially a kind of concerned reflection about one's actions, it becomes less compelling that this must precede the act of confession. As a first step, we might indeed suggest at once that self-knowledge is not the source of confession so much as what confessing expresses. It is not the content but the act of confessing that expresses self-knowledge in SK's sense. If so, plainly, self-knowledge could not precede confession or cause it. For it is only by voluntarily engaging in the act of confession that I show (to myself also) that I have developed a certain concern about myself and my life. My concern is expressed, in part, in acts of confession. And here the idea that confession is essentially inward becomes intelligible. Concern about one's existence is not obviously expressed in the act of confessing to someone else, but it is expressed rather obviously in the act of reflecting on one's life inwardly to oneself. Confession, in the ethical sense, is not so much an act of describing one's life contritely to others as an act of reflecting contritely upon it. Hence, also, SK's frequent emphasis on the intrinsic connection between confession and silence. This could be puzzling if we supposed that by confession he meant giving a contrite account of one's failures to someone else. But it is immediately intelligible if confessing is thought of, rather, as deep and penetrating self-examination.

SK in fact stresses this feature of confession. Even if he speaks of confession, usually, in contexts where he is also speaking of the individual's presence to God, still he takes pains to make it clear that the essential thing about confession is not that it is done *to* God but that on the contrary it is done when and only when the individual is turned inwardly towards himself. That is the force of the idea of being at one with oneself. To confess is to be at one with oneself. And part of what this surely implies is that in confessing I am not essentially with anyone else, even God—unless God be within myself.

We must distinguish two possible claims about confession, one of which SK rejects while accepting the other. He accepts the idea that confession is giving an account of oneself *before* God. But he does not identify this with giving an account of oneself *to* God, and in fact he rejects that as a definition of confessing. Of course, the individual who gives testimony before God may also give it to God; but the first condition by no means involves the second, and the absence of the second does not rob the first of its character as confession.

5

What kind of testimony about oneself does one give in making a confession? SK's answer is, a kind of testimony about oneself that rests on understanding one's life as a whole, a "continuity." Thus, he says, "whoever apprehends his sin in this manner, and wishes in stillness to learn the art ... of sorrowing over his sin, he will discover that confession is not merely an enumeration of particular sins, but is an understanding before God, of the continuity of sin itself" (*TTL*, 30). He adds that "sin is a continuity" (*TTL*, 33). The same idea turns up again in *SD*.

How rare is the man who possesses continuity with respect to his consciousness of himself! Generally men are only momentarily conscious, conscious in the great decisions, but the daily things are not computed at all; such men are spirit (if this word may be applied to them) once a week for one hour—of course that is a pretty bestial way of being spirit. Eternity, however, is essential continuity and requires this of man, that or requires that he shall be conscious of himself as spirit and shall have faith. (P. 104)

   To understand one's life as a continuity, whether in success or failure, is to use the idea of continuity as a measure for one's life. It is to measure one's life, one's self, against some standard of continuity—which one then inevitably finds that one has failed. More precisely, one inevitably discovers that one has in failing to achieve one kind of continuity achieved a quasi-continuity of a different and so deplorable sort. Of course; for one has achieved a continuity in failing to achieve the continuity one ought to have achieved. The discovery is not just that I have failed to win this continuity but that my failure itself has been continuous, continuous because inevitable.

   The continuity that the individual ought to achieve is "eternity"; the opposing continuity that he has achieved is "sin." The passage that I have quoted from *SD* comes from the latter part of the book, in which SK is already discussing Christian ideas.

6

There are no doubt many kinds of testimony that human beings can and do give about themselves. The first that SK considers worth taking seriously is the Socratic. Already here the individual is using a serious conception of the ethical measure for his life. He is not, for instance, measuring life simply by the achievement of happiness; still less, wealth or fame (other Aristotelian criteria). Even Socrates measured his life against a conception of truth. But the Socratic conception of truth is, according to SK, not one but two steps lower than the Christian conception. For in between the two comes a conception of truth that, like the Socratic, makes no reference to a personal god who is regarded as himself *being* the truth but that, unlike the Socratic, considers truth as something absolute and eternal and transcendent with regard to man. SK himself often makes the point that, from the Socratic perspective, truth is immanent within human beings. He means, among other things, that all of us are in principle capable of discovering the truth (the eternal truth) merely by going down within our own minds. And there, in "memory," *anamnésis*, the eternal truth that we have been carrying unconsciously within us all our lives will be uncovered. The paradigm SK appeals to is the *Meno*. For the

Christian, of course, the truth is not to be discovered thus. Already in *PS*, SK is making the point that truth, in the Christian sense, requires a revelation; for it requires a "teacher" who can not only reveal the truth but also make men capable of receiving the revelation. But there is a position intermediate between the Socratic and the Christian. It is the view that truth is absolute but at the same time transcendent. It is the view that there is a standard for human lives that is objective and absolute but at the same time transcendent. This standard SK often calls "the eternal."

SK makes two claims about deep self-knowledge. The first is that we discover that, measured against a certain standard, we can do nothing. The second is that we discover that we are nothing. The second is a deeper discovery than the first. "He who truly knows himself, knows precisely that he can do nothing of himself" (*T*, 164). Let us consider this claim.

One part of it is the truism, repeated again and again in SK's works, that the results of our acts are not wholly within our powers. For results are dependent also on contingencies in the external world. What lies within our powers is, strictly speaking, only our intentions. I can be certain only of the direction in which I am facing; I cannot be certain that I will be able to move one step in that direction. If so, plainly, ethical demands cannot be demands for achievements in the external world. They can be demands only for the effort, the direction, the turning, of our ethical wills in a certain direction. That is all that a human being can guarantee being able to achieve. This doctrine does not imply, however, that we should make no efforts to carry out our ethical intentions in actuality. On the contrary.

The idea that the results of our own acts are not within our powers is connected with another characteristic claim: that ethical consideration cannot be concerned with "rewards" or "punishments." Such a concern is the paradigm of doublemindedness. It is doubleminded for the following reason. If ethical demands are demands on the will, not demands upon our achievements, then ethical concern is concern about one's will, about its direction. So concern about the result of one's action is concern of a quite distinct kind. This is not to say that, ethically, I should not be concerned whether my actions do good or harm to others. Of course I must be, and of course I must make every effort to try to do good to others. It is just that whether I actually do benefit or harm others by my actions is not wholly within my powers. For the part of the outcome which is not within the scope of my own unaided powers, I am not responsible. The will acquires ethical standing not through actually producing good or harm for others but through being turned in one direction or the other.

However, SK is making a deeper point as well: that one result of a deep self-examination is the discovery of radical self-deceit and self-temptation within oneself. It is the knowledge that I can "do nothing of myself" in the direction of making myself wholly truthful, wholly turned in the direction of the truth, completely self-transparent. It is the discovery of an essential "inward struggle." SK remarks that "the man who fails to discover the existence of this inward struggle is involved in a misunderstanding, and his life is consequently imperfect. But if he does discover this struggle, he will here again be made to understand that he can do nothing of himself" (*T*, 164). The inward struggle is simply the struggle between the will to know oneself transparently and a will, deep within each of us, to remain obscure to ourselves. Failing to recognize this inward struggle must mean that a man remains in the "misunderstanding" that he can in principle achieve self-knowledge by himself—and no doubt often in the worse delusion that he actually has achieved it. The discovery that we cannot achieve full transparency by our own efforts, since there is in all of us some universal will to obscurity, is connected with SK's conception of eternity.

At each stage of self-examination, a man uses a particular concept of truth as the measure for his inquiries. This measure serves as his criterion for self-knowledge, self-ignorance, and self-delusion. At the stage we are discussing, the measure for knowledge is a conception of truth as absolute, or eternal. Now "truth" here does not primarily mean the truth of abstract or even empirical propositions. It means the kind of truth which characterizes knowledge of oneself, regarded as the product of a moral self-inquiry. We might call this "ethical truth." It is the kind, or sense, of truth, for instance, which characterizes a man's ethical understanding of his own character, his life, his actions. It is therefore also an ethical standard or goal. This is why SK remarks, in *SD*, that "each thing is qualitatively that by which it is measured; and that which is qualitatively its measure is ethically its goal" (p. 79).

In adopting an absolute conception of truth as the standard for my self-examination, then, I am at the same time adopting a conception of moral truth as absolute, or eternal. This claim is merely the inverse of a definition given by SK himself. "For what is *eternity*? It is the distinction between right and wrong" (*CT*, 215). The same idea is repeated in *OTAr*: "It must, by an eternal separation, cut off the heterogeneous from itself in order that it may in truth continue to be one and the same thing..." (p.

66). It might be objected that this is only one particular conception of moral truth; but that is a crucial part of SK's own theory. For it is essential to the whole theory that at different stages in our journey of self-examination we shall inevitably form different conceptions of the requirement and the possibility. We shall inevitably form different conceptions of the nature of ethical standards, goals, and truths. It is not to be wondered at, then, that most people have conceptions of ethical truth which are not SK's. The understanding of ethical truths as eternal, of the distinction between right and wrong as absolute, is in SK's view quite naturally one that a man can come to only after a long inward journey, a journey that has taken him through many deep varieties of illusion and self-deception.

There is, however, an obvious difficulty about the conception of ethical truth as absolute and eternal, as transcendental. It is just that if truth is like this, then no man can ever know that he has achieved truth. But this is the heart of SK's argument. To adopt a transcendental standard for ethical truth is to adopt a standard which guarantees that I can never be certain that my understanding of myself is the truth or merely another deception.

This claim alone would establish that no man by his own unaided powers can achieve self-understanding. It would not, perhaps, establish that all men essentially resist the deepest self-understanding. For that SK tacitly appeals to the idea that the eternal and the temporal are essentially resistant to, in conflict with, one another. It is one thing to adopt an eternal measure for one's self-understanding—which is also a measure for one's will, actions, and life. It is quite another to live up to such a measure. There will, for this reason, be in all of us an inescapable resistance to adopting an absolute conception of ethical truth. Thus, for example, Anti-Climacus remarks that "there are very few men who live even only passably in the category of spirit. . . . They have not learned to fear, they have not learned what 'must' means, regardless, infinitely regardless of what it may be that comes to pass" (*SD*, 57).

7

The recognition that I can essentially do nothing might seem to be simply recognition of a matter of fact, a fact about the absence of internal connection between the will and the actual world. As such, there seems to be no reason why such a discovery should have any particular effect upon a man's attitudes towards life, feelings about himself, and so on. Yet plainly it does, and ought to. This is because recognizing that I can essentially do nothing is recognizing, among other things, that I cannot by myself achieve the ethical goals and standards I have come to set for myself. It is coming to see that I cannot, except by accident, achieve the life for myself that I have come to will to achieve. Thus grasping that I can do nothing is essentially expressed in a form of sorrow. It is the sorrow of repentance and resignation.

Let us first consider the idea of resignation. This is a central theme of the last part of AE. Here, Johannes Climacus argues that resignation is a fundamental form of any religious view of life. "Resignation" simply means giving up all claims on any object, person, or achievement in this world. It is the exact correlative of the discovery that I can essentially do nothing. For it is the form in which this discovery is expressed in the will. To discover that I can do nothing is to detach my will from all possible results of my acts, all possible achievements. It is, among other things, to cease to be influenced in my decisions by any desire for worldly achievable goods and any fear of worldly ills. This does not entail ceasing to desire and fear. It only requires that my decisions no longer be determined by such motives.

Similarly for possessing worldly goods and being free from worldly ills. It is normal and natural to want to possess, and to enjoy possessing, worldly goods like health, friends, love, intelligence, and so on, and to reject their contraries. But to understand that no actual achievement is essentially within my powers is to understand that it is not essentially in my powers to possess any actual good or to be free from any actual ill. It is simply a matter of contingency—good or bad luck, providence, etc. —whether as a matter of fact I come to possess the good things I want to possess and to be free of the ills I want to be free of. To see this is to detach one's will from the actual possession or non-possession of anything worldly. SK emphasizes that such detachment of the will need not necessarily be expressed in a life of asceticism. On the contrary, it is a running theme of his work that asceticism is all too often a mistaken response to the ethical or religious requirement, a response of "enthusiasm." The King in *AE* does not give up his throne in fact; he only remains always aware that he does not essentially possess it, that it is his only by chance—and that therefore it is not in itself to be desired or gloried in. "Resignation" therefore means an attitude of detachment from the objects and events of a man's actual life. It is to possess the goods I possess, be free of the ills I am free of, in such a way that losing the former or gaining the latter does not cause me the particular suffering of feeling that I am undergoing something I ought not to be undergoing. I do not imagine I have a right to possess the goods I possess; therefore, I do not imagine that when I lose them I am being deprived of something I have a right to—still less, something essential to my identity.

There is a further, and extremely important, implication that SK does not spell out. For what is the natural response to possessing something good? It is happiness, joy. This natural response is not, presumably, dimmed or destroyed by the habit of resignation. The happy lover who possesses his loved one in marriage, but resignedly, is not supposed to have resigned in any way the natural human response of joy. It is just that his joy is now detached from any conception of having his right, or his due. Similarly, although loss of his loved one will quite naturally cause him grief—he does not transcend this response either—it will not be mixed with any feeling that he has lost something he had a right to.

Resignation, in other words, entails *humility*. Thus, in *KG*, SK writes as follows: "When, on the other hand, a man thinks only one thought, he does not have an external object, he has an inward direction towards self-deepening, and he makes a discovery concerning his own inner situation, and this discovery is at first very humbling" (p. 332). And on the next page, he adds that "when one thinks only one thought, one must in relationship to this thinking discover self-renunciation. . . ."

8

I want to think a little more about the individual who has reached the stage in self-understanding at which he recognizes that he can essentially do nothing, so that whatever he possesses and achieves is essentially independent of his will and desire. Such an individual has effectively renounced the world, because he has adopted a measure for his life and will that is eternal. No standard of achievement or willing that is marked in terms of worldly goods can serve him any longer as his standard. For no such worldly standard can be accepted as an ethical measure. Such a man is at the stage "when the earthly is taken away from the self and a man despairs . . ." (*SD*, 62). The same moment appears in *EE2*. Such a form of despair is the obverse of the discovery of the self's existence before eternity.

For in discovering that I exist before eternity, before the eternal measure of the ethical, I am simultaneously discovering that my true self requires to be measured against an eternal measure. But this could not be understood unless my true self was understood to be somehow eternal itself. My own self, and its fate, is involved in that separation between right and wrong which is eternity—or the judgment. "For immortality is the judgment," SK remarks in *CT* (p. 212): "immortality is the eternal separation between the just and the unjust." In coming to understand that the measure by which I am to account myself either good or evil is an eternal measure, I come to understand that I am myself eternal. This is not so much a discovery as an achievement. It would be a discovery about myself only if we imagined that the human self, so to speak, existed at all times in essentially the same form. But this is not so. In SK's view, the self is at any time what it is essentially engaged upon: its will, its goals, its projects, its understanding and penetration of itself. A man's self is thus continually changing not only in content but also in metaphysical status. The deeper my self-understanding penetrates, the deeper the self which in that penetration I acquire. For the self which I am penetrating is also the self that is doing the penetrating! This is why SK remarks several times that immortality is an achievement. In *AE* and *CT* alike, immortality is presented as a qualification that can be won—or lost—in a man's own lifetime, by his own efforts.

The heart of SK's argument is that in coming to understand oneself in terms of the idea of eternity, one necessarily adopts a measure for the self which not only makes the self eternal (immortal) but also at the same moment makes it nothing. In any terms that the individual has so far had available to him the essential and eternal self can only be identified as nothing, as wholly empty. For the only terms that I possess so far are the terms of the world and its contents. And all such terms have been rigorously excluded from my conception of the ethical measure. I come to see that all my life, up to this moment, I have identified my self with external contingent things. For my psyche has been filled with images taken from actuality: desires, hopes, memories, ideals, measures of achievement, conceptions of my self. But now all such images must be rejected. The concrete empirical contents of my intellect and my will and my emotions must be recognized as essentially alien to my true self. So whatever my true self is, it must be essentially distinct from any of its concrete empirical contents and qualifications. I shall therefore define it, as far as the terms I have available to me go, wholly negatively. (This manoeuvre plainly recalls the Hegelian concept of freedom. But it is in fact basic Christian teaching about prayer.)

The individual, at the stage I am discussing, has gone so far as to reject all measures for the ethical other than the absolute measure, which SK calls "eternal." This involves recognizing that no worldly good is in itself an ethical good, no worldly ill in itself an ethical evil. In making this distinction, the individual detaches his ethical will from his natural desires and projects. That is, he reaches a point at which his ethical decisions are no longer determined by natural rewards and punishments. Moreover, his whole attitude to the world and life is qualified in the same way. He sees his possession of any worldly good as, ethically speaking, wholly irrelevant and accidental. This is "resignation." But this is only one half of his ethical achievement. The other half is his recognition that, given an ethical measure that is absolute, his power to achieve his goals by willing alone is nil. He can essentially do absolutely nothing. Moreover, the self that stands as the correlate of such an ethical demand, that is capable of being bound by an eternal requirement, must itself be in some sense an eternal self. It must be a self to which ethical possession of the ethical good is essential, but to which possession of every non-ethical and worldly good or ill is essentially accidental. It is a self that cannot be described at all in any terms taken from experience of the actual world. It is, so to speak, in terms of the world a point which vanishes—a mere power of rejection and resignation. But even this power is illusory. For the individual recognizes that he does not even have the power of "negating" the world wholly within his control. He recognizes that this deep essential power of detachment is itself controlled by the powers of attachment, of worldly desires and projects, that characterize and qualify our empirical and superficial selves—the selves which most of us mistakenly identify ourselves as.

The self, to use an image, becomes at this point wholly empty and transparent. In looking inwards, the individual looks past all the experience-given contents of his psyche, passing beyond these and detaching his true mind and will from them and refusing to identify them with his true self. He looks, as it were, not at but through his mind, his achievements, his life. These are understood no longer to be himself but to be barriers to his coming to see his true self, still more, barriers to his becoming his true self. The self becomes a glass; but nothing is visible through that glass. I look for myself, and what I see is wholly transparent. I look at myself, and what I see vanishes into a disappearing point. I can now see absolutely nothing at all when I turn inwards. For what I am looking for is a transcendent will. But that cannot be seen.

What I used to identify as myself (my ego, "I") is revealed here as psychophysical: real in its own proper terms, but not identifiable as a self, as I now understand this idea. My empirical ego is (as Hume recognized) just a bundle of psychic phenomena—desires, beliefs, memories, habits, etc.—which no doubt manifest some underlying psychophysical mechanism (as Freud postulated). But *I* am neither the phenomena nor the mechanism, nor both together. Now, and only now, when I abandon and reject my empirical ego, is it possible for my true self to emerge. It first emerges, necessarily, in negative form, in the conscious act of abandoning and rejecting my ego, the act of saying, "*I* am none of this; none of this is *me*." But this act is not just the rejecting of a belief, the abandoning of a conception, of myself. For I am not, for myself, just an object in my world of vision, my field of beliefs and conceptions. This is because I am not, and am not for myself—do not appear to myself to be—just an observer, believer, understander. I am an agent: I make decisions, I engage my will in intentions and actions. Therefore, I am *for myself* an agent, a willer. Whatever I identify as myself, as "I," it is part of the sense of the identification that the "I" is a willer, the source of a will. For it is part of the sense that "I" carries that it connotes "willer, source of a will." Pithily, and ungrammatically, I has a will; perhaps I *is* a will. If so, in refusing a theoretical identification of my true self with my empirical psychophysical organism, I imply that nothing in that organism is my will, that my will is distinct from each and every part of that organism. (It also follows that any decision, any action, which has its source within the psychophysical organism thereby has a source wholly outside my will, did not originate in my will. That is another way of saying that it is not my action.) This is the negative sense of "transcendent will." Later, a positive sense may emerge. But that requires existing in a world which is not restricted to the psychic and physical. It requires existing in a world which, so to speak, also contains God. It requires that I come to exist before God. Then I may begin to know what I positively am. (And from *this*, all that is my empirical self has been excluded and rejected.)

IX

Ways of Existing before God

IN THIS CHAPTER I shall describe some of the important ways in which a human being can exist before God, as SK identifies them. I shall not analyse them in detail or explain their relations to each other. This chapter is only a rough long-distance sketch of a wide and complex conceptual landscape.

The discussion of existing before God is many things at once. It is a partial theology (Christology). It is also a partial human psychology. With SK, we cannot separate these two kinds of analysis. There is within his works, in principle, a systematic and precise parallel between the kinds of reality that can be ascribed to God and/the possible conditions of the human psyche. Such a position is obviously Hegelian. But it also has much older roots, for it is a basic principle of neo-Platonic—for instance, Augustinian—theology.

I quote three familiar passages from *SD* to indicate the general assumptions that underlie this position.

Generally speaking, consciousness—that is, self-consciousness—is decisive with regard to the self. The more consciousness, the more self; the more consciousness, the more will, the more will, the more self. A person who has no will at all is not a self; but the more will he has, the more self-consciousness he has also. (P. 29)

The criterion for the self is always: that directly before which it is a self, but that in turn is the definition of "criterion." (P. 79)

But this self takes on a new quality and qualification by being a self directly before God. This self is no longer the merely human self, but is what I, hoping not to be misinterpreted, would call the theological self, the self directly before God. And what infinite reality the self gains by being conscious of existing before God, by becoming a human self whose criterion is God! (P. 79)

I

(1) The first stage in the consciousness of existing before God is negative. In
     SD, it is referred to as "a self that is won by infinite abstraction from every
     externality, this naked abstract self, which, compared with immediacy's
     fully dressed self, is the first form of the infinite self and the advancing
     impetus in the whole process by which a self infinitely becomes respon-
     sible for its actual self..." (p. 55).

This passage recalls *EE2* in its use of a metaphysical language. SK is not
primarily concerned with pure metaphysics. What really matters is that
"abstraction" indicates a psychic process or activity: the activity of
"abstracting" oneself from the immediate, whether external or internal.
An earlier pseudonym called this activity "infinite resignation" (*AE, pas-
sim*; see also *FB* and *EE2*). This is, in the first place, a mode of recognition
of elementary facts (a *prise de conscience*). It is the recognition of one's
essential nothingness.

The recognition of one's nothingness has two parts: recognizing that
one *can do* nothing and recognizing that one *is* nothing. Thus "he who
truly knows himself, knows precisely that he can do nothing of himself"
(*T*, 164). Moreover, "in so far as a man does not know himself, nor
understand that he can of himself do nothing, he does not really become
aware, in any deeper sense, that God exists" (*T*, 167). "But whoever
knows in himself that he can do nothing, has each day and each moment
the desired and indubitable occasion to experience the living God" (*T*,
168). As SK stresses, this discovery is essentially humbling: it can be
made only in humiliation. In *TTL*, SK says that "the more profound the
sorrow, the more will the individual find himself to be nothing, less than
nothing, and this is precisely because the sorrow is that of a seeker who
begins to take cognizance of God" (p. 26); (see also *EOT*).

The discovery that one is essentially nothing also requires one's coop-
erative activity; in this case, the activity is that of self-renunciation. In *KG*,
we find that "when one thinks only one thought, one must in relationship
to this thinking discover self-renunciation, and it is self-renunciation
which discovers that God is" (p. 333). So recognizing that one is nothing
is really better described as wholly renouncing all that one appears to be
and to have.

I emphasize that this requires humility. "The less a man thinks of
himself, not as a man in general, or about being a human being, but of
himself, as an individual, and not with respect to his talents, but with
regard to his guilt, the more significant God becomes to him" (*TTL*, 27).

Similarly, in analysing a profound form of despair in *SD*, SK writes: "But when having to be helped becomes a profoundly earnest matter, especially when it means being helped by a superior, or by the supreme one, there is the humiliation of being obliged to accept any kind of help unconditionally, of becoming a nothing in the hand of the 'Helper' for whom all things are possible..." (*SD*, 71). In this work, Anti-Climacus stresses how often despair involves the lack of humility, that is, pride.

But not all despair involves pride. Anti-Climacus indicates other possibilities. "The despair that is the thoroughfare to faith comes also through the aid of the eternal: through the aid of the eternal the self has the courage to lose itself in order to win itself" (*SD*, 67). Earlier, he declares: "But if repentance is to arise, there must first be effective despair, radical despair, so that the life of the spirit can break through from the ground upward" (*SD*, 59). (See *EE2* for another version of the claim that repentance presupposes despair.)

What is the internal connection between the ideas of "being nothing" and "being able to do nothing" and repentance? And what establishes these conditions as ways of existing before God? It is that one is nothing in comparison with another being, and can do nothing because only that other being can do anything, and that humble repentance is the proper expression of seeing one's true relationship to that being. That being is God, the Creator, the omnipotent.

The stage I am discussing is the first in the process or activity of "acquiring one's soul." SK says that the soul, or spirit, "must at the same time be owned and acquired; it belongs to the world as its unlawful possession; it belongs to God as his true possession.... Consequently he then acquires, if he actually does acquire it, *his soul from the world, of God, through himself*" (*T*, 199). Similarly, he writes: "*before God* to be oneself—for the accent rests upon 'before God', since this is the source and origin of all individuality. He who has dared to do this has authentic individuality and has come to know what God has already given to him..., for individuality is not mine but is God's gift by which he gives me being and gives being to all..." (*KG*, 253). A particular form of despair is described thus: "he does not want to put on his own self, does not want to see his given self as his task—he himself wants to compose his self..." (*SD*, 68).

Recognizing that one is nothing is recognizing that one is wholly the creature of a creator; that one is nothing apart from what the Creator has created and continually now keeps in being; that one's very being, from moment to moment, is wholly dependent on the will of one's creator. It is recognizing that one is created by the Creator out of nothing (*ex nihilo*).

Recognizing that one can do nothing is a consequence of this understanding. For the Creator is omnipotent. His creatures can do nothing of themselves; and all they can do is the result of powers that he has given them, and really the product of his creative will. SK often makes the point that we can never be certain of the future. In his works, this is not a tired Stoic adage. It expresses the thesis that the world which contains the outcome of my act of will is wholly a creation of God in the moment, and that God's creative will is wholly undetermined by anything that happened in the previous moment.

In one reading, this thesis is the final truth expressed in the Book of Job. However finely Job responds to his trials at first—and SK devotes one of his edifying discourses to this subject—it is not until God reveals himself as the omnipotent creator that Job finally recognizes the ultimate truth: "Behold, I am vile" (*Job* 40:4). "I know that thou canst do every thing, and that no thought can be withholden from thee" (*Job* 42:2). And he adds: "Wherefore I abhor myself, and repent in dust and ashes." It is only now that he really acquires the first mode of existence before God, reaches the first stage of true consciousness of God.

2

But D / Can be via

(2)

The second stage, or way, of existing before God is having a conscience. There is a problem here. The concept of having a conscience does not seem to presuppose that one recognizes a creator. Is not there a concept of conscience purely within a moral existence? SK, on the other hand, writes in *SD*: "The point that must be observed is that the self has a conception of God and yet does not will as he wills, and thus is disobedient. Nor does one only occasionally sin before God, for every sin is before God, or, more correctly what really makes human guilt into sin is that the guilty one has the consciousness of existing before God" (p. 80). Conscience, as SK might say, *sensu eminenti*, is therefore essentially God-consciousness. This is, at any rate, what I shall now discuss.

his 2nd :

(2v libe

SK constantly uses two transferred terms in speaking about conscience. They are "silence" and "transparency." In this expository method he is not original. The idea of silence is a commonplace of mystical writings and those about prayer. And the idea of transparency is also a commonplace; it occurs, for instance, early in St. John of the Cross's *Ascent of Mount Carmel*.

—silence

"For without stillness, conscience cannot exist" (*TTL*, 4). The same point is made often in *OTA1*. Conscience is here pictured as a kind of voice, which can be heard only when the "voices" of the world—internal as well as external—are silent. In *KG*, SK writes: "The mark of maturity and the dedication of the eternal is to will to understand that this *I* has no significance if it does not become the *you*, the *thou*, to whom the eternal incessantly speaks and says: '*You* shall, *you* shall, *you* shall'" (p. 98).

The idea of transparency refers primarily to the activity of trying to penetrate one's own self with an essentially truth-seeking reflection. As such, it occurs already in the pseudonymous, and purely ethical, writings. Thus, in *EE2*: "Let us now for once compare an ethical and an aesthetical individual. The principal difference, and one on which everything hinges, is that the ethical individual is transparent to himself.... He who lives ethically has seen himself, knows himself, penetrates with his consciousness his whole concretion..." (pp. 262–63). Similarly, in *AE*: "Existence makes the understanding of the simplest truth for the common man in existential transparency very difficult..." (p. 228). And Climacus explains this task as continuously penetrating one's existence with reflection. One's "existence" is one's deeds and projects, but also one's thoughts, wishes, and acts of will.

The pseudonyms are, from a Christian standpoint, very optimistic about the powers of self-penetration. A more accurate estimate of the possibilities of transparency is given in the late discourse *GU*. Here SK writes as follows, speaking about God.

In altered clearness—aye, this is precisely why He is unchanged, because He is pure clearness, a clarity which betrays no trace of dimness, and which no dimness can come near. With us men it is not so. We are not in this manner clear, and precisely for this reason we are subject to change: now something becomes clearer in us, now something is dimmed, and we are changed; now changes take place about us, and the shadow of these changes glides over us to alter us; now there falls upon us from the surroundings an altering light, while under all this we are again changed within ourselves. (P. 242)

God is "eternal clearness." Again, this is wholly traditional. "Light" is one of the divine names discussed in Pseudo-Dionysius, and it is characteristic, of course, of St. John's Gospel.

Within the two ideas of silence and transparency SK groups several other concepts which help to constitute his idea of conscience as a way of existing before God. These include sincerity, eternity, continuity, and individuality. "But this I know, that with an *insincere* man God can have nothing to do.... There is one sin which makes grace impossible, that is

TRUTH is meta criterion over:
Ethical & Good (purified..)
Aesth~ BEAUTIFUL

for: must love the
TRUTH for its own
else you do not love it.

cp. 199: "truth" is Kierkegaardian

insincerity; and there is one thing which God must unconditionally require, that is, sincerity" (*CT*, 195). These words may strike one as hard.
But they express SK's view that one cannot even be genuinely conscious
of God unless one has an essentially truth-seeking spirit. As he elsewhere
puts it, "no man can see God without purity" (*TTL*, 9). God can come to
exist as a reality for one, only in consequence of one's seeking purification
of one's psyche: mind, heart, and will.

n.b. truth

What kind of self-consciousness is required for sincerity (transparency)? "This sincerity is not a perpetual enumeration of particulars, but
neither is it a mere signature on a piece of white paper, an admission of an
empty generality over one's name . . ." (*TTL*, 33). We are not required to
be able to give clear, detailed accounts of every single word and deed and
thought. That is impossible. But we are required to do more than simply
acknowledge our faults and sins in quite general terms. We are required to
recognize the essential continuity of our lives in sin and to strive for a life
which is essentially continuous in the absence of sin.

cf. Kant

In *SD*, Anti-Climacus writes thus: "Every unrepented sin is a new sin
and every moment that it remains unrepented is also new sin. But how
rare is the person who has continuity with regard to his consciousness of
himself! . . . But eternity is the essential continuity and demands this of a
person" (p. 104). And he continues, discussing the sinner (all of us): "In
his lostness, he is blind to the fact that his life has the continuity of sin
instead of the essential continuity of the eternal through being before
God in faith. In the world of spirit continuity is not only a joy but it is
spirit itself, that is to say, continuity is spirit . . ." (*OTA*, 141).

- eternity and continuity

n.b.

If so, it is not particular sins so much as the condition of sinning which
matters. "The particular sins are not the continuance of sin but the expression for the continuance of sin" (*SD*, 106). It is just this that is revealed to
the truly sincere person. "Whoever apprehends his sin in this manner . . .
will discover that confession is not merely an enumeration of particular
sins, but is an understanding before God, of the continuity of sin itself"
(*TTL*, 30).

A condition of sin

What is the alternative? "Every existence that is within the qualification
spirit . . . has an essential interior consistency and a consistency in something higher, at least in an idea. . . . The slightest inconsistency is an
enormous loss, for, after all, he loses consistency. . . . The believer, one
who rests in and has his life in the consistency of the good, has an infinite
fear of even the slightest sin, for he faces an infinite loss" (*SD*, 107).
Having one's life in the consistency of the good seems to be another

sin

identification for the idea of willing one thing, discussed in *OTA1*. Both
are "purity of heart."

I am not going to discuss in detail SK's concept of the eternal. Here I
want to illustrate only one aspect of this concept. There is an essential
connection between the idea of eternity and the paired ideas of good or
evil. Of the absolute good, for instance, SK writes that "it must, by an
eternal separation, cut off the heterogeneous from itself in order that it
may in truth continue to be one and the same thing and thereby fashion
that man who only wills one thing into conformity with itself" (*OTA1*,
66). Again, in *CT*: "For what is eternity? It is the distinction between
right and wrong.... But how can eternity be a distinction? To be a
distinction—is not that far too imperfect a mode of being to be the
eternal? Well, it isn't that eternity is the distinction, eternity is righteous-
ness" (p. 216).

We can put SK's idea thus. The concept of eternity *is* the concept of an
absolute Good. To have the concept of an absolute Good, and to "have
one's life in the consistency of" the idea of absolute Good, is to relate
oneself essentially to the eternal. It is to exist before the eternal. Now,
existing before the eternal is not, it seems, necessarily a way of existing
before God. Why could one not have a non-theistic understanding of the
idea of the eternal, that is, the absolute Good (a Platonic understanding,
for instance)?

I think SK's answer is that one can easily have such an understanding. It
is essentially the position he ascribes to Socrates. "Socrates explains that
he who does not do what is right has not understood it, either; but
Christianity goes a little further back and says that it is because he is
unwilling to understand it, and this again because he does not will what is
right" (*SD*, 95). But, as SK immediately points out, this implies that the
Christian view is essentially offensive to natural reason. It must therefore
be believed; it cannot be understood. Why should it be believed? Simply
because or in so far as it is revealed. But it can be revealed only to
individuals, one by one, not to groups or to the human race as a whole. It
follows that the non-theistic concept of the eternal is exactly what we
should expect people to have and that existing before eternity can become
a way of existing before God only to the individual to whom the truth is
revealed.

Before discussing this argument further, I want to say something about
the idea of judgment. In *CT*, SK says that "immortality is the Judgement.
Immortality is not a life indefinitely prolonged, nor even a life somehow

prolonged into eternity, but immortality is the eternal separation between the just and the unjust" (p. 212). To exist before the eternal is to exist before the idea of an absolute good. But the idea of good or evil functions essentially within judgment—judgment of deeds, words, thoughts, life as a whole. So, existing before the eternal is having a life which is essentially judged. This is the concept of conscience. Conscience is the voice of eternity, the voice of the eternal within one. "It must be heard by the individual, for the individual has become (sc. in eternity) the eternal echo of this voice" (*OTA1*, 186).

Now, just like the concept of the eternal, the concept of judgment has a non-theistic sense besides its theistic, or specifically Christian, sense. A non-theistic conception of judgment is the conception that human actions must be measured against objective standards, which exist—whether we like it or not, whether indeed we know it or not—as the proper standards for human actions. In SK's early works, all the varieties of the ethical have this in common: they are ways of existing before objective ethical standards.

In the Christian understanding, things are very different. Here the idea of judgment is understood in terms of the idea of a judge. And judgment is essentially connected with the idea of the individual. Thus, in *SD*, Anti-Climacus says that "this is why God is 'the judge', because for him there is no crowd, only single individuals" (p. 123). Already Socrates had insisted on the fact that judgment is essentially passed on individuals.

But "judgment," in a Christian understanding, is not just measurement against objective ethical standards. It is measurement against the idea of sin. And it is measurement by the individual himself or herself. "Christianity begins here—with the teaching about sin, and thereby with the single individual" (*SD*, 120). Even more strikingly, "the category of sin is the category of individuality" (*SD*, 119). These words imply quite unambiguously that it is not conceptually possible to have the idea of individuality outside the Christian understanding of things. So, for instance, Socrates could not have had a true idea of individuality, nor Kant either— unless these men were, without knowing it, within a Christian understanding.

One reason why SK makes this strong point about the idea of individuality has been sketched earlier. It is because, he claims, the true idea of individuality is the idea of particular creation *ex nihilo*. It is the correlative of the idea of a creator. SK seems, therefore, to be implying that unless one has the idea of a creator, one cannot have a genuine concept of individuality. Whatever conceptual complexities are here latent, we can say at least this: what makes real individuals genuinely distinct from one another is, quite simply, that each is the creature of an individual and distinct creative act by a creator.

That is an ontological condition. There is also an equally simple psychological condition. It is the simple fact that to be a genuine individual is to have a conscience; and a conscience is essentially one's own. One's own conscience cannot either be heard by or speak to anyone but oneself. Having a conscience, then, is a mark of true individuality.

Individuality, it follows, is not something that all human beings automatically possess. It is an achievement. (SK occasionally seems to suggest that it can also be lost.) For we do not automatically have consciences. Well, what of the person who never manages to get a conscience? From one point of view, such a person thereby manages to escape judgment. For judgment is carried in the voice of conscience. On the other hand, if the judgment is eternity's—in fact, God's—the person without a conscience may still be subject to judgment whether or not he knows it. In *SD*, Anti-Climacus says that

the person sitting in a showcase is not as embarrassed as every human being is in his transparency before God. This is the relationship of conscience.... The situation of the guilty person travelling through life to eternity is like that of the murderer who fled the scene of his act—and his crime—on the express train: alas, just beneath the coach in which he sat ran the telegraph wires carrying his description and orders for his arrest at the first station. When he arrived at the station and left the coach, he was arrested—in a way, he had personally brought his own denunciation along with him. (P. 124)

(Shades of Kafka!)

Existing before God at this stage, therefore, is existing before a judge. It is existing before a god whom one is conscious of as essentially judging one; before the judgment of God. In SK's scheme, this is by no means the highest or final mode of existing before God. This idea of God is by no means the highest idea of God. Still, it is an essential part of the Christian idea of God; existing before God's judgment is an essential component of the truly Christian existence. It is also probable that in SK's view other religions might share the same general understanding.

The most obvious thing to be said about the idea of God as the judge is that it is independent of, and does not imply, any belief which is essentially Christian. One can exist before God as one's judge without having any of the essentially Christian beliefs about Jesus. These beliefs will help to constitute deeper ways of existing before God, which I have not yet come to. I recall Job once again. In *G*, Constantine Constantius asks, "Did Job lose his case? Yes, eternally; for he can appeal to no higher court than that which judged him. Did Job gain his case? Yes, eternally . . . for the fact that he lost his case *before God*" (p. 117).

At the end of *KG*, SK offers the puzzling idea that God is the "like-for-like, the pure rendition of how you yourself are. . . . God's relationship to a human being is the infinitizing at every moment of that which at every moment is in a man" (p. 352). God is the Judge *for* any person who exists before God in the particular mode of conscience—and that should be all of us.

In the same discourse, SK writes about God as the judge and the merciful. It is one thing to have God as one's own judge, another to require God to judge someone else. "It does not help any that you intend that he shall judge someone else, for you yourself have made him your judge, and he is, *like-for-like*, simultaneously your judge, that is, he judges you also. If, on the other hand, you do not engage in accusing someone before God or in making God into a judge, God is then a merciful God" (pp. 349–50). One's own conscience cannot legislate for anyone else. But if one pretends to use one's own conscience to legislate for others, then, whatever one thinks, the god before whom one exists is a judging god—which means a god "before whom we are all guilty."

For SK, the distinction between God as the judge and the merciful can be clearly and intelligibly made only in Christianity. Existing before a god who is essentially merciful is existing before a god who is loving or is love. And, according to SK, it is only a Christian who can fully believe in a god who is love. I shall try to show why below.

There seems to be something unstable, unsatisfactory, about existing before God in this second way, about recognizing a god who is one's creator and judge. For one must be conscious of oneself as essentially sinful and thus deserving of whatever sin deserves. If God is recognized *only* as creator and judge, must this not cause despair? For the judge *judges*. He does not *as judge* have mercy and forgiveness. Certainly, non-Christians as well as Christians believe in a god who is merciful. But "merciful" is a different name from "judge," and its use expresses a different way of existing before God—just that way which I am about to describe. The point is simply that the forgiveness of sins is not an attribute of God that is contained within the definition or consciousness of God purely as creator and judge.

3

The third way of existing before God is existing before Christ. SK makes it quite clear that existing before Christ—acknowledging Christ as God— is distinct from merely existing before God. Thus, he writes that "at this point the intensification of the consciousness of the self is the knowledge of Christ, a self directly before Christ" (*SD*, 113). And he adds, emphatically: "As stated previously, the greater the conception of God, the more self; so it holds true here; the greater the conception of Christ, the more self. Qualitatively a self is what its criterion is. That Christ is the criterion is the expression, attested by God, for the staggering reality that a self has, for only in Christ is it true that God is man's goal and criterion, or the criterion and goal" (pp. 113–14).

What is the intensification of self at this stage? "A self directly before Christ is a self intensified by the inordinate concession from God, intensified by the inordinate accent that falls upon it because God allowed himself to be born, become man, suffer, and die also for the sake of this self" (*SD*, 113).

First, we must consider the fundamental idea of Christ: that Christ was born God and man, the God-man, God become man. We must also consider the ideas of offence, faith, and being a contemporary. What, in SK's view, is this fundamental idea? "The God-Man is not the unity of God and Mankind. Such terminology exhibits the profundity of optical illusion. The God-man is the unity of God and an individual man. That the human race is or should be akin to God is ancient paganism, but that an individual man is God is Christianity, and this individual man is the God-Man" (*IC*, 84). The God-man is in the fullest sense both God and an individual man. According to Anti-Climacus, the highest intensification of sin consists precisely in denying one or the other side of the crucial identification, "so that either Christ does not become an individual human being but only appears to be, or he becomes only an individual human being..." (*SD*, 131).

Now, "the God-Man is the paradox, absolutely the paradox" (*IC*, 85). But what sort of paradox? It is not the sort of paradox that a proposition, or theory, might embody. For the God-man is not a doctrine. In general, "Christianity is not doctrine" (*IC*, 108). Anti-Climacus echoes his pseudonymous predecessor, who wrote that "Christianity is therefore not a doctrine but the fact that God has existed" (*AE*, 290). (On the same page Climacus actually makes one of his extremely rare references to "the God-Man.") The paradox of the God-man is the paradoxicality of a particular being, not a proposition.

offence

To this sort of paradoxicality we can attach the concept of offence, being offended. "That an individual man is God, declares himself to be God, is indeed the 'offence' κατ᾽ ἐξοχην" (*IC*, 28). SK adds later: "Offence has essentially to do with the composite term God and man, or with the God-Man" (*IC*, 83). Offence is at Christ.

faith?

Of course, Christ is not necessarily a cause of offence. But he is necessarily a cause of the possibility of offence. "From the possibility of the offence a man turns either to offence or to faith" (*IC*, 83). Anti-Climacus consistently says in *SD* that both having no opinion about Christ and not being able to have faith in Christ are forms of offence—except, of course, if one has never heard of Christ.

contemp?

If offence at Christ and faith in Christ are not kinds of belief or disbelief in a proposition or theory, then what are they? Here we must discuss the idea of contemporaneity. Already in *PS*, Johannes Climacus makes the elementary distinction between "immediate contemporaneity" and "non-immediate contemporaneity" (see, for instance, pp. 84, 87). Thereafter, SK seems to take this distinction for granted. It allows him to say two things: that an immediate contemporary may not be a "non-immediate" contemporary and that an immediate non-contemporary may be a "non-immediate" contemporary. So, not all the actual contemporaries and neighbours of Jesus were necessarily his spiritual contemporaries, and later generations are not debarred from being his spiritual contemporaries.

df.
1-3 you
cf.
=present

However, there is a deep analogy between the two concepts. It emerges in SK's use of the idea of a situation. "No, the *situation* is inseparable from the God-Man, the situation that an individual man who stands beside you is God-Man" (*IC*, 84). He adds that "no relationship with the God-Man is possible except by beginning with the situation of contemporaneousness."

We should take quite seriously SK's use of this term. It implies that, in his view, the relationship of the Christian to Christ is that of one individual to another "who stands beside him." The Christian is not primarily related to any proposition or doctrine about Christ. He is related to Christ—in exactly the kind of way an individual is related to any other individual who "stands beside him," that is, who is part of the situation in which he finds himself. To be a Christian is to find oneself to be in the same situation with Christ, in a situation together with Christ. This view has alarming consequences. It implies, for instance, that the Christian's relationship to the Atonement is not to a doctrine about the Atonement (see *IC*, 109) but is finding oneself to be in the same situation as someone who is being crucified out of love for oneself. This experience must plainly be more intense than just entertaining a dogma, especially since it includes the recognition that one is oneself responsible for crucifying this person (see *CT*, 180).

Saying that the situation is inseparable from the God-man is also saying that Christ, as the God-man, cannot be the object or result of any sort of proof whatever. It is saying that Christ is necessarily the object of faith. In fact, "this contemporaneousness is the condition of faith, and more closely defined it is faith" (*IC*, 9). "Nor must we with impious heedlessness fancy presumptuously that we know as a matter of course who He was. For no one *knows* that, and he who *believes* it must be contemporary with Him in His humiliation" (*IC*, 143). So "non-immediate contemporaneity" is just another description of faith.

One further point about contemporaneity. To be contemporary with Christ is not *simply* to find oneself standing beside a particular man who (*NARR*) was and is God. It is to find oneself beside a man who, like all human beings, had a particular life, said particular things, and did particular things. Being Christ's contemporary, therefore, is being contemporary with the whole of Christ's life. The whole of Christ's life constitutes the "situation" of contemporaneity.

This explains why, in *IC*, Anti-Climacus talks in such detail about Christ's life. It explains why *CT* so frequently draws on particular episodes of Christ's life. It explains the lengthy discussion in *DS*. It also explains why SK emphasizes the Gospels throughout his religious writings. For the Gospels display the situation, namely, Christ's life; and meditating on the Gospels is therefore an essential part of the activity of being contemporary with the God-man.

And it is because Christian faith is contemporaneity with Christ, and this means being situated together with Christ in all his life, that the whole of Christ's life constitutes our paradigm (the Pattern, the Way). It is in this sense, finally, that Anti-Climacus says: "only in Christ is it true that God is man's goal and criterion" (*SD*, 114). God can be the "measure" for a human being, for his or her life, only if God is also a human being, whose life thereby constitutes just such a measure.

In this section I have discussed existing before Christ only in its most abstract form: existing before Jesus identified as God. I say abstract, because it is impossible to believe in the divinity of Jesus without also ascribing to him certain other and specific names. These names correlate with the concrete forms of existing before Christ; and to them I turn now.

4

SK's works contain many of the traditional names of Christ. I shall divide these names into two groups. The first group consists of the following names: Teacher, Communicator, Mirror, Pattern, Way, and Truth.

SK uses the name "Teacher" to refer to Jesus already in *PS*. In this work, Climacus claims to be offering a hypothesis, a thought-experiment; and the origin from which the experiment derives is Socrates. It would be reasonable to infer from all this that "Teacher" is an unilluminating, even perhaps a misleading, name for Jesus. But such is not the case. For the name occurs significantly in many of SK's most important Christian works.

For instance, in the introductory section of *CT*, SK writes that "it is true enough that the Gospel itself is the real teacher, that He is 'the Teacher'..." (*CT*, 13). Again, in *IC*: "They have nonsensically forgotten that here the Teacher is more important than the teaching...; they take Christ's teaching and do away with Christ. This means to do away with Christianity, for Christ is a person, and He is the Teacher who is more important than his teaching.... Only of a man can it be said that his teaching is more important than he himself is; to apply this to Christ is a blasphemy, it is to make Him a mere man" (p. 123). (Anti-Climacus here echoes Climacus's experiment.)

DS makes the point clear: "The Saviour of the World, our Lord Jesus Christ, did not come to the world to bring a doctrine; He never lectured.... His teaching in fact was His life, His presence among men" (p. 200). So, it is only the individual who is contemporary with Christ's life who can "learn" from this "teaching," to whom Christ can be a "teacher."

CT connects this idea of teaching with the Johannine names of Way, Truth, and Life: "He is 'the Teacher'—and the Way and the Truth and the Life in the instruction..." (p. 13). So does *IC*: "to be a teacher, especially a teacher of the race, 'the teacher of mankind', answers to the conception of truth as 'the way'" (p. 203). Here is a conceptual connection I shall come back to later.

SK also calls Christ "the Communicator," in both *FV* and *IC*: "the modern confusion has succeeded in transforming the whole of Christianity into direct communication by leaving out the Communicator, the

God-Man. As soon as one does not thoughtlessly take the Communicator away, or take the communication and leave out the Communicator, as soon as one takes the Communicator into account (the Communicator who is the God-Man, a sign, and the sign of contradiction) direct communication is impossible, just as it was in the situation of contemporaneousness" (*IC*, 127).

Indirect communication and the concept of faith are directly related. "The God-Man must require faith and must refuse direct communication" (*IC*, 142). Anti-Climacus points out, however, that the resulting relationship is not maieutic. For no man has a right to make himself into an object of faith for another (*IC*, 142).

Indirect communication and the possibility of offence are therefore also directly connected (see *IC*, 139). But why either? "The possibility of offence...is in the deepest understanding of it an expression for the necessity of calling attention, or for the fact that there is required of man the greatest attention possible...with respect to the decision to become a believer" (*IC*, 140). As Anti-Climacus also remarks in *SD*, "when God lets himself be born and become man, this is not an idle caprice.... No, when God does this, then this fact is the earnestness of existence. And, in turn, the earnestness in this earnestness is: that everyone *shall* have an opinion about it" (*SD*, 130).

It is in this sense that Anti-Climacus applies to Christ the name "Sign" (*IC*, 124). "Immediately He is an individual man, just like other men, a lowly, insignificant man; but the contradiction is *that He is God*" (*IC*, 125). Thus Christ is a sign of contradiction.

The name "Mirror" is often given to the Gospels, the stories of Christ's life (see the first part of *TS*). For Anti-Climacus writes that "a contradiction placed directly in front of a man—if only one can get him to look upon it—is a mirror" (*IC*, 126). For a contradiction "puts a choice before one, and while he is choosing, he himself is revealed" (*IC*, 126). But in this case the contradiction is the God-man himself. "And why? Because, replies the Scripture, He shall reveal the thoughts of hearts" (*IC*, 126). For the presence of Christ reveals either offence or faith in the individual who has become contemporaneous with him. So, we can call not only the Gospels but also both Christ's life and Christ himself a mirror. How do the concepts of teaching and communicating relate to these twin realities?

Although Anti-Climacus says that Christ's person is more important than his teaching, he does not say that Christ's teaching is unimportant. Of course, it is not and for a Christian cannot be unimportant. Consider, to take just one instance, the first part of *TS*. The whole argument is summed up in these words: "when thou readest God's Word, it is not the obscure passages which impose a duty upon thee, but that which thou understandest, and with that thou must instantly comply" (p. 54). And a few pages later SK remarks that "it is only too easy to understand the requirements contained in God's word—'give all thy goods to the poor', etc." These requirements are 'God's Word' not only in the sense that the Bible is seen as God's Word, but in the more literal sense that they were uttered by Jesus—who is God. So, quite plainly, the person who exists before Christ the Teacher also exists, so to speak, before Christ's teaching: the requirements that Christ sets out, as reported in the Gospels. One cannot recognize the Teacher but not the teaching.

Could one receive and respect the teaching, but not recognize Jesus as the Teacher, that is, as God? On the face of it, this is not impossible. One might accept Jesus as a great moral teacher, a holy man, a prophet—but not as God. However, of this kind of position Anti-Climacus says, almost at the end of *SD*: "In this denial of Christ as the paradox lies, in turn, the denial of all that is essentially Christian: sin, the forgiveness of sins, etc." (p. 131). He is pointing out that a good deal of Christ's teaching is about himself—and that it asserts of him precisely what people who deny Christ's divinity deny. So anyone who does not recognize Christ as God is forced to reject a good deal of his teaching as simply false (at best). One who does not recognize "the Teacher" can accept only some parts of the teaching.

The concept of communication relates differently to Christ and to his teaching. What can be communicated only indirectly is Christ's being, the fact that he is God. But his teaching is not in this sense only indirectly communicable. Much of it is "only too easy to understand." (This has nothing to do with the difference between direct and parabolic teaching. Parables can be just as easy to understand as direct teaching.) It may be argued that all moral teaching as such necessarily requires indirect communication. But this view belongs only to Johannes Climacus—not even to Judge William. Certainly all moral teaching requires appropriation by the hearer if it is to be effective, and it is in this sense necessarily indirect. But I see no evidence that SK himself shared Climacus's view. In any case, even if moral teaching by human beings must be indirect, there is a good reason why Christ can teach directly. He has the authority.

Still, Anti-Climacus points out, to receive the teaching without recognizing the Teacher leaves one in sin. "Very often, however, it is overlooked that the opposite of sin is by no means virtue. In part, this is a pagan view, which is satisfied with a merely human criterion and simply does not know what sin is, that all sin is before God. No, *the opposite of sin is faith*, as it says in Romans 14:23 . . ." (*SD*, 82).

5

"Pattern" and "Way" are two of SK's most familiar names for Christ. I do not believe that the implications of these names are sharply distinct, except that to "Way" there attaches a concept of "Truth." "Pattern" answers to the idea that we should *imitate* Christ; "Way," that we should *follow* him. But imitating Christ and following him are the same.

In *IC*, for instance, Anti-Climacus writes: "Christ came to the world for the purpose of saving the world, and at the same time (as was implied in His first purpose) to be 'the pattern' to leave behind him footsteps for those who would attach themselves to Him, who thus might become followers, for 'follower' corresponds to 'footsteps'" (p. 232). Again, in *DS*, SK himself: "Yet Thou didst leave behind Thee the trace of Thy footsteps, Thou the holy pattern of the human race . . ." (p. 161).

To exist before Christ as the Pattern is to have God for one's pattern. "As a man he was not created in the image (pattern) of God, but as a Christian he has God for a pattern!" (*CT*, 44). Moreover, "for the lowly Christian the pattern is in existence, and he is in existence for his Pattern. . . . The lowly Christian who is himself before God is as a Christian *in existence for his Pattern*" (*CT*, 45). SK wants to stress the connection between the Pattern and lowliness. "The lowly man believes that this Pattern exists expressly for him who is in fact a lowly man" (*CT*, 45). For "here on earth the Pattern can only be in lowliness and can only be seen in lowliness" (*CT*, 55).

The idea of the Pattern is also expressed in the terms "paradigm" and "ideal." Thus, "imitation must be introduced, to exert pressure in the direction of humility. It is to be done quite simply in this way: everyone must be measured by the Pattern, the ideal" (*DS*, 207). Note again the reference to humiliation. Again, imitating and following are conjoined. For SK goes on: "Christ no more desires now than He did then to have admirers (not to say twaddlers), He wants only disciples. The 'disciple' is the standard: imitation and Christ as the pattern must be introduced" (*DS*, 207).

The sense in which Christ is the Pattern is that his life is the pattern. "Christ's life here on earth is the paradigm; it is in likeness to it that I alone with every Christian must strive to construct my life" (*IC*, 109). SK even says that "this life of His is the Pattern" (*IC*, 198). So, imitating

Christ means in fact imitating Christ's life. This is what having God for
one's pattern really means. And this is what one is measured by: the
criterion and goal. Existing before Christ as one's pattern is therefore
trying to live a life which measures up to the life of Jesus, as recorded in
the Gospels.

For SK, imitation of Christ has two principal marks: humiliation
(humility) and suffering. Almost the whole of *IC* is devoted to stressing
that the Christ whom we are to take as our pattern is Christ in his
humiliation, not his exaltation. Thus, "every word He has uttered was
uttered in His humiliation" (*IC*, 162). Christ's humiliation was, quite
centrally, a matter of the circumstances of his life: that he chose to live in
lowliness. Anti-Climacus distinguishes this fact as a potential cause of
offence: "the fact that one who gives Himself out to be God shows
Himself to be the poor and suffering and at last the impotent man" (*IC*,
105).

In *DS*, SK states that "Christ is the Pattern, and to this corresponds
imitation. There is only one true way of being a Christian—to be a
disciple. The 'disciple' has this mark among others, that he suffers for the
doctrine" (*DS*, 215).

One might wonder here how imitating Christ's life is related to obeying his requirements. For, in the case of any other human being, we can
distinguish between imitating and obeying. It is one thing to follow
Socrates's teachings, quite another to imitate his life. In Christ's case the
distinction cannot even be made. For his life perfectly exemplified his
teachings; his teachings perfectly expressed his life. Yet SK thought that
one could understand the teachings fully only by reflecting on the life that
exemplified them. If so, Christ is fully the Teacher only for a person for
whom he is the Pattern. Conversely, to take Christ for one's teacher but
not one's pattern must entail a failure to understand the teaching fully.

I shall say little about the idea of Christ as the Way. Once again,
however, we have to consider Christ's life. The point which SK stresses is
that the Way is "narrow" (see, for instance, *OTA3* and *TS*). "His life,
every blessed day, every hour, every instant, expresses the truth that the
way is narrow" (*TS*, 28). Moreover, this way gets narrower and narrower; harder, more full of suffering. To say that the way is narrow is just
to say that it is essentially suffering. And that means suffering in the
specifically Christian mode (see part 2 of *CT*). Thus, in *DS*: "What is
decisive for Christianity . . . the notion of suffering because one adheres to
God, or, as we say, suffering for the doctrine, which properly is the
following of Christ" (p. 196).

The name "Way" is closely connected with the name "Truth," and also with the name "Life." In *IC*, Anti-Climacus explicitly identifies all three: "But when the truth is the way, when it is being the truth, when it is a life (and so it is Christ says of Himself, 'I am the way, the truth and the life')..." (p. 202). "Christ is the truth in such a sense that to *be* the truth is the only true explanation of what truth is.... That is to say, the truth, in the sense of which Christ was the truth, is not a sum of sentences, not a definition of concepts, etc., but a life.... And hence, Christianly understood, the truth consists not in knowing the truth but in being the truth" (*IC*, 200–201).

The name "Truth" is not restricted to the Anti-Climacus works and so is genuinely Kierkegaardian. In *CT*, SK asks, "Did Christ ever undertake to prove some truth or other, or to prove the truth? No, but He made the truth true, or He made it true that He is the Truth" (p. 104). This remark occurs in a passage in which SK considers what proving an eternal truth might mean; and he remarks that the highest thing a man can do is to *make* an eternal truth true, to make it true that it is true. And how does one make it true that some "eternal truth" is true? "By doing it, by being himself the proof, by a life which also perhaps will be able to convince others."

This activity is "reduplication," in one of that word's many senses. "Truth in its very being is the reduplication in me, in thee, in him, so that my, so that thy, that his life, approximately, in the striving to attain it, expresses the truth, so that my, that thy, that his life, approximately, in the striving to attain it, is the very being of truth, is a *life*..." (*IC*, 201). Rather more simply, SK remarks of Christ "that what He said, He was" (*DS*, 170). Certainly there are Hegelianized overtones in Anti-Climacus's statement, just as in his predecessor Johannes Climacus's use of the same word. But the point can be made without them and is SK's own.

Thus, "Truth" and "Life" denote the same attribute. "Christ's life upon earth, every instant of his life, was the truth" (*IC*, 199). Similarly for "Truth" and "Way." Anti-Climacus distinguishes between truths of such a kind that the truth (as a result) is distinct from its proof (the way of reaching the result): "When the truth itself is the way, the way cannot be shortened or drop out, without the truth being corrupted or dropping out" (*IC*, 202). This is precisely the case for Christianity, which is truth in the sense of "the Way," not in the sense of a result—or of a doctrine (see *IC*, 203).

I now repeat in the present terminology a point I made earlier. "Only then do I truly know the truth when it becomes a life in me" (*IG*, 202). SK adds that this explains the meaning of Christ's comparing truth with food: "so also is truth, spiritually, both the giver of life and its sustenance; it is life." This passage has been referred, quite correctly, to *John* 6:51, and presumably to the Dominical utterances that surround this verse. It is therefore interesting to turn back to *IC*, 100, where Anti-Climacus briefly discusses the utterances. He appears to signal that he wants to dissociate them from the interpretation that connects them with the Mass and to give them a different interpretation.

The epistemological point is strongly made. Anti-Climacus says that "knowing the truth is something which follows as a matter of course from being the truth, and not conversely; and precisely for this reason it becomes untruth when knowing the truth is separated from being the truth . . . ; no man knows more of the truth than what he is of the truth" (*IC*, 201). And he goes on, logically enough, to infer that, strictly speaking, "one cannot know the truth."

I want to make a final connection. "In this world truth conquers only by suffering, by defeat" (*IC*, 192). Why is this? Because this world is *this world*. "And to will to resemble the truth . . . in the world of untruth, that must bring one to lowliness and humiliation . . ." (*IC*, 191). Or, in other words, "he cannot in any wise escape suffering as long as he cannot persuade himself to escape from the picture; for since the picture he would resemble is the picture of perfection, and since the reality in which he finds himself and in which he would express this resemblance is anything but perfect, suffering is assured and unavoidable" (*IC*, 188–89). Again a frequent Kierkegaardian theme.

6

I want to begin this section by quoting once more an important remark by Anti-Climacus: "A self directly before Christ is a self intensified by the inordinate concession from God, intensified by the inordinate accent that falls upon it because God allowed himself to be born, become a man, suffer, and die also for the sake of this self" (*SD*, 113). I am now approaching the heart of SK's conception of God, the deepest way of existing before God. Here, the accent falls on the Atonement, the forgiveness of sins, God's unchanging unmerited creative love for mankind.

The accent falls, increasingly, on the individual who exists in this way before God. Anti-Climacus writes:

Christianity teaches that this individual human being—and thus every single individual human being . . ., this individual human being exists *before God*, this individual human being who perhaps would be proud of having spoken with the king once in his life . . . , this human being exists before God, may speak with God any time he wants to, assured of being heard by him—in short, this person is invited to live on the most intimate terms with God! Furthermore, for this person's sake, also for this very person's sake, God comes to the world, allows himself to be born, to suffer, to die, and this suffering God—he almost implores and beseeches this person to accept the help that is offered to him! (*SD*, 85).

Obviously, this is SK himself speaking out of his own heart. But at the same time, he is speaking for everyone. He is stressing the increasing and astonishing *reality* that God comes to have for one if one's experience of God is centrally defined as the experience of Christ's love and death and the forgiveness of one's sins through Christ. "Contemporaneity" becomes more and more literal in its application to the believer; his life takes place more and more in the "situation" with Christ.

In this section, I am going to discuss SK's uses of the ideas of redemption, atonement, forgiveness, and love as elements of the deep way of existing before God. I begin by, once more, quoting two passages in which SK links the name "Redeemer" with the names "Pattern" and "Way." In *IC*, he writes that "Christ came to the world for the purpose of saving the world, and at the same time (as was implied in His first purpose) to be 'the pattern', to leave behind Him footsteps for those who would attach themselves to Him, who thus might become followers, for 'follower' corresponds to 'footsteps'" (p. 232). In *DS*: "Thou who art both the Pattern and the Redeemer, again both the Redeemer and the Pattern, so that when the striver sinks under the Pattern, then the Redeemer raises him up again, but at the same instant Thou art the Pattern, to keep him continually striving" (p. 161). And he makes a similar point later: "Meanwhile we constantly recall to mind that Jesus Christ was not only a pattern but also the Redeemer, in order that the Pattern may not alarm us to desperation" (*DS*, 171; see, also, p. 217 for the same point again).

SK stresses the fact that "Pattern" and "Way" are to be understood essentially in terms of humiliation and suffering. The passages quoted above make a stronger point. To take Christ as one's pattern is to have a measure, and ideal, which one cannot possibly achieve. For Christ's life was perfection, being sinless. But no human being can be without sin. The consciousness of Christ is born within and from sin-consciousness. So, to exist before the Pattern might well create a kind of despair. And so it would, if the Pattern were not also the Redeemer. We should be unable to exist before the Pattern if we did not also believe that our pattern is our redeemer too.

"He whom the race crucified was the Redeemer" (*CT*, 287). This remark may introduce SK's understanding of the Atonement. In order to grasp what kind of understanding this is, we must recall SK's fundamental assumption that "the *situation* is inseparable from the God-Man" (*IC*, 84). It follows that the Atonement itself is not to be understood as a theory or historical claim—although the crucifixion of Jesus may be taken to be a historical event. The Atonement is, for the believer, a *situation*. It is the centre of the believer's experience of the reality of Christ. To exist before the Redeemer is to exist before the redeemer of one's own sins—not just a redeemer of the sins of mankind in general, and certainly not a redeemer of the sins of other people but not oneself.

This understanding has a very important implication. The believer does not need to have a doctrine of the Atonement. The believer need not understand *how* Christ's death atones for our sins. He or she need only believe that it does. If so, it follows that we need not expect to find anywhere in SK's works a doctrine of the Atonement. I emphasize this negative principle of interpretation, because it allows us to refrain from imposing on SK a doctrine of the Atonement which is familiar, traditional, and not clearly tenable. This is the doctrine of substitution.

There are several passages in which SK speaks in the language of substitution. For instance, in *CT* he says that "this death of His upon the cross is the sacrifice of propitiation for the sin of the world..." (p. 288). In *YTS1*, he writes: "For when He, when the suffering and death of the Atoner is the satisfaction for thy sin and guilt—being a satisfaction it assumes in fact thy place, or He, the Substitute, steps into thy place, suffering in thy place the punishment for sin, that thou mightest be saved...did He not put Himself entirely in thy place?" (p. 368). Again, in *TAF2*: "Though justice were to rage, what more can it want? For satisfaction has indeed been made...a satisfaction, a vicarious satisfaction, which covers thy sin entirely and makes it impossible to see it, impossible for justice..." (p. 22). And so on.

I am not arguing that we should not take the language of substitution seriously. We should—only not as expressing a *doctrine* of substitution. In SK's works, substitution represents an experience, part of the way in which the believer experiences Christ. Substitution is part of the Christian's situation.

This is an inescapable aspect of *TAF2*. That discourse is headed, as usual, by a prayer. The prayer ends with these words: "And so today Thou art still the hiding-place; when the sinner flees to Thee, hides himself in Thee, is hidden in Thee—then he is eternally defended, then 'love' hides the multitude of sins" (p. 18). These words do not express a doctrine. They express, powerfully, an experience: the experience of being hidden within and defended by Christ.

SK writes in the same discourse: "He hides them (sc. sins) quite literally.... Jesus Christ covers with his *holy body* thy sin.... He covers over thy sin just by covering it with His death..." (pp. 22–23). In these typical remarks, he is describing parts of the experience. I am going to try to elucidate the experience a bit, considering it from two aspects. First, the believer is *before* Christ. But second, the believer is *within* Christ. One is *before* Christ in the experiences of the forgiveness of one's sins, of Christ's love for one, and of judgment. I mean only that in these experiences Christ is experienced as *other*—which, of course, he is.

Let me begin by recalling Anti-Climacus's statement that to despair of the forgiveness of sins (one's own sins) is itself a sin. SK frequently stresses that the condemnation from which Christ delivers the believer is not primarily God's but the believer's own. It is the condemnation of one's own conscience, which is also God's voice. To be able to believe that one's own sins may be forgiven is not just to believe that God may forgive them. It is to experience their possible forgiveness *within oneself*; to cease to feel that they are unforgivable, to cease to feel the condemnation of one's own conscience as inescapable.

The woman who was a sinner (Luke 7:37) is here a pattern for all of us. "The test by which this woman was tried is: to love her Saviour more than her sin" (*YTS*, 385). This is hard; for "there is nothing to which a man holds so desperately fast as to his sin." We all love our sins. Thus we do not wholeheartedly want to give them up. If so, how can we wholeheartedly desire them to be forgiven—and forgotten?

Once more: "She loved much, hence she forgot herself entirely; she forgot herself entirely, 'hence her many sins were forgiven'—forgotten..." (*YTS*, 384). The key idea is "forgotten." For there is a paradox about the idea of forgiveness of sins. If one is conscious of one's sins, then how is it possible to feel that they have been forgiven? If one is still aware of them as sins, then surely they must still weigh on one's conscience; if they are felt as forgiven, then surely they cannot be felt at all any more. How can there be "a pardon which does not make me increasingly sensible of my sin, but truly takes my sin from me, and the consciousness of it as well" (see *TAF*, 21)? It is this paradoxical forgiveness which is Christ's, the forgiveness of authority. To be able to believe in this forgiveness is the only condition on which one can dare to believe oneself able to be justified and pure (see *TAF*, 21–22). So "sin is transformed into purity."

Now I turn to SK's conception of love: the divine love, *agapé*. First, a general remark. The conception of love became increasingly central in SK's thinking the more deeply he reflected. It is explicit in *KG*. But it is the central theme of many of his deepest writings: *CT4*, *YTS*, *EOT*, and *GU*. The last reference is particularly illuminating. For it shows that SK conceived of God—not, *sit venia verbo*, only of Jesus Christ—increasingly as love. In *TAF1*, he writes that "God is unchanging love" (p. 14). Love is the essence of God's creativity, as also of his relationship with each individual. "Even his omnipotence is under the sway of love" (*CT*, 132). "The omnipotence which creates out of nothing is not as incomprehensible as the almighty love which out of this, which for omnipotence is nothing, is able to make something which exists independently for love" (*CT*, 132). And "Christianly, every man (the individual) ... absolutely every man is equally near to God. And how is he near and equally near? Loved by him" (*TAF*, preface). Now the last sentence of *GU*: "he always finds Thy love equally warm. ... O Thou who art unchangeable!" (p. 240).

Recall that in *KG* SK conceives of God as the "like-for-like," the infinitizing of what is in one. God is love for the individual who loves and forgives others, judgment for the individual who judges and condemns others. Now SK makes a different and deeper point. Instead of separating the ideas of judgment and love, he brings them together. God's love is itself judgment. This is a theme of *TAF1*. Thus, "The severest judgment ever passed upon the world ... was it not Christ's innocent death, which yet was love's sacrifice? And what was this judgment? Surely this, that 'love' was not loved."

The judgment of love falls on the loving and the unloving, although differently. For the judgment of love is simply forgiveness—Christ's forgiveness. Yet: "when love judges thee, and the judgment is (oh, horror!), 'Thy sins are forgiven thee!' Thy sins are forgiven thee—and yet there is something ... in thee which makes thee sensible they are not forgiven" (*TAF*, 12). That is one's lack of love. But everyone lacks love more or less. However, let us recall that God is *unchanging* love. It is true that every Christian must experience the divine love as a judgment on himself or herself. It is Christ's suffering which reveals the guilt of every believer. It reveals that he or she essentially shares in the guilt of having crucified God. Yet it is also true that the divine love and forgiveness are unchanging. So whatever one's sins have been and are, there is always a hope for forgiveness in the future. For there is always the possibility that one may come to love, or love more.

"When thou dost love much, much is forgiven thee—and when much is forgiven thee thou dost love much" (*TAF*, 15). To this we can add a sentence out of the prayer that introduces *YTS3*: "Thou art love of such a sort that Thou Thyself dost woo forth the love which loves Thee, dost foster it to love Thee much" (p. 379). To exist before Christ, at this depth, is to exist before a God who is loving—who is in fact love. But one can exist in this way only in virtue of the love within one. On the other hand, love is possible for a human being only in so far as he or she exists before a God who is love. It is a constant theme of *KG* that the love that is within us flows from God's love. Thus, "a human being's love is grounded, still more deeply, in God's love. If there were no spring at the bottom, if God were not love, then there would neither be a little lake nor a man's love" (*KG*, 27). And the outpouring of God's love is a free gift.

I am now reaching the limits of this study. But there are still two ideas that I must mention. First, there is the experience of finding oneself not before but *within* Christ. SK describes this way of existing at the end of *TAF2*, that discourse on the Atonement. Since Christ *is* the Way, the Truth, and the Life, the believer can be and remain in the way, truth, life, only by being and remaining *in* Christ. So SK speaks of "the communion which thou shalt endeavour to maintain in thy daily life by more and more living thyself out of thyself and living thyself into Him, into His love..." (*TAF*, 25). I believe SK means these words to be taken literally. He is talking about a spiritual, not spatial, relationship.

In *KG*, SK explicitly identifies the idea of spirit with love: "Only in love to one's neighbour is the self, which loves, spiritually qualified simply as spirit..." (p. 69). Love to one's neighbour is a reflection of one's love to and from God. "Spiritually understood, what are the ground and foundation of the life of the spirit which are to bear the building? In very fact it is love; love is the deepest ground of the life of the spirit.... And the edifice which, spiritually understood, is to be constructed is again love..." (*KG*, 204–5). Anti-Climacus, too: "In the relationship to God, where the distinction of man-woman vanishes, it holds for man as well as for woman that devotion is the self and that in the giving of oneself the self is gained" (*SD*, 50n). The self can be literally *within* Christ because the self is essentially love, and Christ is pure love.

The second idea that I must mention is the idea of the Holy Spirit. But I can say almost nothing about SK's understanding of this idea. This is a serious lacuna in the present study. For presumably, the deepest of all ways of existing before God is existing in the Holy Spirit.

I believe there is only one text in SK in which he explicitly discusses the idea of the Holy Spirit. That is the third and final discourse of *TS*. Here SK enforces one belief: "in a spiritual sense it is true that the communication of the life-giving Spirit begins with death" (p. 96). It begins, that is, with the believer's "dying from" the world, which means the natural self. It is then that the Holy Spirit comes, the Comforter, the Paraclete. In a striking passage, SK echoes the traditional teaching of mysticism: "when all confidence in thyself or in human support, and also in God as an immediate apprehension, when every probability is excluded, when it is dark as in the dark night—it is in fact death that we are describing—then comes the life-giving Spirit" (*TS*, 101). The Spirit gives us life. SK means spiritual life, the life of the spirit.

X

Christ as "the Truth"

I

SK THOUGHT CONSTANTLY about the words of Jesus: "I am the way and the truth and the life" (John 14:6). This remark is the coping-stone in SK's theory of truth, in his understanding of moral and religious belief.

Plainly the word "truth" is not being used here in anything like the sense familiar to logicians and epistemologists. It is tempting to suppose that it is being used in a wholly distinct sense, so that it is straightforwardly ambiguous. But this is not how SK saw the case. For him, there is a real and crucial connection between the present idea and the idea of truth required within a theory of knowledge.

Let us think about the claim "I am the truth." This is some kind of identity-claim. That is the simplest and most natural reading of it, although it is also perhaps the strongest and least directly intelligible. What could possibly be meant by this identity-claim?

In SK's view, what characterizes morality—including the moral requirements which are a central and integral part of any religious faith and life—is the presence of standards or a standard. This general point is urged in *SD*, when Anti-Climacus writes: "The criterion for the self is always: that directly before which it is a self, but this in turn is the definition of 'criterion'. . . . everything is qualitatively that by which it is measured, and that which is its qualitative criterion is ethically its goal; the criterion and goal are what define something . . ." (p. 79).

I write "standards" because ordinarily a man's morality is embodied in a number of more or less distinct principles and ideals. And I write "a standard" because, as Anti-Climacus implies and as SK argues in *OTA1*, if his morality is coherent, the various apparently distinct elements in it can be seen as derivatives—applications—of one very general conception of the good. So, I take Anti-Climacus's statement to boil down to this: a man's self is his conception of the good. In Kantian language: a man's self is the formal object of his will. As Anti-Climacus also says: "The more consciousness, the more will; the more will, the more self" (*SD*, 29).

This last remark, however, must be treated carefully. It might perhaps be taken in a Nietzschean sense. But any such reading is the exact opposite of the truth. For *OTA1* makes it plain that SK is not talking about relative *strength* or *grasp* of will. He is talking about the idea of *purity* of will. And "the more will" means *not* the stronger will or the more embracing will, but the purer will. In *OTA1* this idea is partly explained through the idea of transparency, or a constantly self-examining awareness; and the same idea is visible everywhere in *SD*. Does not Anti-Climacus explicitly say, "The more consciousness, the more will"? In his terms, it is the consciousness within a man's will that gives his will substance and reality; so that however strong a man's will appears to be, if the man lacks fundamental consciousness—consciousness of himself—his will has little or no substance and reality. We cannot say of such a man that he has a *will* at all—however overbearing, assertive, and generally obnoxious he is.

For SK, we can understand the words of Jesus as a way of making the claim, "I am the criterion, the standard." That is, (*a*) "I am the standard by which every human being should come to measure himself"; (*b*) "I am the standard by which every human *is* in fact measured, whether or not he is conscious of it"; and (*c*) "I am the ultimate and perfect standard—that is, the *absolute* truth."

Claim *a* is supported by a remark Anti-Climacus makes in *IC*: "The highest examination is this: whether one will be in truth a Christian or not" (p. 184). A man's moral standard, his criterion, his conception of the Good, is not only a standard by which *he* measures and examines deeds and lives, his own as well as other people's. It is also a measure of the man himself. The higher the measure, the higher a man's vision of the Good, the higher, in one sense, the man—the higher the moral and religious level of his life. This is not to say the better the man. On the contrary, the higher we set the measure for a man, or a man sets the measure for himself, the lower and worse he is likely to appear. Hence a heightening of the conception of the Good naturally goes with a deepening humility and self-abnegation.

Implicit in *b* is the claim that there is at least one standard which is *objective.* It is central to SK's whole epistemology of morality that moral standards and standards for religious faith are generally *not* objective. Yet, as he writes in *JSK*: "Here, quite certainly, we have inwardness at its maximum proving to be objectivity once again" (p. 355). For moral and religious beliefs generally there are and can be no external, objective, standards—no criteria for rightness and wrongness, truth and falsity. So the search for such criteria must be directed inward, upon a man's sincerity, self-understanding, purity, and so on. Yet this is not the final truth, since the final truth is that there exists God; and the deepest achievement of inwardness is penetration to a vision of God, a hearing of God's voice.

As for claim *c*, the idea that there is an absolute truth is ultimately derived from Plato. "Absolute truth" in the present context means absolute criterion for truth, that is, for the rightness of moral and religious beliefs. This is to say, after all it *does* make sense, finally, to measure moral and religious beliefs for truth against an objective standard. There *is* a criterion for truth for such beliefs.

The criterion for truth is simply Christ's way of life. Confining ourselves to moral principles and ideals, a principle or idea is *true* if it was an essential element of Christ's way of life. If and only if Christ's life expresses and conforms to a certain principle or a certain ideal, then that principle or ideal is *true*. For example, if we say that Christ's life was essentially an exhibition of the two commandments he states in *Matthew* 22 (to love God and to love one's neighbour as oneself), then we are implying that these two commandments are *true*—and thus also the criteria for the truth or falsity of all other moral principles and ideals.

It is no accident, seen in this light, that Jesus puts together the ideas of "way" and "life" with the idea of truth. For it is not what Jesus said, or taught, that stands as the criterion of truth; it is how he lived. It is his life. But this does not mean what he did, that is, what he observably and externally performed. As his own words often make obvious, external performances cannot be taken as a secure guide to the spirit within. And it is precisely the spirit of a man's performances—his intentions, his motives, his understanding, his desires—that is the point.

That is why it is a complete misunderstanding of all that Jesus tried to teach to infer that external conformity to the words and deeds of his life is what is required. External conformity does not in the least guarantee conformity to the spirit within his life, the *way* in which he lived. So it is not the external facts of his life which constitute the real criterion of truth for moral requirements. It is the spirit of that life, the way in which Jesus lived and died. This is what SK means by "imitating," by the imitation of Christ, which is a central theme in the later, more rigorous, works.

2

Here are three remarks from different works in SK's Christian corpus.

O Lord Jesus Christ, Thou who indeed didst not come to judge, but wilt come again to judge the world, Thy life on earth is in reality the judgment by which we shall be judged. (*IC*, 180)

The severest judgment ever passed upon the world . . . , was it not Christ's innocent death, which yet was love's sacrifice? And what was this judgment? Surely this, that "love" was not loved. (*TAF*, 11)

If . . . you do not engage in accusing someone before God or in making God into a judge, God is then a merciful God. (*KG*, 350)

To be judged means either of two things. Usually it means to be measured by some person against a standard used by that person for measurement, for instance, in moral judgment. But, as SK uses the idea, it often has an objective sense. It means to be measured against an *objective* standard, whether or not you are aware of the fact, whether or not you are aware of or accept the standard, and whether or not anyone actually does the measuring. In this sense, the very existence of an objective moral standard is in itself a "judgment."

SK often and characteristically associates the idea of judgment, in this objective sense, with the idea of God. That is the gist of the third remark above—in which God, or this idea of God as essentially the judge, is explicitly distinguished from Christ, that is, God as essentially loving, self-sacrificing, and forgiving. Thus, in *CT*, SK writes: "For what is eternity? It is the distinction between right and wrong. Everything else is transitory. . . . But the difference between right and wrong remains eternally, as does He, the Eternal, who fixed this difference *from eternity* . . ." (p. 215).

On the other hand, the distinction between the idea of God as judge and the idea of God (in Christ) as loving is purely notional. It signifies a distinction between two kinds of conception of God. But this distinction is not thereby made out to be unimportant. On the contrary. For a man's conception of God—supposing he has arrived at any conception of God at all—is presumably his way of conceiving of the Good. The conception of God is the conception of the measure and standard. So a man's conception of God is the conception of the measure and standard. So a man's conception of God (if any) is also the measure for him—for *his* self, his will.

The conception of God as judging, in a sense of "judging" distinct from "loving," or "constituting the objective judgment by the fact of loving," is inadequate when placed beside the conception of God as essentially loving; or as judging in and through his loving. This conception is, for SK, the *true* conception of God; the other only partly true. That is, the Christian conception of God is for SK the *true* conception of the Good. We can put it very simply: God *is* The Good (see *CT*, 230). God is the unchangeable Good. (See *GU*, as well as the passage from *CT* just cited; also the remark about the Good in *OTA1*, 57.)

But this unchangeable and absolute Good can be identified with love. Therefore, after all, we do not have to hold apart the two conceptions of God as essentially judging and as essentially loving. For God's love, manifested in the life and death of Jesus, *is* his judgment. This is SK's real point. It is utterly mistaken, in SK's view, to think of God's judgment in anything like human, or subjective, terms. In particular, it is utterly wrong to connect this idea of judgment with any idea of reward or punishment. (That is why the ideas of eternal happiness and eternal misery, heaven and hell, play absolutely no part whatever in SK's account of *judgment*.)

It is not that God judges individuals—presumably by means of some standard or standards which we all more or less fail to achieve. On that assumption, it is then a real question where, so to speak, God gets these standards. Are they there already, independently of even God's will, or are they simply the standards that God wills? Neither answer makes any sense in a Christian understanding, though both have often been tried. God's judgment is simply the measuring of a man against God's love, that is, against the love that was the substance of Jesus' life.

SK emphasizes that the Christian understanding of judgment is not more lax, not more mild, than, say, the Judaic or Islamic conception of judgment. On the contrary, it is much more rigorous and severe. The standard which is given in the life of Jesus—absolute love—is the highest and most rigorous that can be imagined. SK does not therefore see the replacing of the law by love, the law's fulfilment in love, as a relaxation of standards. On the contrary. In *TAF1*, for example, he writes: "Love says, 'Everything is forgiven thee—if but little is forgiven, it is because thou dost love but little'" (p. 11). If the standard by which a man is measured is love—whether and how and how much he loves—then if he loves little, he has failed to meet the standard. And this is just how it is, whatever "forgiveness" may be offered. If we imagine God's judgment as having consequences—reward or punishment—then it is easy to imagine God as able to tamper with the proper consequences, for example, to forgive a ~~man~~ who fails the judgment. But if, like SK, we see the judgment as *objective*, as the simple existence of God's love as a measure for human lives, then forgiveness becomes irrelevant. God can be imagined as foregoing a man's deserved punishment. But not even God can be imagined as letting a man off the measurement which exists in the very fact of God's unchanging absolute love. The punishment lies simply in the man's failure to meet this standard to be loving. (Forgiveness here could mean only God's making the unloving man loving.)

However, it would be wrong to think that SK's moral theology stopped here. Consider just the two following, and extremely characteristic, remarks: "Christ came to the world for the purpose of saving the world, and at the same time (as was implied in His first purpose) to be 'the pattern', to leave behind Him footsteps for those who would attach themselves to Him, who thus might become followers, for 'follower' corresponds to 'footsteps'" (*IC*, 232). "Meanwhile we constantly recall to mind that Jesus Christ was not only a pattern but also the Redeemer, in order that the Pattern may not alarm us to desperation..." (*DS*, 171).

These remarks show that, in SK's mind, Christ's function as the "pattern"—the measure, the standard—is analytically inseparable from his role as redeemer. And the connection is elsewhere, as one might expect, shown to lie in the Atonement. For the purposes of the present argument, I want only to point out that both of Christ's functions are implications of God's love. It is in a life and death which were expressions of absolute love that Christ is our "pattern"; but of course this same absolute love is also the source of our redemption. The fact that God is absolute love is both the judgment and the "redemption" from the judgment.

3

Now I must say something about the idea that *love* is in some manner the absolute Good: the highest principle of morality, the measure and standard for life. There has always been a temptation to contrast "love" with "law," and ethics of love with an ethics of law. But SK takes pains to make it plain that he sees no such contrast and that he thinks that Jesus saw and made no such contrast either. I want to briefly consider a section of *KG*: the first part of chapter 3 (part 1), called "Love Is The Fulfilling Of the Law."

SK makes, among others, these points. First, Christ's love "was the fulfilling of the law" (p. 106)—not the abolition of the law but its "destruction," in the sense that because in his life Jesus perfectly fulfilled the law, the law now and henceforth exists essentially not in the form of a demand but in the form of a life positively fulfilling the demand. We, therefore, are now confronted with the law in a form in which it does not stand to us as a demand so much as a pattern, an ideal.

Second, *this* contrast must not be seen as a contrast between rigour and relaxation, or precision and vagueness, or the external (activity) and the internal (spirit). In SK's view, matters are in fact almost precisely the reverse. "Love is the fulfilling of the law, *for in spite of all its many provisions the law is still somewhat indeterminate.... Thus the law is a sketch.... In love the law is completely defined*" (*KG*, 110). The ideal, or pattern, of absolute love does not pick out an ethics in which activity is unimportant. On the contrary. Although love is itself, of course, an inner quality (like faith), it is for SK essentially manifested outwardly, in action. This thesis does not imply that action is a completely adequate expression of love, nor that action by itself is a sufficient substitute for love (works without faith). As SK says of Jesus, "Love in him was pure action" (*KG*, 106); not "the inactivity of feeling." These views imply that an ethics of love does not and cannot abolish the requirements on activity which are the characteristic feature of an ethics of law. An ethics of love cannot substitute for, or do without, principles. Nor can we wholly replace principles by ideals.

Third, SK says that Christ was the law's "*explanation*" (*Forklaring*) (*KG*, 108). And he goes on: "Only when the explanation *is* what it explains, when the one who explains is that which is explained, when the explanation is the transfiguration [*Forklarelse*] only then is there the right relationship. Alas, we are not able to explain in this way.... Our earthly life, which is weak and infirm, must distinguish between explaining and being..." (p. 108). By the law's explanation SK means an answer to the question, Why is this the law? Why does the law comprise these requirements? Or, an explanatory account of the principles of morality. But how was Christ that?

In his life, Jesus perfectly expressed the law in perfectly fulfilling it. But he did so precisely in loving and acting with absolute love. His life, therefore, reveals that there is an essential identity between what the law requires and what absolute love performs. And it reveals also that if there is a rationale for the law, the rationale is just that if the law requires performance *P*, it is because *P* is the expression of love. (foreshadowed in *EE2*: "Duty is only one: to love truly with the inward movement of the heart; and duty is as protean in its forms as is love itself..." [p. 151]).

This identity, which constitutes the explanation of the law, can be expressed in another way. If we think of the law as the expression of God's will, then we can say that there is an essential identity between God's willing *these* things and God's being absolute love. If God wills X, that is because God is absolute love, loves absolutely, because to will X is characteristic of absolute love, and because X is itself love's work. *By living in such a way as to show that "love is the fulfilling of the law," Jesus explained the law.*

The conception of law as the expression of God's will has an important role within SK's theory. For it allows him to move from the idea of morality as a system of principles to the Christian idea that "morality" is summed up and revealed in the life of Jesus, without abandoning the characteristic ethical concepts of principle, standard, ought–ought not, right-wrong, conscience, judgment, and so on. In moving to an ethics of love SK thinks of himself not as abandoning the characteristic standpoint of *morality* but as developing and fulfilling the implicit meaning of the moral standpoint.

Therefore, to balance the move from God-as-judge to God-as-love, we must, in SK's view, never forget that everything has still to do with the concepts of ought–ought not, right-wrong. This particular aspect of the total theory is stressed, following *KG*'s exposition of the ethics of love, in *CT*, which thus forms the third wing of the triptych whose first wing is *OTA1*. So, for example, we find SK saying such things as these: "For immortality is the Judgment" (*CT*, 212). It is "the eternal separation between the just and the unjust." Eternity "is the distinction between right and wrong. Everything else is transitory.... But the difference between right and wrong remains eternally..." (*CT*, 215). Christ did not abolish the difference between right and wrong; he did not abolish right and wrong, ought and ought not. Rather, in his life and death he revealed, "explained," the what, the how, and the why of fulfilling the requirements implicit in these concepts.

Now, just as it is, in SK's view, utterly mistaken to try to separate a judging god from a loving god, so here once again there is a serious mistake awaiting us. This is the mistake of separating, even conceptually, God's will and God's love. If we try to distinguish these functions, we shall be liable to invent a picture of God which, though familiar, is crazy: a schizophrenic, or split-vote, god, where one person sets rules which he wants us to keep, and another constantly lets us off the consequences of not keeping the first person's rules.

For SK, as for all orthodox Christians, God's will *is* his love—his love *is* his will. So, if we imagine morality to be the expression of God's will, it is just as much the expression of his love for us. If we imagine God's mercy and forgiveness as expressions of his love for us, they are equally expressions of his will. The conclusion of *KG* is mainly devoted to urging this identity. SK makes the point in his concept of the "like-for-like" (*Lige for Lige*). "God's relationship to a human being is the infinitising at every moment of that which at every moment is in a man" (*KG*, 352).

If so, we can argue in the following way. If morality is the expression of God's will, then the question why God, so to speak, selected just *these* rules and not others to be the content of morality can now be answered by saying that since he is essentially loving, in selecting just *these* rules for us God is selecting rules to fulfil which is itself to be loving. What God really wills is that we should be loving creatures; and he does so because he is essentially loving himself—because he *is* love.

Now, why should loving someone mean wanting that person to be loving? Because loving someone means wanting the Good for that person. Now, there are numerous different conceptions of the Good. So, we can distinguish the level and kind of love by seeing what conception of the Good is present. To want someone to be rich and powerful is a pretty poor sort of loving; to want him to be happy—in the ordinary worldly sense—is better, but still not very enlightened; to want him to be good, virtuous, is still better.

God's conception of love—if I can so speak—must necessarily be the true conception. So, in loving us, God wishes us to possess the Good, that is, the true and ultimate Good. *But the true Good is love—loving.* (This identity does not, of course, contradict the earlier identification of the Good with God, since God *is* love.)

This identity is rock bottom. For SK it is the foundation-stone of all thought about morality and religion. He says in *KG*, for example: "to love is the greatest happiness" (p. 134). And he connects love with the concept of *joy* (*Glaede*; see, for example, *KG* 75–76). However, we cannot necessarily understand that God's will is his love for us; for his will seems to us to impose requirements which are very different from anything we can understand as an expression of *love*. That is because our conception of the Good, and so of our own Good, is inadequate: corrupt and sin-penetrated. As a result, we do not see that our Good lies simply in love, in absolute sacrificial love. In fact, this ideal of love necessarily appears to our corrupted consciousnesses as the exact opposite of a good to its possessor. Hence God's love, in willing that we imitate Christ's absolute sacrificial love, necessarily appears to us as a will for our self-destruction, self-annihilation of what we naturally but corruptly conceive as our selves—all that is selfish, self-isolating, and self-destroying inside us. In a word, we cannot see that our true deep selves are pure love. It is only when the individual begins to see this that he can begin to recognize God's will for him as being essentially and purely loving.

Appendix

READING ABOUT KIERKEGAARD

THIS IS NOT a Kierkegaard bibliography. There is a good one in Josiah Thompson's *Kierkegaard: A Collection of Critical Essays* (Garden City, N.Y.: Doubleday, 1972). I list here only such books and articles as I have found specially helpful in thinking about the subjects in the present book.

First, philosophy. Plato is closer to SK, and throws more light on his thinking, than all other philosophers put together. For this book, the relevant dialogues are the *Apology*, *Phaedo*, *Gorgias*, *Meno*, and *Symposium*, particularly the *Apology*. SK's general conception of "the Good" descends from Aristotle's *Nicomachean Ethics*, his general conception of the human mind from the *De Anima*, and his logic from the *Metaphysics*. Kant offers a deeply illuminating foil to SK's Christian stance in *The Doctrine of Virtue* and *Religion Within the Limits of Pure Reason* (parts 1 and 2). Much of Hegel's *Early Theological Writings* is remarkably close to SK, while in the later *Philosophy of Right* Hegel advances (or retreats) to an ethics totally antithetical to SK's own. Bradley's *Ethical Studies* is constantly question-provoking.

Contemporary philosophy hardly touches SK or the problems that concerned him. The great exception is Wittgenstein. His "Lecture on Ethics" runs close to some of the pseudonyms. SK's epistemological probings will be understood better after working through *On Certainty*, and *Philosophical Investigations* explains a good deal of what SK is trying to do as he argues. For SK's characteristic scepticism, Richard Popkin's *History of Scepticism from Erasmus to Descartes* (New York: Harper and Row, 1968) is profoundly revealing. The central issues are probed with extraordinary lucidity by Michael Dummett, in his state-of-the-art *Truth and Other Enigmas* (London: Duckworth, 1978). Nor should Heidegger's *What Is Thinking?* be passed over.

Next, theology. SK's acknowledged works cannot be understood unless they are put in the right context, which is theological, not philosophical. Their topics are commonplaces of moral theology and mystical theology, their contents usually traditional and orthodox in doctrine and also in presentation. SK's Christianity is often close to Saint Augustine's, as in the *Confessions*, for example. The classics are constantly illuminating: Pseudo-Dionysius in *The Divine Names* and *Mystical Theology*, Eckhart's *Detachment*, *The Cloud of Unknowing*, and *The Imitation of Christ* (particularly close to SK). SK stands so near the centre that Catholic and Orthodox writing is often equally relevant. Saint Teresa's *Way of Perfection*, Saint John of the Cross's *Ascent of Mount Carmel*, and P. de Caussade's *Abandonment*, plus many of the Fathers anthologized in the *Philokalia* (trans. E. Kadloubovsky and G. E. H. Palmer, vol. 1 [London: Faber & Faber, 1951]), bear profoundly on SK, not least because they treat the same psychological issues as he does. Among more recent theological writing, I have found special help in George MacDonald (*Unspoken Sermons*) and Simone Weil (*Gravity and Grace, Waiting on God*). In the history of theology, Anders Nygren's *Eros and Agape* stands out as a treatment of a subject central in SK's thought from a stance close to though not identical with SK's. Evelyn Underhill's classic *Mysticism* shows how SK fits into the wide Christian tradition; especially part 2, chapters 3, 6, and 9, which suggest that we read him as a theologian of the *via negativa*. I need not, but still shall, mention that it is impossible to study SK's acknowledged works without a copy of the *New Testament* at hand—preferably in Greek.

SK's remarkable psychological insight is often compared with modern psychoanalytic theory. In fact, the two are quite different. Nearly all psychoanalytical theorizing is about the hypothetical underlying mechanisms, whereas SK's analyses are of the phenomena, and belong in the tradition of psychological analysis that attaches to Christian writings about sin, temptation, prayer, and purification. But Marion Milner's two books, *A Life Of One's Own* (Harmondsworth: Penguin, 1952) and *On Not Being Able to Paint* (New York: International University Press, 1967) are quite exceptionally clear, deep, honest and provoke reflections about the whole subject of self-knowledge.

Among the many studies of SK himself, I have found none more illuminating and thought-provoking than the series of articles coming from Alastair McKinnon. He is using newly developed statistical techniques to provide mathematically encapsulated information, enormously dense and rich, about SK's actual texts—in Danish, *bien entendu*. These articles do not, and are not meant to, stand as statements of results. They are research tools of a unique and irreplaceable kind, though useful only to someone who either already knows SK's writings thoroughly or is ready to use the articles in constant reference to the writings and to whatever specific questions he is putting to the writings. I list here a few of these articles.

"The Central Works in Kierkegaard's Authorship," *Revue Internationale de Philosophie* 26 (1973).
"Kierkegaard's Remarks on Philosophy," *Journal of the History of Philosophy* 11 (1973).
"Theological Focus in Kierkegaard's *Samlede Vaerker*: Some Basic Data," *Studies in Religion* 4 (1974).
"Most Frequent Words and the Clustering of Kierkegaard's Works," *Style* (1974).
"Aberrant Frequencies as a Basis for Clustering the Works of a Corpus," *Cirpho* 2 (1975).
"Kierkegaard and His Pseudonyms: A Preliminary Report," *Kierkegaardiana* 10 (1977).
"Kierkegaard's Perception of the Bible," *Kierkegaardiana* 11 (1980).

I have also found constantly useful the following article by McKinnon and Niels Jørgen Cappelørn: "The Period of Composition of Kierkegaard's Published Works," *Kierkegaardiana* 10 (1977). And I have frequently consulted the *Samlede Vaerker*, available in paperback (ed. Peter Rohde, 20 vols. [Copenhagen: Gyldendalske Boghandel, 1962–63]).

Finally, the paperback editions of the standard English translations of Kierkegaard that I have quoted from.

Attack Upon Christendom, trans. W. Lowrie (Princeton: Princeton University Press, 1944).
On Authority and Revelation, trans. W. Lowrie (New York: Harper and Row, 1966).
Christian Discourses, trans. W. Lowrie (Princeton: Princeton University Press, 1971).
The Concept of Dread, trans. W. Lowrie (Princeton: Princeton University Press, 1967).
Concluding Unscientific Postscript, trans. D. F. Swenson and W. Lowrie (Princeton: Princeton University Press, 1941).

Edifying Discourses, trans. D. F. Swenson and L. M. Swenson (London: Collins, 1962).

Either/Or, vol. 1, trans. D. F. Swenson and L. M. Swenson, vol. 2, trans. W. Lowrie, rev. H. A. Johnson (Princeton: Princeton University Press, 1944).

Fear and Trembling, trans. W. Lowrie (Princeton: Princeton University Press, 1954).

For Self-examination and *Judge For Yourselves!* trans. W. Lowrie (Princeton: Princeton University Press, 1974).

The Gospel of Suffering, trans. A. S. Aldworth and W. S. Ferrie (London: James Clarke, 1955).

The Journals, trans. A. Dru (Oxford: Oxford University Press, 1938).

The Lilies and the Birds, trans. W. Lowrie (London: Oxford University Press, 1939).

Philosophical Fragments, trans. D. F. Swenson, rev. H. Hong (Princeton: Princeton University Press, 1962).

The Point of View For My Work as an Author, trans. W. Lowrie (New York: Harper and Row, 1962).

Purity of Heart, trans. D. V. Steere (New York: Harper and Row, 1956).

Repetition, trans. W. Lowrie (Princeton: Princeton University Press, 1941).

The Sickness Unto Death, trans. H. Hong (Princeton: Princeton University Press, 1980).

Stages on Life's Way, trans. W. Lowrie (New York: Schoken, 1967).

Thoughts on Crucial Situations in Human Life, trans. D. F. Swenson, ed. L. M. Swenson (Minneapolis: Augsburg Publishing House, 1941).

Training in Christianity, trans. W. Lowrie (Princeton: Princeton University Press, 1944).

Two Ages, trans. H. Hong (Princeton: Princeton University Press, 1978).

The Works of Love, trans. H. Hong and E. Hong (New York: Harper and Row, 1964).

Index